"Lars Erslev Andersen and Jan Aagaard
IN THE NAME OF GOD

Lars Erslev Andersen
and Jan Aagaard

IN THE NAME OF GOD

– The Afghan Connection and the U.S. War against Terrorism. The Story of the Afghans veterans as the masterminds behind 9/11

Foreword by dr. Rohan Gunaratna

University Press of Southern Denmark 2005

Published with the generous support of
The Nordic Summer University (NSU)
Ingeniør N.M. Knudsens Fond
The University of Southern Denmark

© The Authors and the University Press of Southern Denmark 2005
Set and printed by Narayana Press
Cover design by Anne Charlotte Mouret, UniSats
ISBN 87-7674-060-9

Cover photo:
U.S. President Ronald Reagan and spokesman for the Afghan Resistance Alliance, Burhanuddin Rabbani, in the Oval Office of the White House circa mid-80's (AP Photo/Dennis Cook).

The translation of the international edition of this work:

Coordinated by the Danish House of History
Translated by Cindie Margaard
Editor and proofreader: Tony Wedgewood

University of Southern Denmark Studies in
History and Social Sciences vol. 307

University Press of Southern Denmark
Campusvej 55
DK-5230 Odense M
Phone: +45 6615 7999
Fax: +45 6615 8126
Press@forlag.sdu.dk
www.universitypress.dk

Distribution in the United States and Canada:
International Specialized Book Services
5804 NE Hassalo Street
Portland, OR 97213-3644 USA
Phone: +1-800-944-6190
www.isbs.com

CONTENTS

Contents 5

Preface 11

Foreword 15

1. In the name of Civilization
   – U.S. Middle East Policy from Reagan to W . . 19
   Reagan between idealism and realpolitik:
   The civilization-conservative strategy 22
   Bush's international pragmatism:
   The civilization indifferent strategy 25
   Clinton – dialogue and a democratic mission:
   The civilization-promoting strategy 30
   Clinton's universal concept of civilization 32
   Bush – Neoconservative activism in the Middle East:
   Resumption of Reagan's civilization-conservative
   strategy 38
   Bush's Grand Strategy in the Middle East 40
   The Bush Doctrine: Civilization war and defense
   of American values 49

2. The concept of terrorism, questions
   of legitimacy, rights and power 52
   Terrorism in Denmark 53
   Freedom-fighter or terrorist? 54
   The branding of opposition groups by states . . . 57
   The Oslo process 1993-2000 58
   From civil justice system to foreign defense action . . 60
   The message drowns in apocalyptic horror 62
   A pragmatic definition of terrorism 64

3. Globalization, networks and cyberwar
   in the postmodern world 67
   Weapons of mass destruction on the black market . . 68
   The oil-for-food agreement 71
   The background to anti-Americanism 72
   Pakistani intelligence in collusion with the USA 75
   Networks 77

4. Islamic Fundamentalism 80
   A modern concept 80
   Inequality and the lack of political influence 82
   Fundamentalism – a product of secularization 85
   Economic and cultural globalization 87
   New religious movements 89
   Salafiya and global jihad 90
   The Salafiya movement 92
   Da'wa 93

5. Saudi Arabia's globalized dilemma 97
   Power struggles in Saudi Arabia 98
   Bush's turnaround on the Palestine conflict 99
   The USA turns a deaf ear 100
   The export of jihad 102
   The young exert pressure 105
   Rebellion by cassette tape 106
   The alliance between al-Sheikh and al-Saud 107
   With Wahhabism as a building block 109
   Islamic fundamentalism and the Gulf War 110
   The opposition sounds off 112

6. Egypt: A historical setting for militant Islam . . . 116
   Moderate and militant wings 117
   Sayyid Qutb and the state of jahiliya 118
   The ideology is realized 121
   The assassination of Sadat 123
   New tensions between the government and opposition 126

7. The Soviet invasion of Afghanistan 129
   The Iranian revolution 130
   The Carter Doctrine 130
   Coup in Afghanistan 131
   The question of Pashtun 132
   The Communist Party 133
   Popular uprising 135
   The Russians arrive 136
   The Persian Gulf and Iran 137
   Excerpt from the magazine of the Soviet Army 138
   The Indian Ocean and Pakistan 139
   Regional ambitions and China 140
   The anti-Soviet alliance 141

8. The Mujahideen and the Arab Brigade 143
   Hekmatyar and Rabbani – two key figures 144
   Pakistan's involvement 144
   Egypt's role 146
   China and Iran as players 147
   Recruitment 149
   Hamas 150
   Financing 152
   Abdallah Azzam 153
   From training to combat 154
   Estimated American military aid to the Afghan
   resistance movement 157
   The Arab Brigade in numbers 157
   Outside the superpowers' searchlight 158
   The Taliban 161
   Unemployed Afghan veterans 162

9. The Afghan veterans, national terrorism
   and international networks 164
   Egyptian Afghan veterans on new missions 165
   More violence across borders 167
   The Danish connection 168

A fundamentalist speaks	171
History repeats itself in Algeria	174
GIA escalates violence	176
The unsuccessful dress rehearsal for 11 September	177
Kabul – London – Amman – Aden	179
The British connection I	180
Yemen: A den of terrorists	180
The British connection II	181
The Filipinos offer their services	182
Afghan veterans and the Dayton Agreement	184
Salafiya followers establish themselves in the Balkans	185
The boomerang effect in China	186
Al Qaeda gets involved in the Caucasus	187
From Brønshøj, Denmark via Grozny to a jail in Moscow	188
The Diary of Abdul Aziz	189

10. Osama bin Laden
– portrait of a leader and his organization 191

Source credibility	192
Bin Laden	193
More in spirit than in body	195
Al Qaeda is organized	196
The financing of terrorism	198
To war with the USA	200
The Americans wake up	202
The essential requisites for a network	203
The Hebron Agreement	206

11. Pax Americana
– or "the axis of evil" as new world order 206

The Wye Memorandum	207
A world of intractable centers of unrest	208
The Clinton plan	210
The responsible superpower	210
A revival of Cold War strategy	212

Postscript to the international edition:
   International terrorism and weak states 214
      Al Qaeda is back in business 215
      Terror and weak states 216
      A mistaken strategy 218

Bibliography 220

Notes 232

PREFACE

In mid-June 2001, barely three months before 11 September, Lars stood at the top of the World Trade Center in New York City and wondered what would have happened if the terrorists had succeeded in their attempt to level the building in 1993. The prospects were frightening and it was natural to compare them to Pearl Harbor, both because that attack on an American naval base had been a trauma in American history ever since its occurrence, and because in the summer of 2001 Americans marked the sixtieth anniversary of the event with a new epic film and a wealth of new books on the subject.

The speculations at the top of the World Trade Center became part of the research for a book on the history of terrorism. It was planned to begin with precisely those same deliberations of what would have happened if the twin towers had been brought down in 1993, as the terrorists clearly had intended.

That chapter was made unnecessary by the events of 11 September. Our preoccupation with the events of 1993, however, was not. Since that day in February when the world first heard about "Ground Zero," each of us has been concerned with trying to understand what the attack in New York in 1993 was actually about, what led to it, and what implications could be deduced from it. Our interest in these questions is closely related to the fact that, in one way or another, both of us came to be occupied with the terror attack when the investigations in the USA produced an offshoot in Denmark; in 1993, three Egyptians were arrested and later charged with planning terrorism on Danish ground. Jan was involved in the investigation of the case, while Lars appeared as a prosecution witness at the trial in Århus. The case ended with an acquittal, which did nothing to diminish our interest in the World Trade Center incident, its background in Afghanistan and the Middle East, and it's ushering in of a new type of global terrorism. For Jan it meant that a period of leave in 1997 resulted in a Master's thesis in History at the University of Copenhagen on the Afghan veterans and their role in the escalation of Islamic-based terrorism in the 1990s; for Lars it led to a new research project in January 2000 on the concept of terrorism in American security policy from Carter to Clinton. It was in the light of these events that we decided, in the fall of 2001, to write this book, in which we tell the story of the Afghan connection.

We would like to underline that this book was written before the outbreak of the Iraq war in March 2003 as well as before the terror attacks in Madrid, Spain March 2003.

Although the book is a result of teamwork each chapter has its own author: Lars Erslev Andersen has written chapters 1, 2, 3, 4, 5, 10, 11, and the Postscript while Jan Aagaard has written chapters 6, 7, 8, 9. Chapter 1 is new and especially written for the international edition of this book.

We are of course grateful for the helpful and qualified advice we have received along the way from colleagues in the Danish Police, the Armed Forces and the University of Southern Denmark. We owe them many thanks.

We would like to thank our translator Cindie Maagaard, and editor Tony Wedgwood for their kind cooperation as well as the Danish House of History for great help with the production of the international edition, and University of Southern University Press for competent support in publishing the book. We are also grateful for the funding provided by Ingeniør N.M. Knudsens Fond and University of Southern Denmark. We would like to express our gratitude to Dr. Rohan Gunaratna, Head, International Centre for Political Violence and Terrorism Research, Institute of Defense and Strategic Studies, Singapore for his kind and useful advices and comments!

Finally but not least we express our gratitude to the Nordic Summer University for co-funding the international edition and for organizing seminars and a Summer Conference. The Nordic Summer University (NSU) is a long-established institution within the Nordic intellectual arena. During more than 50 years of existence it has provided a lively forum for academic and intellectual debate, and involved many leading academics, politicians, and intellectuals from all the Nordic Countries. The NSU has always been at the forefront of intellectual thinking, juxtaposing views from the international and Nordic academic arenas, and introducing new thinking and influences into the Nordic Countries. The NSU is not a dusty relic of a bygone age, but a dynamic space where intellectuals from different age groups meet to share their thoughts and test out their arguments. It constitutes a forum for intellectual thought where narrow academic disciplines are replaced by thematic topics, creating an interdisciplinary space where academics and intellectuals with various backgrounds can interact. Several of this book's chapters came into being as papers presented and discussed in the wonderfull forum that NSU is organising, and in a world of academic uniformity and competition the existence of NSU should be highly appreciated as an alternative and productive intellectual setting. We certainly do.

For the record, we must emphasize that all the information in this book has been gathered from open sources and that no classified material on Danish or international matters has been used. We must also stress that we have sole responsibility for the book's content and analyses.

Copenhagen and Odense, July 2004
Lars Erslev Andersen and Jan Aagaard

FOREWORD

In the Name of God, Jan Aagaard and Lars Erslev Andersen discuss the evolution of the global terrorist landscape during the past three decades. The most profound developments they identify are, first, the shift in the gravity of terrorism from the Syrian-controlled Biqa' Valley in Lebanon to Afghanistan; second, the background for the shift in the epicenter of international terrorism from Afghanistan to Iraq, and third, the newest land of jihad; and fourth, the morphing of Al Qaeda from a group into a global movement.

When the security and intelligence service of Denmark disrupted a terrorist operation by a jihadi cell planning to strike targets in Denmark in 1993, Aagaard and Andersen distinguished themselves as counter terrorism practitioners and scholars. Although the word *al-Qaeda* was unknown to the Western services, the disrupted attack in a planning stage bore the hallmarks of Al Qaeda. The Egyptian jihadists had identified Western and Israeli targets in Denmark and the attack was most likely to coincide with the bombing of the first World Trade Centre attack of February 1993. Learning from the coordinated simultaneous attack against US and French targets in Beirut by the Lebanese Hezbollah a decade earlier, Afghan-trained jihadists realized the value of such high impact operations across the Atlantic. Although the Afghan-trained jihadists were not as well organized and led at that time, subsequently they gained substantial expertise and experience in the conduct long range deep penetration operations such as 9/11. The authors Aagaard and Andersen followed the trajectory of the jihadists, both in the territorial conflict zones that produced the terrorists as well as in the West where their supporters and operatives built state-of-the-art networks.

The authors present a rich history that enables both the generalists and the specialists to understand the politico-religious ideology that drives the contemporary jihadists to kill and die. They discuss in detail, the formation of that powerful belief system, the key ideologues, the financing, the training, and most importantly, the terrorist. The two pivotal events that led to the formation of the contemporary Jihad networks – first, their defining Afghanistan experience and second, the international neglect of Afghanistan – are chronicled. The perception of the political leaders, bureaucrats and the public to the emerging threat including the intervention of Afghanistan and the strategic arguments for the invasion of Iraq are discussed.

Today, the world faces an unprecedented threat. Even four years after 9/11, the threat has not receded but surged. Our response has been sufficient to prevent several terrorist attacks but insufficient to end terrorism. Although governments have thwarted mass fatality terrorist attacks that would have otherwise killed several thousands of innocent citizens and foreigners, the threat is present and persistent. The research by the authors demonstrates that we must now steadfastly move beyond prevention into ending the threat. To meet the challenge of threat of this scale and magnitude, the authors call for a political response beyond the overwhelmingly kinetic reaction of the Western states. To their minds, investing in operational counter terrorism - targeting cells planning and preparing attacks – will not reduce the strategic threat of terrorism. It will certainly prevent attacks, weaken the group in the short term but, to neutralize the real threat, we must weaken the terrorist capacity. Especially after the US invasion of Iraq, the terrorist capacity to replenish those killed or captured; to raise funds, to procure supplies, to collect intelligence and mount attacks have increased. Unless we develop an unprecedented global response, that is to fight the terrorist capacity to regenerate, we will suffer from terrorism for the next 100 years. How do we rise to this monumental challenge?

First, ideologically challenge the extremism prevent in our societies, in our schools, and in our houses of worship. We must work closely with the religious leaders, the educators, and the elite of our countries to create a societal norm and an ethic against the use of violence.

Terrorism is a vicious by product of extremism. Unless we develop a zero-tolerance attitude against terrorism, we will always suffer from terrorism.

Second, reform the educational institutions by prosecuting teachers who preach violence, and make the curricula more relevant to modern day living.

Third, reform our financial institutions, banks and charities. We must work closely with the financial sector to prevent the terrorists from abusing and misusing the banks. Most banks have indicators to detect criminal money but not terrorist money. As charities continue to be used by terrorists to sponsor and to move money to execution cells, we must call for greater transparency especially of the Gulf based charities.

Otherwise, the money we donate to alleviate poverty, build schools, and improve health and sanitation, will be used to kill innocent men, women and children. Unless a charity is responsible for the end user, the charity must be shut down.

Fourth, we must work with the international, domestic and local media organizations to ensure that they do not disseminate the terrorist message. Some of these media outlets have done more damage to politicise and radicalize youth than the terrorist ideologue themselves. Media personnel and media owners must exercise greater self regulation and restraint in reporting the clarion call of terrorists to strike.

Fifth, most countries seek to fight terrorism using the penal code. To effectively combat terrorism, governments must develop specific counter terrorism legislation. Without designating or proscribing terrorist groups, we cannot effectively weaken these groups, especially their support functions such as propaganda, recruitment, fund raising, procurement, safe houses, transport, intelligence gathering. We must encourage countries that suffer from terrorism to draw from global best practices in counter terrorism legislation.

In this important work, Aagaard and Andersen provide the background information, both the understanding and the knowledge for the West to formulate and develop a response beyond operational counter terrorism.

We have to constantly learn from our successes and failures and more importantly from the successes and the failures of others. Until now, the west has failed firstly to understand and then decisively respond to the challenge before us. We have a responsibility to this generation and to the next generation to understand the threat and respond resolutely to this challenge. I recommend this important work for both the generalist and the specialist.

Rohan Gunaratna
Singapore, 2005

Rohan Gunaratna is Head of the International Centre for Political Violence and Terrorism Research at the Institute of Defence and Strategic Studies, Singapore, and Senior Fellow, Combating Terrorism Centre at the United States Military Academy at West Point.

I. IN THE NAME OF CIVILIZATION — U.S. MIDDLE EAST POLICY FROM REAGAN TO W

> *There is a value system that cannot be compromised, and that is the values that we praise. And if the values are good enough for our people, they ought to be good enough for others, not in a way to impose because these are God-given values. These aren't United States- created values. These are values of freedom and the human condition and mothers loving their children*
>
> George W. Bush interviewed by Bob Woodward, November 19, 2002[1]

Values are important in foreign policy, asserted Condoleezza Rice, George W. Bush's security policy advisor, in an article from October 2002.[2] If, she continued, the Soviet Union had won the Cold War, the world would look very different today. With this in mind, she rejected the old debate between "realists" and "idealists" which in her opinion had characterized research in international policymaking too long.

In the realist school, values and ideology are granted low priority in favor of power as the key to stability and the protection of national security interests. The idealists, on the other hand, emphasize the necessity of a clearly articulated value base for formulating the necessary foreign policy for the achievement of peace and security. According to Rice, the debate is of purely academic interest because power and values are, in reality, always closely intertwined.

Although Rice may be right on this point, the rhetoric of successive American administrations has been seen to interpret and attach importance to the issue of values quite differently, with a tendency to downplay idealism during times of peace while in times of war playing an openly activistic role on the moral stage. What a specific administration emphasizes naturally has consequences for how important it conceives international cooperation and alliances to be.

In American contexts one can discern three main foreign policy strategies: two which place heavy emphasis on an idealistic, value-oriented foundation, and one which can be described as pragmatic internationalistics. This last type is represented by a group of policy makers and scholars (realists and neorealists) who advocate a strategy that can be termed the "civilization-indifferent strategy": protection of national security interests through a balance of power, deterrence and containment, with emphasis on international alliances and cooperation. Cultural values are completely subordinate to issues of power and security.[3]

In the history of ideas the tenets of the civilization-indifferent strategy hark back to a conception of state found in the English philosopher Thomas Hobbes (1588 – 1679), known for the expression bellum omnium contra omnes, "the war of all against all": in a state of nature the individual human being would be at the mercy of his instincts and focused solely on selfpreservation in a fight for life and death. In the state of society, the natural right to selfpreservationis surrendered to the state, after which the individual must renounce his uniqueness and submit to the rule of the state.[4] In a similar way, the international system of states can be seen as a society in which the individual state submits itself to an international order without any regard for what makes the state distinctive in its own right other than what is determined by its potential for power.

In opposition to the civilization-indifferent strategy are the two value-oriented strategies(constructivism), each of which in its own way attaches great importance to cultural values, though with points of departure in two very different interpretations of civilization. The first, the"civilization-conservative strategy," operates with a cultural relativist concept of civilization like that known from the work of Samuel P. Huntington: civilizations are different and mutually exclude each other, which means that they can only exist in the same world in accordance with the motto that each is self-contained and minds its own affairs

– that is, as long as states are not engaged in competition or conflict over power, values or resources. If conflict arises, the sole strategy for survival is to wipe out the other, if necessary, by war. This strategy is, in other words, based on shifts of regimes by which "the other" is eradicated and replaced by someone made in one's own image.[5]

The third strategy is referred to as the "civilization-promoting strategy" here. It is based on a universal concept of civilization according to which there are in principle no fundamental oppositions among cultures, only differences which can be overcome through dialogue. Within a civilization extremists can be found in the form of states as well as groups and individuals, and these must be fought through missionizing or through international and national systems of justice. While war is a necessary and preferred defense strategy in the civilization-conservative strategy, the civilization-promoting school primarily as a punitive measure in connection with diplomacy and international cooperation uses military might.[6]

The two value-oriented strategies can be traced back to ideologies expounded by the earlypioneers of North America, according to Carl Pedersen, a scholar of American culture and history, in his book Den sårbare nation [The Vulnerable Nation] from 2002: "The pioneer mentality that developed throughout the nineteenth century is the seed of the present unilateralism with its emphasis on traditional American virtues and resistance to cultural exchange with corruptive foreign countries. This contrasts with the more multilateral traditions of the east coast, which in accordance with a puritanical, missionizing self-conception had to come in contact with the outside world, in order thereby to improve it."[7]

The former has in recent times been represented by administrations such as Ronald Reagan's (1981 – 1989) and George W. Bush's (2001 –), while Jimmy Carter's (1977 – 1981) and, mutatis mutandis, Bill Clinton's (1993 – 2001) are examples of the latter understanding of foreign policy, although one has to admit that it is difficult to see Clinton as a puritan. If one replaces the idea of an "evangelical enthusiasm for the mission" with such concepts as human rights, democracy, market economics and free trade, it is probably easier to connect the idea of a "missionizing self conception" with Clinton the libertine.

I. IN THE NAME OF CIVILIZATION

Both Reagan's and George W. Bush's ideologically anchored conservatism and Clinton's liberal internationalism build on a large investment in the concept of civilization, which nevertheless is promoted and interpreted very differently according to whether one belongs to the Republican right wing or sees oneself as a modern, liberal Democrat.

REAGAN BETWEEN IDEALISM AND REALPOLITIK: THE CIVILIZATION-CONSERVATIVE STRATEGY

The Reagan administration, which regarded the Cold War as an actual war that had to be won at any price, attached great importance to an ideological value base, which meant that security policy was explicitly formulated in clear – some might say dogmatic – moral concepts: the Soviet Union was the "Evil Empire," Libya's President Kadafi was, according to Reagan, a barbarian who was part of the worldwide Islamic fundamentalist movement, and George Bush's Vice President, Dan Quayle, in a speech in Maryland in 1990 could see a direct link between "the rise of Communism, the rise of Nazism and the rise of radical Islamic fundamentalism."[8]

Reagan's uncompromising and confrontational attitude towards Islamic fundamentalism and states in the Middle East which challenged American interests was followed up by a foreign policy in which the USA was willing to go alone in defending the free world. This was clearly evident in the case of Libya: the USA had Britain's permission to use English bases as points of departure for bombings but disregarded protests from NATO allies such as France and West Germany.[9]

Despite Reagan's many attacks on Islamic fundamentalism, which was, according to Shultz, identical with "radical extremism,"[10] the Reagan administration never formulated an actual policy towards political Islam, but devoted all its attention to the Cold War against the Soviet Union.[11] It was this evil that it aimed to eradicate, and this was to be done through uncompromising confrontation with the Communist superpower and its proselytes around the world, including the Middle East.

It is interesting to see how the strong emphasis on and defense of

American virtues and values and their superiority in relation to political Islam was completely transformed into "cool realpolitik" under Reagan, becoming a matter of finding alliance partners in South Asia and the Middle East in the fight against Communism. It was the conservative Islamic states, such as the fundamentalistic Saudi Arabia and the Emirates in the Persian Gulf on which Reagan relied in the containment of the Soviet Union.

Even the Islamic Republic of Iran was an object of Reagan's realpolitik, since it was believed that the Republic could be won over to the side of the free world in the fight against Communism. And at the same time, the USA could obtain the release of the American hostages held captive in Lebanon by the Iran-backed Hizbollah group. To make accounts balance, the USA sold arms to Iran, which was officially prohibited by an arms embargo, while profits were secretly to be sent to the militias in El Salvador fighting the socialistic Sandanist regime in Nicaragua, which likewise was contrary to a Presidential order explicitly prohibiting the overthrow of foreign governments.[12]

The plot, with its mix of value-driven combat against Communism and power-oriented realpolitik, was further complicated by the fact that in the Iraq-Iran war from 1980 to 1988, Reagan and his special Middle East envoy, Donald Rumsfeld, officially supported the otherwise Soviet-friendly Iraq with arms, and also – unofficially, of course – turned a blind eye to Iraq's production and use of chemical weapons.[13] Their support of Iraq was a result of the fact that the USA had gotten on a regular collision course with Iran following the Islamic revolution in 1979 against the country's American-backed regime, the kidnapping of a good 50 Americans through the occupation of the American embassy from November 1979 to January 1981, and the fear that Iran would export the revolution to the entire region.[14]

Political Islam may have been an evil, but from the perspective of the Reagan administration, it was a lesser evil than Communism; therefore, allying oneself with Islamists was acceptable, if the purpose was to keep the Evil Empire down and prevented from accessing the oceans via the Gulf as well as the oil resources that provide the free world with cheap energy. With regard to Iran, Reagan's realpolitik ended in scandal, while support for the most radical Mujahidin bore fruit in the beginning when the Soviet Union gave up and withdrew completely from the Afghan mountains in 1989.[15]

The history of this, in brief, is that in December of 1979 the Soviet Union invaded Afghanistan in order to help the socialist regimes there remain in power. The invasion provoked strong reactions in the USA, which feared that the Kremlin's intentions were first to gain control over Afghanistan, which lies in an area of interest to the Soviets, in order then to continue along the 400 kilometers to the Persian Gulf and secure the attractive access to the ice-free ports. The USA's persistent efforts since World War II to keep the Soviet Union away from precisely the Gulf are due to the conviction that if the Communists were to gain access there to the seas, they could secure dominance over the world seas and thereby achieve global power.[16] Naturally, the fact that two-thirds of the world's known and easily accessible high quality oil resources were located in the Gulf region also played a crucial role in American geopolitical interest there. Since the Eisenhower Doctrine of 1957, therefore, the USA has reserved the right to employ military force should the superpower's national security interests be perceived as threatened.

Via the Muslim country of Pakistan and the Islamic fundamentalistic Saudi Arabia, Reagan implemented a campaign that involved training Mujahidin in guerrilla warfare and supplying them with effective weapons. As of 1986, these included the Stinger missile, which was capable of shooting down the Soviet Hind helicopter, and thus were of vital importance for the fact that the luck of war turned to the advantage of the Mujahidin. In all, the USA sent 900 Stinger missiles to Afghanistan in the period 1986-1987, and in the years 1980-1989, the USA backed the Islamic resistance movement with more than $2 billion.

The goal of the support was achieved with the withdrawal of the Soviet Union in 1989, but at the same time, Reagan's policy in Afghanistan contributed to the building of the Islamic networks that both throughout the 1990's supplied the conflicts in the Middle East, Central Asia, the Caucasus, Africa and South East Asia with Mujahidin and were behind terrorist attacks on the USA – not least the attacks on September 11th, 2001.

Ronald Reagan's foreign policy was fundamentally determined by his simple but unshakable faith in the time-honored, conservative, American values that were threatened by Communism, which therefore was the enemy against which all efforts were made to fight. In the service of this primary cause, the USA thus allied itself with groups and states which ideologically certainly were not apart of the American civilization, but which could be used in the fight against the Evil Empire – a conflict which in Condoleezza Rice's formulation actually had to be seen as a fight for survival.

Thus the USA appeared on the one hand to have both great moral integrity and military might in the unwavering fight against Communism, and on the other hand to be shady and vulnerable to both critique and asymmetrical threats with regard to the ad-hoc alliances. The Mujahideen, for example, were an excellent ally in the fight against the Soviet Union, though it would subsequently be seen that the USA had at the same time nourished a viper at its own breast, so to speak. This fedanti-Americanism in the region and was used by USA-critical intellectuals and scholars in Europe to call up an image of the superpower as a giant, which stumbled around, aimlessly in the regional conflicts of the world. This is a criticism, which of course only holds up when the primary role of the USA in the Cold War – facilitating the triumph over Communism – is ignored.

BUSH'S INTERNATIONAL PRAGMATISM: THE CIVILIZATION INDIFFERENT STRATEGY

Policy makers who adhere to a pragmatic activism in international politics can be found particularly among middle-ground Republicans who desire to promote American interests, whether economic or in matters of security, through international cooperation. And here, greater weight is given to loyalty than to values. In spite of a harsh attack on Saddam Hussein comparing him with Adolf Hitler, the Bush administration from 1989 to 1992 – with people such as Secretary of State James Baker and National Security Advisor Brent Scowcroft in leading positions supported by Joint Chief of Staff Colin Powell

– was largely characterized as taking a pragmatic and international-alliance-oriented course.

In their views of the Middle East there was little if any worry that close allies like Egypt and Saudi Arabia had major problems with the practice of democracy, as long as they loyally supported American policy. At the same time, Bush and Baker did not refrain from putting pressure on Israel when they deemed it necessary.[17] In extension of Condoleezza Rice's remarks, it can be said that Bush stood for a realistically oriented foreign policy, but because of the war against Iraq and the burgeoning crisis in Algeria he was pressured into formulating value-oriented principles regarding democracy and political Islam which nevertheless had little influence on policy actually implemented. Greater importance was attached to security interests than to ideological principles.

Ronald Reagan's Vice President, George Bush, took office at a time when the Cold War was rapidly coming to its end and when expectations for the future were marked by belief in peace and cooperation. The free world had triumphed; it was time to cooperate, within a framework provided by the UN, on the resolution of international conflicts as they might arise in the future. Internationalists thus dominated foreign policy.

Bush himself had a career as ambassador in China and Director of the CIA behind him. Secretary of State James Baker and Security Adviser Bent Scowcroft also belonged to the internationalistic wing of the Republican Party and gave high priority to cooperation rather than to an ideologically cemented unilateralism in pursuit of American security interests. Scowcroft also held the position of National Security Advisor in Gerald Ford's administration, but under Bush assumed a much more prominent and influential role.

The will to cooperate internationally was demonstrated clearly in connection with the political handling of Iraq's occupation of Kuwait August 2nd 1990. The entire course of events was managed by the book, from the first resolution in the UN Security Council, which condemned the Iraqi aggression, to international support for submitting Iraq to economic sanctions and making it clear that the UN would play a leading role in military action if Saddam Hussein did not withdraw from Kuwait, to the actual war and subsequent resolutions.

Particularly the formation of the international alliance in 1990 stands out as an exceptional diplomatic achievement in which Bush and Baker succeeded in getting such normally irreconcilable countries as Iran and Saudi Arabia, Syria, Israel and Egypt to join the alliance and thereby de facto to cooperate. The demands on the various countries differed: Israel, for example, was to refrain from military reaction to the 29 Scud missiles fired by Iraq at Tel Aviv and Jerusalem, and it was vital for Iran to remain neutral in the conflict.

The success of the alliance was owed to the fact that the individual countries had more to gain by not creating obstacles to American efforts to build alliances than by the reverse – which Jordan and Yemen were to discover after the Gulf War. Both countries were at risk of internal unrest and destabilization if they backed the USA and the West in a war against an Arab country, so they opposed military action against Saddam Hussein. The USA and its European allies perceived this as support for Saddam Hussein, with the result that they were penalized after the war both economically and by international political isolation.

The same fate befell the Palestinian Liberation Organization (PLO), whose leader, Yassir Arafat, had paid a heartfelt visit to Saddam in Baghdad at the highest point of the conflict. Then, when the war came, Palestinians in the occupied areas on the West Bank and in Gaza could be seen on the roofs of their ramshackle buildings cheering each time Iraq managed to strike Israel with a Scud missile. For the PLO, too, isolation and economic punishment were the result of support for the loser of the war.

A key reason that Baker and Bush could with few exceptions keep the alliance together was the general expectation that the USA along with the Soviet Union would sponsor a comprehensive peace process in the Middle East when Iraq had been driven from Kuwait. This expectation came after Saddam Hussein had pointed out the double standard according to which Israel had been able to occupy Palestinian land since 1967 despite the UN Security Council's repeated orders for Israel to withdraw. The orders did not result in threats of military force from the USA, the West or the UN, although it was precisely such threats to which Iraq was subjected after the occupation of Kuwait.

Saddam, in other words, wanted answers to questions which to most people seemed reasonable, and Bush's reaction was to guarantee that the USA and the Soviet Union would take the initiative in a "comprehensive peace process in the Middle East" following the Gulf War.[18]

When the war ended, diligent diplomatic efforts by the Americans were seen, and James Baker in particular worked hard to get the parties to agree to participation in a peace conference for the Middle East that was held already in Madrid in November 1991. The PLO was in a weak position, and Yassir Arafat had to agree to the Palestinians' being represented by policy makers from the occupied areas and not from the PLO's headquarters in Tunis. The Palestinians, moreover, did not get their own delegation but were included in Jordan's.[19]

By the same token, Israel was under intense pressure to accept not only the participation of a Palestinian delegation but one that counted members from Jerusalem, including the spokeswoman Hanan Ashrawi from the city's Palestinian elite and political top. The Israelis' objection to the participation of Palestinians from the Holy City stemmed from the fact that they had formally annexed East Jerusalem in 1981 and therefore resisted the symbolism inherent in the representation of Palestinians from Jerusalem. The USA and the Israeli government were also at odds with each other over the conditions of the loan for which Israel applied, and which Bush and Baker granted on the condition that "not one cent would go to settlements."[20]

The Bush government also succeeded in persuading Syria to participate at Madrid and begin bilateral negotiations with Israel. It had always been Israel's strategy to negotiate individually with its opponents in order thus to split the Arab world; this had succeeded with Egypt in the Camp David peace in 1979, but now Syria, one of the most radical Arab states in relation to Israel, sat alone at the table in direct negotiations with its arch enemy.

The Bush government thus displayed impressive diplomatic performance both in the Persian Gulf and in Israeli-Arab relations, including the conflict over Palestine. For the USA, the Gulf and Israel have in the past as well as the present formed the two pillars of American Middle East policy, in relation to which each new administration in Washington has had to formulate a political strategy. In both areas Bush, with his pragmatic policy of alliance building, was seen in 1991 to turn conflict – Iraq's occupation of Kuwait and the Palestinian uprising of 1987 – to negotiations with broad international backing.

About the time that the Cold War was coming to a close, a new phenomenon was making itself felt with increasingly greater importunity, necessitating an actual political stance in Washington. This phenomenon was political Islam.

It was certainly not entirely new, because for years Egypt had been familiar with the challenge – which both was political and manifested itself in political violence and terrorism – from Islamic fundamentalism. It was precisely an Islamic group, al-Jihad that was behind the assassination in 1981 of the country's President, Anwar Sadat, as punishment for his entering into the Camp Dave peace with Israel.

It was also an Islamic revolution in Iran in 1979 that with one stroke made one of the USA's closest allies in the region its greatest enemy. In addition to the breaking off of diplomatic relations between the USA and Iran, the change of political system in Iran led to the hostage crisis at the American embassy, an issue that particularly influenced American relations to Iran. The revolution also produced offshoots in Lebanon and Hizbollah's kidnappings in Beirut during the 1980's.

After having been overshadowed by the Cold War for years, the Islamic challenge began to stand out in the light of the new world order – not least because on the one hand it focused attention on the lack of political reforms in the Middle East, and on the other schematized the relationship between Islam and democracy.

Because the war against Saddam Hussein was finally waged in the name of democracy and the free world, it became more and more difficult to disregard the fact that the countries the West was defending were actually among the most undemocratic countries in the world. This was the case not least with Saudi Arabia and the smaller Gulf states, which is why an increasingly great demand for political change there was seen.

CLINTON — DIALOGUE AND A DEMOCRATIC MISSION: THE CIVILIZATION-PROMOTING STRATEGY

Despite his successes in foreign policy, George Bush did not succeed in getting re-elected as President during the 1992 elections. Yet the international arena that Bush left to his successor, Bill Clinton, was characterized by optimism and belief in progress in all areas: Bush was on good terms with the Soviet General Secretary, Mikhail Gorbatjov, and it was allegedly in council with him that Bush formulated his vision of the New World Order on September 11th, 1990.[21] The following year the Soviet Union was gone; the Berlin Wall had been dismantled in 1989, the UN had led a – by all appearances – successful campaign in the Gulf, and in 1991 it had actually been possible to hold a major conference on peace in the Middle East that introduced negotiations between Israel, the Palestinians and their Arab neighbors.

Everything at the beginning of the 1990's indicated that the world was heading towards better times in which the UN and the USA would be able to work together to tackle the conflicts that might arise in the future. The world picture, however, was not, of course, entirely rosy – especially not if seen from more peripheral areas in Africa, South America and Asia, where poverty, misery and armed conflicts could in fact be found.

Nor in those regions favored by the Western states and their media was the world free of conflict: civil war had broken out in Algeria in 1992 and many feared that it could spread to other countries in North Africa, perhaps even to southern Europe. From 1992 radical Islamic groups in Egypt were seen targeting terrorist activities against Western tourists. And in the Balkans the situation threatened to develop into war, conflict and ethnic cleansing after the Soviet Union had dismantled and no longer held the region in its tight grip. From Washington in 1992 and 1993, however, these problems were seen as being limited and manageable, and in any case did not pose the level of threat that had been felt during the Cold War.

Understandably, the Americans began to look inward and grant higher priority to domestic problems than to problems outside of home. This was the agenda on which the Democrat Bill Clinton had focused in his triumphant election campaign in 1992. After his entree into the White House, it was on such typical domestic issues as education and health that the Clinton administration concentrated, and according to rumors in Washington, Clinton appointed Warren Christopher as Secretary of State with an order not to "put foreign policy in the headlines."

It was noticed that Clinton somewhat uncustomary chose less well-known people for national security advisors, since neither Anthony Lake nor his deputy and later successor Sandy Berger had had major profiles in Washington's security-political jet set before their appointments to office. In a way it seemed as if Clinton only wanted to support the positive momentum that characterized foreign policy by using the potential in the possibilities created by globalization for economic integration and the free movement of goods. In brief, it was a geoeconomic strategy that saw free trade and market economics as the path to stability and international cooperation based on the selfdetermination of nations, respect for human rights and the promotion of democracy.

This "new Wilsonism," named after President Woodrow Wilson – who precisely during the peace settlements following the First World War insisted on the idea of the self-determination of nations – was summarized in Clinton's A National Security Strategy of Engagement and Enlargement from 1996.[22] Instead of pointing to the strategic threats against the USA, the paper argued for market economics and enlargement of the group of democratic countries as a basis for global security – incidentally, resembling closely the philosophy which in the fall of 2002 was behind the EU's historic expansion towards the East with the admission of ten new countries from the previous Soviet bloc.

CLINTON'S UNIVERSAL CONCEPT OF CIVILIZATION

In the context of the history of ideas, Clinton's enlargement strategy was based on a universal concept of civilization: that is, in principle we all inhabit the same civilization, though this takes many cultural forms, without, however, standing in the way of possibilities for dialogue and solidarity. Time and time again Clinton and his advisors rejected Samuel P. Huntington's thesis of the "clash of civilizations" and pointed instead to a universal understanding of dialogue. Or put another way: dialogue is principally always a dialogue within a civilization and not among civilizations.

The American social scientist and professor Francis Fukuyama had already in 1989 argued for the same idea under the heading "The End of History," an article for The National Interest which was later developed into a book.[23] The idea here was not of course that history would come to a halt, in the sense that events would no longer take place, but that history would at some point in time achieve the ultimate goal, which would occur, according to Fukuyama, when all the countries in the world had developed into liberal democracies. With the fall of the Berlin Wall and the dissolution of the Soviet Union and the Eastern bloc, this goal seemed within reach and, one could add, Clinton's idea of "enlargement" would push the process forward.

In his book, Fukuyama drew on the idea put forth by the German philosopher Immanuel Kant of the eternal peace that could be achieved in a global community consisting of democratic states.[24] Yet it was especially Kant's German heir in idealism, George Wilhelm Friedrich Hegel, who provided the philosophical foundation for Fukuyama's ideas on history: in spite of war and conflict, oppression and exploitation, we are all part of the unrolling of history, which in Hegel's interpretation is defined as the long road from the birth of the concept of freedom as an abstract idea in the East to its concrete unfolding in the West with the development of the modern state.[25]

There is a direct connection between the thought of Fukuyama, Hegel and Kant and the French Enlightenment philosophy from the middle of the eighteenth century that formulated precisely the idea of civilization as the norm for the social life of human beings. With the concept of civilization, the Enlightenment philosophers created a unified vision of human beings' relation to nature, their relations with each other and with themselves individually as being determined by reason or rationality in accordance with the French world for reason, raison.[26]

Human beings' relation to nature was to be determined by dominance over nature through the development of technology and science.

Human beings' relations with each other, according to the vision, were to be regulated through a rationalization of rights and ethics, whereby actions would be evaluated on the basis of concepts of "right" and "wrong" rather than "good" and "evil."

Finally, the human being in relation to himself should have the opportunities for selfexpression through art or by other means, written or spoken.

This conception had significance both as a vision for the future and in relation to "the others," those who did not (yet) belong to civilization, but who, through a civilizing process, could come to do so. The enlargement of civilization could thus both occur over time, namely in the form of progress toward increasingly more civilization, and in space, namely by civilizing "the wild."

France's policy in Algeria emerges here as something close to a paradigmatic example, as the country, following the French victory, was annexed and transformed to a French county and subjected to French norms and the French language, French schools and an insistent French secularization. In the form it took in French Enlightenment thought, civilization was thus a normative concept, but it must also be pointed out here that at the same time, an interpretation of the concept of critique, with Jean Jacques Rousseau as the most famous critic of civilization, was being developed. That civilization was understood as normative means that the concept established norms for human beings' relation to nature as one of dominance over it; human beings' relations to each other through as based on ethical rules founded on reason and a system of justice; and the human being's relation to himself as an autonomous and authoritative individual, as in Kant's definition.[27]

The fact that critique formulated specifically as a critique of civilization gained footing at the same time reflected the way that civilization not only was an expression of progress but could also contain its darker aspects in the form of humans' alienation from nature, the marginalization of minorities from the common good and the leaving of individuals to their own isolation.

Although the concept of civilization in the plural, "civilizations," did occasionally occur in the work of the French philosophers, it was characteristic to think of civilization in universal terms, which meant essentially that everyone could engage in dialogue with everyone else. Civilization was something one could learn. In this regard, a crucial point is that actions were to be judged according to concepts such as "right" and "wrong" because they could thereby be influenced and changed; this was obviously important in designing foreign policy: it is possible to influence and change states and nations in order that they can comply with the fundamental norms governing ideas about civilization, simply because they all take part in the universal civilization, regardless of where they are.[28]

The conclusions of this kind of thought are there do not exist several civilizations and that the idea of a Judeo-Christian or an Islamic civilization is simply wrong; yet cultural and religious differences can of course be identified within civilization. There is thus a difference between civilization and culture, where culture can come to expression in many ways but is principally changeable and adaptable.

This understanding of civilization was a guiding force in the Clinton administration's efforts to formulate a policy with regard both to political Islam and to the conflicts in the Middle East on which the government initially could not avoid taking stance, and which later became one of Clinton's primary areas of concern. While Reagan had not formulated a unified policy and Bush made do with his Assistant of State for Near East Affairs Edward P. Djerejian's speech[29], it was practically a must for Clinton and his security advisors to take a position on the Middle East, including Islamic fundamentalism. A good part of the way they continued along the course plotted by Djerejian, distinguishing between moderate and radical/extremist Islamic groups. In the beginning this actually led Clinton and his staff to initiate a dialogue with the groups they viewed as moderate, such as the Muslim Brotherhood in Egypt and FIS in Algeria.[30] But following severe criticism from the governments of the two countries, Washington discontinued the dialogue, though in the years that followed Clinton encouraged France and Algeria to engage in dialogue with the moderate Islamists.

The fundamental view was that the USA had no issue with Islam, but that on the contrary, devout Christians and faithful Muslims had many attributes in common, such as temperance, high moral standards and strong family ties. The radical Muslims behind terrorist activities did not really have anything to do with Islam but exploited the religion for political purposes, or, as Clinton said, "The Traditional values of Islam – devotion to faith and good works, to family and society – are in harmony with the best of American ideals. Therefore, we know our people, our faiths; our cultures can live in harmony with each other".[31] A great deal of reserve was displayed when explaining terror and Islamic violence in cultural terms, and they were viewed as a result of the social problems brought about by processes of modernization everywhere.

Security Advisor Anthony Lake expanded Djerejian's framework of understanding to categorize Muslim states as either radical or moderate. The former, called "backlash" states in a well-known article by Lake in the journal *Foreign Affairs*, had to be contained, while dialogue and cooperation with the latter should be encouraged by the USA. Rogue states were countries like Iran, Iraq, Sudan and Libya, while Egypt and Saudi Arabia belonged to the moderate group.[32] The idea was that extremism could be fought by means of a double strategy entailing first and foremost the promotion of the process between Israel and the Palestinians. Progress in this area would weaken political motives for joining the radical groups and would release economic resources – there was talk of a peace dividend – which would improve socioeconomic conditions and thus remove the recruitment base for extremist Islamists.

Secondly, the strategy entailed isolating or encapsulating the radical states, where attention was focused particularly on Iran and Iraq. As early as in 1993, the same year in which Clinton moved into the White House, Martin Indyk, the Director of the Middle East office in the National Security Council, formulated a strategy on double containment in the Gulf: consistent sanctions and military pressure on Iran and Iraq. The rogue states lay out of reach in relation to the civilization-promoting project, but this did not mean that they did not possess the necessary civilizing potential to develop into full-blooded members of the universal civilization. Containment and sanctions by way of the international justice system would serve to promote democratic forces.[33]

Clinton attempted to incorporate the European NATO countries as well as Russia and China in his Middle East policy, but without success. He had difficulty living up to his own rhetoric, for although the headlines spoke of dialogue and combating terrorism, Clinton's policy remained for the most part on the level of realpolitik without achieving results in the Middle East.

In spite of the fact that Middle East-based terrorism pursued Clinton – with attacks on Americans in the Gulf, Yemen and East Africa and with sabotage against the peace process from his first days in the White House until he handed the office and a Middle East in deep crisis over to George W. Bush in 2001 – Clinton maintained a policy for fighting terror that gave priority to the civil justice system. It is true that he had sent cruise missiles towards Osama bin Laden's camps in Afghanistan in 1998 and, as revenge for the terrorist attack on the embassies in East Africa, bombed a factory in Sudan that the USA believed produced chemical weapons. But these were limited actions, "bombs in the sand," that were exceptions to Clinton's rule to prosecute terrorists as he had done with the persons behind the World Trade Center attack in 1993 and those who had been arrested after the bombings in East Africa in 1998.

But precisely this strategy, by which in a best case scenario it is only the actual perpetrators and not the master-minds who are hit, was, along with the fact that Clinton completely gave up on the Iraq problem and failed in the Oslo process, a great source of frustration and critique for his political opposition. When Clinton handed over the White House to Bush, the Oslo process lay in ruins and a bloody conflict between the Israelis and Palestinians with a daily loss of human life had superseded negotiations. In Iraq, Saddam Hussein was more secure in power than ever before, and it was likewise obvious that the sanctions against the country only served to strengthen his hold. And outside the port city of Aden in Yemen an American warship was torpedoed by a rubber boat filled with explosives, which was followed by repeated threats which caused the American forces in the Gulf to remain on the highest state of alert.[34]

Clinton's strategy of containment in the Gulf and the placing of such high stakes on the belief that the peace process in the Palestinian conflict was the key to detente in the Middle East were completely amiss, and it was logical that the new Bush government would try different paths. There are several reasons for Clinton's failure, but there is much to indicate that his government did not have the room for political maneuvering that was necessary in order to carry out the necessary decisions and set forth the visions that could have changed the agenda for Israel and the Palestinians. The President was probably much too limited by the influential Israeli lobby and the interests it shared with the Republican majority in Congress.

Many as the most characterized the Clinton administration Israel-friendly ever, with a large representation by persons affiliated with the American-Jewish interest group, American Israel Public Affairs Committee (AIPAC) in key posts in the State Department and in the White House.

It was people such as Clinton's chief negotiator in the Middle East, Dennis Ross, and Martin Indyk, who under Clinton managed to direct the Middle East Office in the National Security Council and in the State Department and twice function as the USA's ambassador in Israel, who were the architects behind Clinton's Middle East policy. Prior to taking office in the Clinton administration Indyk was employed as the director for the pro-Israeli think tank the Washington Institute for Near East Policy, a post which Dennis Ross took over when he left the State Department at the end of Clinton's presidency. Martin Indyk moved to the Brookings Institute, which in several areas works closely with the Washington Institute, where thanks to a large grant he was able to establish a research program with focus on democratization in the Middle East.

BUSH — NEOCONSERVATIVE ACTIVISM IN THE MIDDLE EAST: RESUMPTION OF REAGAN'S CIVILIZATION-CONSERVATIVE STRATEGY

The speculations began as early as the presidential election campaign in the spring of 2000. The guessing games, not surprisingly, were centered around the standpoints of a coming Bush administration; most people expected a government under Al Gore to continue the line Clinton had laid, concentrating on international collaboration and agreements, and unequivocal support for Israel (with a preference for a middle-of-the-road position in Israeli politics and emphasis on dialogue with the Palestinians).

Whilst there was some nervousness in the AIPAC, certain optimism was evident among Israeli critics with the prospect of a new Republican government. Although it had been Bush Snr who been responsible for Middle East politics before Clinton, many expected the son to follow in his father's foot steps. Quite simply because the only people who were known with any certainty to be guaranteed top positions in a new Bush government were the familiar faces from his father's cabinet.

There was Richard Cheney, Defense Secretary during the Gulf War and candidate for the job of Vice President. Cheney was expected to continue the policy of that time, encouraged incidentally by his barely disguised business interests in the Middle East oil industry.

The coming Secretary of State, Colin Powell, Joint Chief of Staff during the Gulf War, had actually been against the war with Iraq and was known for being a cautious general who placed higher priority on international collaboration than bombers.

Bush's security advisor, Condoleezza Rice was an unknown factor in the Middle East question but had received an excellent reference from internationalists like Bush Snr and his Security Advisor Brent Scowcroft in their joint memoirs.[35] Rice's background was as a researcher in Russian and Eastern European affairs at the prestigious Stanford University in California, where she was professor and provost until she joined Bush's election campaign. On several occasions, Rice revealed, with some unfortunate statements, that there were certain gaps in her knowledge oft he Middle East. Nonetheless, she would turn out to be of great influence in the new Bush administration, where, according to Bob Woodward in his book *Bush at War*, she was the coordinator of foreign policy in the White House.

Among pro-Palestinian and pro-Arab circles, therefore, there was a certain optimism for the new Bush government. But it dwindled somewhat as it slowly but surely became apparent what people were occupying the offices in the National Security Council, the Pentagon and the State Department. Rumsfeld and Wolfowitz were the front rank fighters in the Department of Defence and a minor exodus of people followed them from the neo-conservative think tank, the American Enterprise Institute (AEI).

It fairly quickly became clear that the Bush government had a very different agenda from the one presented by Bush Snr ten years previously. In the Israeli-Palestinian conflict, George W. Bush kept his election promises and left the arena to the belligerents. With the people he had placed in the Pentagon, who in former years had thundered against Clinton's abortive attempts to control Saddam Hussein, it was also clear that a tough and confrontational Iraq policy could be expected.

During his first foreign visit, a courtesy visit to Mexico less than a month after assuming the office of President, Bush's first active step in foreign policy was to order the bombing of Baghdad. His justification in so doing was that Iraq had deployed sophisticated Chinese radar that represented a threat to the American and British fighters that held Iraq under surveillance. The bombs were accompanied by sharp threats that the USA would not hesitate to attack Iraq if Saddam did not stay in line.

So it was plain from the start of Bush's period of office in Washington that he would pursue a hard line on Iraq and both he and the people in the Department of Defense left nobody in doubt that they wanted to see a change of regime in Baghdad. As early as the spring of 2001, many people therefore expected a conflict to arise between the USA and Iraq that would eventually bring about the fall of Saddam, whether that would be the result of a coup or American bombs was irrelevant.

In his relations with Iran, Bush initially showed more compliance than his predecessor Clinton and started by proposing that the so-called

ILSA legislation (Iran-Libya Sanctions Act of 1996), which was to be renegotiated in June 2001, be extended for only one year instead of five. The legislation threatens boycott of anti-American companies that invested more than USD 40 million in Iran. But the Bush government was voted down by Congress who insisted on a five-year period, sticking to the hard line in Iran policy laid by Clinton. Nevertheless, it is worth pointing out that the Bush government, only six months or so before Bush coined the term 'the axis of evil' in his State of the Union speech january 2002, had sent signals of a highly conciliatory policy on Iran.

BUSH'S GRAND STRATEGY IN THE MIDDLE EAST

Prior to 11 September, the world was thus somewhat confused about what to expect from Bush in terms of the Middle East. People's attention was grabbed by the obvious differences in interpretation of the global situation by the Pentagon and the State Department and especially by the political measures that might be adopted. And there was uncertainty about what role Rice played and what line she would support.

But as early as six months after Bush's inauguration it became evident that the new American government was patently more right wing as it was under Bush Snr, and that it would not hesitate to go it alone in international politics when it deemed necessary. Examples that the USA meant what it said are the American rejection of the Kyoto Agreement, the distancing from an international court for war crimes, the plain-text message that the USA, with or without international understanding or support, would abandon the ABM Treaty, and its unshakeable intention to develop a missile defense system, despite uncertainty about which system was regarded as the best.

In addition to these direct signals and despite colossal tax reliefs to the most comfortably off, Bush announced considerable increases in the defense budget.[36] As far back as 1999 negotiations on a new strategic concept for NATO, it had been made clear what were regarded as the greatest threats since the Cold War – rogue states, global terrorism and weapons of mass destruction. It was these threats would equip the American defence structure to face and it was this, even before 11 September that lay behind the weighty demands for an increase in the national defense budget.

"The regimes in control of these "rogue" states – a term used widely before the last administration substituted the flaccid term "states of concern" – pose an immediate threat to the United States. The first priority of American policy must be to transform or destroy rogue regimes." Richard Perle gave this unambiguous recommendation at a Senate hearing in February 2002.[37] This old and bold Cold War warrior is not without a certain status – during the Reagan administration, in which he served as Deputy Secretary of Defense with responsibility for international security policy, he was dubbed "The Prince of Darkness" because of his uncompromising confrontational policy towards the Soviet Union. His recipe for breaking the Communist superpower was continually to increase the military strength of the USA

Under Bush, Perle became Chairman of the Pentagon's Policy Committee, member of a number of highly influential networks with close links to organs such as Middle East Forum, Jewish Institute for National Security Affairs (JINSA) and Center for Security Policy (CSP). He also assumed the role of ideological mentor for the strongly pro-Israeli politicians with close links to Christian fundamentalists on the right wing of the Republican Party. Together with Defense Secretary Rumsfeld, Deputy Defense Secretary Wolfowitz and Vice President Richard Cheney, Perle was the architect behind the new American Middle East policy that became even clearer after 11 September.[38]

The key elements were close ties with the Israeli right wing, support for the Israeli Prime Minister Ariel Sharon's militant policy against the Palestinians and demands for regime changes in the Middle East – in Iraq, Palestine, Iran, Syria, Lebanon or even Saudi Arabia and Egypt, as these latter two seemed unable themselves to implement the necessary reforms that would serve the interests of the USA.

As member of the board of directors of the right-wing Israeli Likud newspaper Jerusalem Post, Perle had close links to the Israeli right wing and never made any secret of the fact that he, like Douglas Feith and

David and Meyrav Wurmser, regarded the Oslo process as a plague that threatened Israel's security and that should be stopped as soon as possible. David Wurmser was director of the Middle East program in the neo-conservative think tank AEI and, together with another of its associated researchers, Laurie Mylroie, had made himself spokesman for the view that the driving force behind conflicts and terrorism in the Middle East was Iraq.

In 2000, Mylroie published the book *Study of Revenge*, in which she made Iraq responsible for the terrorist attack on the World Trade Center in 1993 and claimed that Saddam Hussein and Osama bin Laden collaborated on terrorist activity in the USA.[39] Her book created quite a stir and when it was reprinted after 11 September, it sold like hot cakes. Feith had also worked closely with Perle both in the AEI and the Reagan Department of Defense was also one the movers and shakers in Washington for the passing of the legislation for Iraq's liberation in 1998. This allocated USD 97 million to support Iraqi opposition in a coup against Hussein. When Bush assumed power, Feith was appointed Under-secretary of Defence with responsibility for drafting a national security policy.

It was not just in the Pentagon that Perle's friends from neo-conservative circles had found important jobs. They also occupied posts in the State Department, where, for example, yet another AEI colleague, John Bolton, was permanent Under-secretary of State responsible for arms control. Before his appointment, Bolton was known in Washington as an opponent of the ABM treaty and a critic of the idea of an international war crimes court.

With the massive influx of neo-conservative bigwigs, it could not have come as a surprise to many that the new Bush administration was to follow a very different line from that of his predecessor Bill Clinton. But it did take some unawares that many of the people Bush tasked to steer policy in Defense and State were not recruited from the ranks of his father's henchmen but from those who had wintered on the political sidelines since the Reagan era.

One of their most important issues was fierce criticism of the Oslo process and of Clinton's understanding with the Israeli Labor party of setting any priority at all for negotiations with the Palestinians. If Israel were to enter negotiations, then it would only be from a position of absolute strength, and that was not the case in the 1990s, so ideally the Oslo process had to be stopped.

With the election of Benjamin Netanyahu, a sworn opponent of negotiations with the Palestinians, as Prime Minister of Israel in 1996, Washington neo-conservatives eyed the chance of putting a spoke in the wheel of the Oslo peace process. Shortly after Likud's landslide victory, Perle and his friends wrote a paper that was formed as an actual recommendation to Netanyahu. Apart from Perle, it was signed, among others, by James Colbert (JINSA), Douglas Feith and the Wurmsers, and entitled *A clean Break*, which was to be understood purely and simply as a definitive withdrawal from the Oslo process.[40] On the very first page there was a call for Israel to "work closely with Turkey and Jordan to contain, destabilize and roll-back some of its most dangerous threats. This implies clean break from the slogan, "comprehensive peace" to a traditional concept of strategy based on balance of power". It went on to say that Israel should "change the nature of its relations with the Palestinians, including upholding the *right of hot pursuit* for self defense into all Palestinian areas and nurturing alternatives to Arafat's exclusive grip on Palestinian society" (original's italics).

The paper also recommended that Israel made itself economically independent of the USA, as its safety could only be guaranteed through its own military strength.

Finally, it pointed out the necessity for the USA and Israel to force a change of regime in Syria and Iraq.

The papers's recommendations fell on deaf ears with Clinton in 1996 and even Netanyahu had difficulty in following them. But when Bush took over power and the neo-conservative network moved into the Pentagon and the White House, it was exactly the policy that George W. Bush and Ariel Sharon agreed Israel should implement in tackling Palestinian resistance. When that paper is read together with the sundry recommendations that Perle and his colleagues presented at countless hearings in the American Congress throughout the 1990s and up to the present day, a clear picture is painted of a Middle East policy based on close Israeli-American cooperation and military superiority.

Firstly, American security policy was to give defense of the homeland the highest priority by continuously developing, modernizing and extending American forces. In other words, a focus on missile defense, reorganization of the defense system to flexible hi-tech units that could be deployed as and when needed and the clear will to use its military superiority.[41]

Secondly, the enemy was to be beaten on his own ground, before, that is, the USA came under threat. So the concept idea of a preventive strike became a cornerstone, which meant that the USA should eliminate threats before they reached the USA. This 'strike first' doctrine was to be adopted whether USA's coalition partners were players or not. As Perle put it so succinctly in an interview on the TV program Frontline in October 2001, "If the coalition is going to protect a terrorist state like Saddam, then to hell with the coalition".

Rumsfeld followed up on this arrogant rhetoric when France and Germany prevaricated in supporting a war against Iraq in February 2003 and called them 'the old Europe'; and later placed Germany in the same group as rogue states such as Libya and Cuba.

Thirdly, the USA was to maintain an unambiguous military strategic alliance with Israel, based on the two countries in fellowship maintaining sovereign military superiority in the region.

Fourthly, the USA was to work to forcing the introduction of democracy in the Arab countries. Democracy should be understood in this context as regimes with transparent decisionmaking structures used to promote American interests. In this connection, the USA, in its efforts to pursue its own interests, should not hesitate in using military force to eradicate regimes in the Middle East and other places where it deems necessary. In short, they should be prepared to bomb democracy into the Middle East.

The framework of a Grand Strategy for the Middle East was thus formed. In the westerly region of the Middle East, close economic and military cooperation with Israel were to be maintained and in the easterly region, the Arab states and Iran were to be put on the right course, which could best happen by the USA enforcing regime changes. Initially in Iraq of course, but thereafter also in Saudi Arabia, considered by the neo-conservatives to be a far greater threat than Saddam Hussein's Iraq.

Indeed, Iraq was referred to as the tactical threat, Saudi Arabia as the strategic threat and Egypt as the prize – a summation attributed to the RAND researcher Laurent Murawiec, later affiliated with the neoconservative think tank, The Hudson Institute in Washington, D.C. It appeared during a briefing on Saudi Arabia that the think tank RAND gave to Perle's Defense Policy Committee in the early summer of 2002.[42]

First Iraq was to beaten into submission, not so much because the country represented any real threat to the USA but because Saddam's policy was one of the most influential factors behind the anti-American tidal wave in the Middle East.

Then, with Iraq in the fold and the Americans able to rely on a new Iraqi regime's help to maintain oil prices at a level acceptable to the west, it would be Saudi Arabia's turn, a country thought to be a major supplier of al-Qaida warriors and main sponsors of the Koran schools around the world that provided the backbone of the militant terror network. Traditionally, Saudi Arabia was the USA's closest ally in the region and if the superpower started applying pressure, in the name of democracy, for reform intended to stop Saudi Arabian export of all kinds of conflict, it would be difficult for the government in Washington to look on silently whilst American citizens, like the leader of the Ibn Khaldoun Center in Cairo, Saad Eddin Ibrahim, was imprisoned in Egypt, merely for allowing himself the freedom to criticize the lack of democracy and numerous violations of human rights. But after regime shifts in Iraq and Saudi Arabia, Egypt would be the prize where political reforms would spead from the Gulf to the greater Middle East.

Now it may smack of exaggeration to give the neo-conservative network all the glory for the new American Middle East policy. As indeed it is, because if everything had gone as they wanted, war with Iraq, by all accounts, would have been declared in the months following 11 September.[43] The policy adopted was naturally an indication of compromise, first and foremost between the Pentagon on the one hand

and the CIA and the State Department on the other, as CIA Director George Tenet's and Colin Powell's understanding of foreign policy lay much closer to theinternational line of pragmatism that colored Bush Snr's policy than the neo-conservative's idealistic activism.

Nevertheless, much suggested that both President Bush and his security advisor Dr Rice listened attentively to neo-conservative recommendations: Bush allied himself closely with Sharon and refused to meet Arafat; clear signal were sent, garnished with threats to Iran, Saudi Arabia and Egypt to follow more closely the American agenda; and in his speech to the newly graduated cadets at West Point on 1 June, Bush launched his idea of a preemptive strike. If The National Security Strategy of the United States, a document of more than twenty pages presented by the White House to Congress on 20 September 2002, is read alongside this speech, the ideas become unified with exemplary clarity.

The government's strategy for the Middle East was far from unopposed in the USA. Warnings against and skepticism for the resurrection of George Shultz's ideas on preventive and preemptive strikes[44] were heard everywhere, from think tanks, universities and even prominent Republicans with current security policy experience. But the neoconservative network clearly had considerable clout and the backing of the voters that belonged to that large group of fundamentalist Christians on the right wing, who both cherish traditional and conservative American values and were greatly influenced by what can be called Christian Zionism. That is, the concept that the second coming of the Messiah would take place only when the Jews had gained a lasting foothold in Israel, which is why the coming could be enhanced through constant support for the state of Israel.

The alliance between right-wing Christians and the Israeli right wing became a concrete reality after Likud's accession to power in Israel in 1977. With an unequivocally pro-Israeli policy, American politicians harvested votes not only from American Jews but also from the Christian fundamentalists that had recently given Bush his election victory in 2000. And there were a great many votes for the harvesting.

The American professor of religion at Chicago university, Don

Wagner, estimated that when Jimmy Carter, another devout Christian, spoke out in 1977 for Palestinian's rights to their country, it cost him 20 million Christian votes at the presidential election in 1980: "During a speech in March 1977, Carter included a statement that the Palestinians had 'a right to their homeland'. The Israeli lobby and the Christian right wing responded a number of very visible actions. Within a few weeks a series of whole page advertisements began to appear in the American media. The copy began with '"The time has come for evangelical Christians to confirm their faith in biblical prophecy and Israel's divine right to its country." Then followed a line aimed directly at Carter's statement – "we as evangelists confirm our faith that the Promised Land belongs to the Jewish people ... we will take very seriously any effort to carve a nation or political unit from the Jewish homeland".

The customary explanation for Jimmy Carter's election defeat by Ronald Reagan is the fiasco attempt to release the American hostages held by Iranian students in the occupied American embassy in Teheran. But Wagner refers to another factor that played a role – "an estimated 20 million evangelical Christians voted for Reagan, many of whom were opponents to Carter's form of evangelical Christianity, which did not propound unconditional support for Israel".[45] It is of course a contentious issue as to how much importance to attach to the Christian right wing in an American presidential election campaign, but there is undoubtedly some influence. Especially when it is a close-run election, as was the case in the fight between George W. Bush and Al Gore in 2000.

The fact that the neoconservatives were able to acquire as great an influence on foreign policy as they did under George W. Bush has several explanations. Bush himself belonged on the right wing of the Republican Party, which upholds traditional conservative family values and was skeptical about the Federal government – "those folks up in Washington," as Bush contemptuously referred to the political machine in the nation's capital during his campaign. Time after time he criticized the Clinton administration and Al Gore for getting involved in hopeless and expensive nation-building projects outside the USA; and he stressed that American soldiers should only be stationed abroad when national security interests were at risk. Subsequently during the election campaign both he and Condoleezza Rice proposed that the USA should withdraw its troops from the Balkans.

Even during the election campaign, Bush stood out as an isolationist who would not get his country inveigled in international disputes unless it was necessary in the defence of American interests. In such a situation he would display "great leadership", as he passionately reassured the voters in the second of the three tradition TV duels with Al Gore. And he would not hesitate to use the armed forces, which he intended to rebuild to past levels of strength and greatness, after Clinton, according to him, had let it decline. He also criticized Clinton's hesitation in implementing the missile defense project and promised to give it top priority. The order of the day for Bush's first six months as President was both isolationism and significant increases in the defense budget.

Bush had presumably learned from his father's mistakes of neglecting domestic policy in favor of involvement in the Middle East, and on several occasions distanced himself from and indeed put pressure on Yitzhak Shamir's government, thereby losing the votes of both the American Jews and the Christian right wing. This latter convinced Bush Jnr that he should not get involved in the Israeli-Palestinian conflict, and if he did nonetheless, then it should be unequivocally on Israel's side.

Meanwhile in the Gulf, American servicemen were facing death threats, clearly evidenced by the attack on the *USS Cole* in Aden on 12 October 2000, right in the middle of the election campaign.17 American sailors lost their lives and the huge hole in her hull prevented the Cole from sailing home to the East Coast under her own steam.

The Navy was in the Gulf because of the two rogue states Iran and Iraq – and Saddam Hussein's regime, promised Bush and his advisors, would come to feel the change of power in Washington. So it was plain for all to see that Bush would turn the Clinton Middle East policy on its head and transfer involvement from the Israeli-Palestine conflict to boost the effort against Iraq.

THE BUSH DOCTRINE: CIVILIZATION WAR AND DEFENSE OF AMERICAN VALUES

With the terrorist attacks of 11 September, the die was cast for a unilateral foreign policy based on strong defence and a consistent policy of containment, accompanied by a tangible will to use military might when necessary in any region where American security interests dictated. These attacks provided the Bush government with a convenient sounding board for its ideological discourse, which from then on stood as an unvarnished resurrection of Reagan-like power politics, in which 'the axis of evil' filled the position that 'the empire of evil' had under Ronald Reagan. Bush could thereby formulate his doctrine – either you supported the USA in the war against terrorism or you supported the terrorists. The use of the moral concepts of good and evil signaled a completely different understanding of civilization than prevailed in the days of idealist Clinton.

Where Clinton's understanding of civilization was universalistic, Bush's was clearly relativistic, completely in line with the theory of The *Clash of Civilizations*. Whereas Clinton saw cultural differences as differences within the same civilization, and hence basically reconcilable through dialogue, the Bush camp tended towards making such differences irreconcilable and immutable contradictions that would only disappear with the one conquering and eliminating the other. In fact, Huntington's comments on Islam in his book *The Clash of Civilization* and there making of World Order were very accurate in their critique of Clinton's strategy – "Some Westerners, including President Bill Clinton, have argued that the West does not have problems with Islam but only with violent Islamist extremists. Fourteen hundred years of history demonstrate otherwise. The relations between Islam and Christianity, both Orthodox and Western, have often been stormy. Each has been the other's Other. The twentieth-century conflict between liberal democracy and Maxist-Leninism is only a fleeting and superficial historical phenomenon compared to the continuing and deeply conflictual relation between Islam and Christianity"[46] Here there can be no reconciliation!

In 2002, Michael A. Ledeen of the AEI, one of the circles of neoconservative ideologists in Washington but who had only occupied minor positions in the Pentagon and State Department, put the cat among the pigeons in a summary of his book *The War Against the Terror Masters*."Behind all the anti-American venom from the secular radicals in Baghdad, the religious fanatics in Tehran, the minority regime in Damascus, and the multicultural kleptomaniacs in the Palestinian Authority is the knowledge that they are hated by their own people. Their power rests on terror, recently directed against us, but always, first and foremost, against their own citizens. Given the chance to express themselves freely, the Iraqi, Iranian, Syrian, Lebanese, and Palestinian people would oust their current oppressors. Properly waged, our revolutionary war will give them a chance. You need only listen to the screams of the Middle Eastern tyrants to prove to yourself that they fully understand the import of the struggle. When the Iranian terrorist leader Rafsanjani announces to the entire Islamic world that President George W. Bush has "the brain of a sparrow inside the body of a dinosaur," – as he did in late February 2002 – you know he is scared. We will succeed, for we excel at destroying tyrannies. The great democratic revolution of the last quarter of the eighteenth century bears an American trademark, and the entire twentieth century shows the awesome power of our revolutionary energies. Again and again we were dragged into war: by the Kaiser into World War I, by Tojo and Hitler into World War II, by Stalin into the Cold War, by Saddam Hussein into the Gulf War, and by Osama bin Laden into the war against terrorism. Each time our enemies chose the time, place, and circumstances under which the war began. They had all the advantages, and we have tossed them all (except al Qaeda, which will soon be tossed) onto history's trash heap of failed lies. We wage total war because we fight in the name of an idea, and ideas either triumph or fail... totally. Ask Mikhail Gorbachev."[47]

Ledeen's interpretation is extreme but there can be little doubt that many in Washington saw the War against Terrorism as a morally justified mission to eradicate evil. Its path of progress was not, like that of the international missionaries of the East Coast, to help others develop the potential inherent in all cultures, but, from a relativist position like Huntington's, simply to remove the hostile and threatening civilizations and replace it with a new one founded on the good old values from the American heartland.

It is possible that Condoleezza Rice was right in her view that discussion between idealists and realists is of mostly academic interest, and also that power and values are always intertwined. Nevertheless, it is a palpable fact that different governments draw up their foreign policy differently with different weightings on the very issues of power and value.

Regain had a clear ideological basis for his confrontation policy with the Soviet Union, which led to his creating a power balance strategy in the Middle East based chiefly on security interests in the overriding struggle against communism. To George Shultz's great displeasure, ideology and values had only any limited consequences for the Middle East policy, which was driven largely by real-political interests.[48]

Reagan never drafted a policy on political Islam but prioritized co-operation with Islamists, whether they were the mujahidin in Afghanistan or the mullahs in Iran, as long as they were of use to overriding objectives.

The Bush government, however, adopted a pragmatic angle on foreign policy, and only with Saddam Hussein's invasion of Kuwait and the Algerian Islamic fundamentalists' display to the world of the West's highly ambiguous relations with the democratic development of the developing nations was the Bush government forced to formulate value-oriented visions for global security.

Clinton adopted Fukuyama's ideas on universal civilization and made expansion of democracy and human rights through dialogue his vision for international politics. Closer analysis, however, shows that he was often forced by circumstance to pursue a security policy of realpolitics rather than an idealistic defense of human rights.

George W. Bush opted for a classical unilateral policy, which ideologically was further enhanced and realized after the events of 11 September, when the neoconservatives arguments on enforced change of regimes in the Middle East – the democracy argument – met with attentive ears in Washington, great scepsis in European NATO countries, with France at the fore, and decided nervousness and fear in the Middle East.

2. THE CONCEPT OF TERRORISM, QUESTIONS OF LEGITIMACY, RIGHTS AND POWER

This chapter takes its point of departure in the debate that took place in Denmark surrounding the concept of terrorism after 11 September. Following a summary of the problems involved in making an unequivocal definition, the concept is discussed in relation to other concepts, such as freedom, legitimacy and power. Terrorism is distinguished from war, and it is argued that terrorism is primarily a matter for the police and the civil justice system. Finally, new terrorism is described briefly and an argument made for the necessity of a pragmatic definition.

If you used the term terrorism before 11 September, you were sure to be met with critical comments in most academic circles, and if you went so far as to link the term with Islamic fundamentalism, you could be fairly certain of being excommunicated from the politically correct circles that characterize Danish Middle East scholarship. Until September 11, making any claims of links between the Palestinian resistance group Hamas and terrorism was generally not acceptable. Although terrorism as term is still taboo in quite influential academic circles, it assumed an almost disproportionate focus immediately after 11 September, just as the image of a terrorist became based more and more stereotypically on Osama bin Laden's appearances in the videos broadcast by the news channel *al-Jazeera*: a terrorist was Muslim, had a long beard, was dressed in Middle Eastern garb, and was a fanatic.

TERRORISM IN DENMARK

When the Sri-Lankan researcher Rohan Gunaratna told the Danish *TV-2 News*[49] that Denmark was a safe haven for terrorists, where they could be granted asylum and live in peace and quiet, and where sympathizers could collect money for international terror networks, the media began a fullscale hunt for terrorists in Denmark – despite the fact that Prime Minister Poul Nyrup Rasmussen categorically denied that there was any substance to Gunaratna's accusations.

In the following months, newspapers disclosed the existence of Muslims who had been granted asylum and who were notorious for having had contact with international terror networks, particularly the Egyptian group al-Jama'a al-Islamiya, which merged with al Qaeda in 1998. "Disclosed" is perhaps too strong a term, because if the said newspapers had checked the archives, they would have found that all the people they had tracked down were well known by the Danish media, and as early as 1994 and 1995 had been mentioned, photographed and interviewed by the country's entire press corps during the prosecution of three Egyptians at the court in Århus for planning terror in Denmark.[50] *The Washington Post* was able to tell of a certain Abu Mujahid, whom the Danish paper *BT* later described as al Qaeda's man in Denmark, without anyone really knowing anything about the man's actions or hide-outs. The Danish newspaper *Politiken*, on the other hand, revealed that a former Iraqi general and defense chief had obtained "tolerated residency" in the town of Sorø. The two major television channels were on the spot immediately and in their news broadcasts showed where the alleged war criminal lived in such a way that anyone who might have an interest, including Iraqi agents, would be able to locate him.

In this case, the difference between the small nation and the superpower became clear: while in Denmark everyone was outraged at the fact that a war criminal could reside in their country, and either wanted him prosecuted or thrown out of the country – without it being clear exactly where to – in the USA this type of person would be debriefed, pumped for information about the Iraqi system, and given a cover identity (and not prosecuted, as some self-classified pundits would otherwise have us convinced), so that the information disclosed could potentially be used in the course of military action in Iraq. But as far as we know the man in Sorø was not a terrorist – simply a war criminal. The case illustrates well the degree to which concepts by then had become mixed up: the distinction was no longer made between war and terrorism. Bush had already foxed this firmly in the public eye the same day the events occurred, by declaring his "war against terror"; it was also confirmed by the European NATO countries who demonstrated their sympathy for the USA by activating Article Five in the NATO treaty: a military attack on one country was to be considered an attack on the entire alliance. Yet there is an essential difference between terrorism and war: the first is a matter for the police and justice system; the second is the responsibility of states and military organizations.

An important consequence of 11 September in Denmark was that both public debates in the media and political discussions in Parliament came to a great extent to revolve around terrorism. Among the concrete results of this was a heavy increase in appropriations for the Danish Defense Intelligence (FE) and the Danish Security Police (PET) for fighting terrorism, and new legislation in the form of what was known as the "terror package". Whereas previously a single, very succinct paragraph (§ 114) in the criminal code had sufficed, the new legislation was as thick as a novel.

With all these substantial measures, which will likely be supplemented by research funding for some of the many experts on terrorism who appeared on the various television stations after 11 September, it is natural that demands are being increasingly made for a definition of terrorism. This, as everyone knows by now, is somewhat easier said than done.[51]

FREEDOM-FIGHTER OR TERRORIST?

The problems with making an unequivocal definition are twofold: the content of the concept itself and its resemblance to other types of violence (crime, guerrilla warfare, freedom and resistance struggles, etc.); and the fact that the concept is used in political justification of the use of force or activities that could potentially have negative consequences for civil rights or international law. The concept is emphatically a political one and its connotation is always negative: if a group is designated "terrorist", it is branded as illegal, dangerous, fanatic and in every sense illegitimate, which means that when a state labels a group as "terrorist", it simultaneously grants itself the right to stop the group's activities with whatever means may be necessary – although naturally methods used by different states vary. Legitimacy, in other words, is distributed in such a way that the state gains it fully, while the group in question loses it completely.

On this basis it is clear where the political dispute lies. This is perhaps best illustrated by the Palestinian and Islamic resistance group Hamas. When Hamas assumes responsibility for a man blowing himself up in a disco in Tel Aviv and killing 19 young Israelis, the general consensus is to define it as an act of terrorism, and a debate as to whether the time has come to classify Hamas as a terrorist organization quickly arises. For although the majority of people – but not all, even in Denmark – would say that the action in the disco can in no way be legitimized, its background can be explained. The result – confusion about the concept of legitimacy.

The fact that Hamas is engaged in a struggle against the Israeli occupying power can be both explained and legitimized, and for some people it can also legitimize the action of the man in the disco, as well as, in a broader sense, the use of random violence against civilians in the service of political struggle. This is an obvious fallacy: the suicide bomber in the disco cannot be legitimized by the fact that Hamas is fighting a legitimate campaign of resistance against an illegitimate occupying power, nor by the fact that, in addition to its armed struggle, it also does a great deal of important social work. The concept of terrorism has, as mentioned, an unambiguously negative connotation and when we designate the action in the disco as "terrorism", it is to demonstrate both a clear condemnation of it and the conviction that it cannot be legitimized in any form or under any circumstances. It is thus quite possible to regard Hamas' fight against Israel as a legitimate freedom struggle (and thus regard Hamas as a freedom movement), at the same time as unequivocally condemning some of the means it employs in its struggle. Similar deliberations were apparently taken up by the EU countries when they produced a list of terrorist groups that was made public at the end of December 2001. Hamas appears on the list, but only under the name of the organization's military branch, the Izz al-Din al-Qassam Brigade. With such a demarcation, the EU signals its condemnation of terrorism while simultaneously acknowledging Hamas's right to oppose Israeli occupation.[52]

In trying to arrive at a definition of terrorism, this leads us to focus intensively on the content of the specific action and its motive. However, this does nothing to dispel disagreement about political definitions of actions as "terrorism", as making the classification will always be the task of those in power. In Denmark it is thus the Folketing [the Danish Parliament] that in the final instance must determine through legislation what actions are defined as terrorism in the penal code. Thereafter it is up to the courts to interpret concrete cases. The difference between a democracy and a dictatorship is namely that democracy acknowledges that there is dispute and conflict over a large number of issues in society, including the concept of terrorism; hence nothing in the political discourse is static but always opens to discussion. This is a concept of governance that provides an important guarantee for the rule of law in our society. In many ways it would actually make more sense to limit the use of the concept of terrorism to situations involving legitimate states, as terrorism could then be defined as an attack on the fundamental values of the legitimate state. Few people would have problems defining the use of violence against civilians ina legitimate law-governed state with the purpose of sending a political message as terrorism; problems quickly arise, however, when the same action takes place in a dictatorship. The objection to reserving the concept of terrorism for legitimate states is, of course, that problems of definition are merely shifted to the concepts of legitimacy and legitimate states. But this is safer ground, since there is both international consensus about and a long tradition of defining the principles of law-governed states.[53]

THE BRANDING OF OPPOSITION GROUPS BY STATES

The confusion surrounding the concept of terrorism arises to a high degree precisely because different governments see great political advantage in labeling resistance and opposition groups as terrorist organizations. This is the case, for example, with Turkey's fight against the Kurdistan Workers' Party (PKK), Russia's fight against the Chechen rebels, Egypt's prohibition of the Muslim Brotherhood, Algeria's fight against the Islamic Salvation Front (FIS) and the Armed Islamic Group (GIA), and Israel's fight against Hamas and Palestinian Islamic Jihad. For all these states, the rhetoric about terrorism has had political objectives much broader than the combating of terror alone. On the one hand, the discourse on terrorism is used to justify a state's use of means that go far beyond what can be accepted by a law-based society to fight its enemies; on the other, states seek international backing for this kind of strategy. This is precisely why Russia – using a choice of words that could have been copied directly from the American State Department's homepage on terrorism – has insisted on calling the Chechen rebels terrorists, and after 11 September has actually received the backing of support from Washington to do so. This must be seen in light of the fact that the USA has profited by the understanding shown by Moscow for the necessity of basing American soldiers in areas of Russian interest in Central Asia.

Another case was seen in Denmark in the summer of 2001, when Israel sent a new ambassador to Denmark; a debate arose as to whether it is permissible for security services to use "moderate physical pressure" in combating terrorism – a number of Danes, following the lead of the then Central Democrat member of the Folketing Arne Melchior, believed that it was. This Danish debate was really an offshoot of a much more serious issue – the very persistent and insistent efforts of the Israelis to delegitimize the entire Palestinian resistance by classifying it as terrorism.

This is not a new strategy and has attended the Oslo process, for instance, from its very beginning in 1993. Yet it became a dominant issue when terrorism expert Benjamin Netanyahu[54] came to power in Israel in 1996, after Hamas had carried out a series of very bloody acts of terror in Tel Aviv and Jerusalem to avenge Israel's murder of a Hamas activist in Gaza earlier the same year.[55] For Netanyahu it was a question of delaying the Oslo process by referring to Arafat's inadequate efforts to combat Palestinian terrorism. This should be seen in light of the fact that from May 1996 until the outbreak of the al-Aqsa intifada in September 2000, no acts of terror was carried out for which Hamas claimed responsibility. After the intifada's outbreak, and especially since 11 September, the Israeli government has been seen to take every opportunity to portray the Palestinian resistance as terrorism that should entitle Israel to do anything in the name of preventing terrorism. In addition to actual acts of terror, such as suicide bombings, the Israelis thus define all acts of violence, including political assassinations and firing at Israeli soldiers in the occupied areas, as acts of terrorism.

The Oslo process 1993-2000

The Oslo process was triggered by the Declaration of Principles, which in turn was the result of a number of secret meetings that took place without the knowledge of political leaders initially but that were later acknowledged by both the Israeli government and the Palestinian leadership. The decisive phase in the process took place in Oslo with the active support of the Norwegian-government – hence the name of the process.

Although the accords met with strong resistance from the Israeli opposition and from nationalistic and Islamic Palestinian groups, as well as from countries such as Iran, Iraq and Syria, they were generally welcomed and promptly received backing from the rich Arab countries, the USA and the EU. And Arafat, Peres and Rabin (but not the Israeli historians Hirschfeldt and Pundak, the PLO's "Minister of Finance" Abu Alaa or the PLO negotiator Abu Mazan) were awarded the Nobel Peace Prize for the accords.

> The signing of the Declaration of Principles in Washington began a process that led to several treaties and to the Israeli withdrawal from parts of the West Bank in 1995 and '96 after partial withdrawal from Gaza in 1994. With the shift of power in Israel in 1996, followed by a number of Palestinian terrorist attacks in Jerusalem and Tel Aviv, the Oslo process stalled. Several attempts to resume negotiations, culminating at Camp David, were without result, and in the fall of 2000 it was clear that the process had not led to the desired peace.

On 24 September 2001, the White House publicized a list of organizations and individuals that the Bush administration claimed had connections to the al Qaeda network. In Jerusalem, Ariel Sharon was furious that Hamas and Palestinian Islamic Jihad were not included on the list. The reason the Americans gave for the omission was that the list only targeted global terrorism and not national, under which the Palestinian groups were counted. After several hearings in the American Congress in October concerning the passage of the annual appropriation to Israel of almost $2.8 billion, the two groups were added to the list. Accordingly, there was no longer any difference between the USA's fight against al Qaeda in Afghanistan and Israel's fight against Hamas and the Palestinian Authority in the occupied areas. The Israeli lobbying organisation the American Israel Public Affairs Committee (AIPAC) had considerable influence on the outcome and triumphantly described the course of events on its web site.[56]

Israel has thus been successful in getting the Israeli-Palestinian conflict depicted as a branch of the war on terror, although, all things considered, the conflict revolves around the Israeli occupation of territory land from which they are obliged to withdraw in accordance with international law. This has meant that in its fight against the Palestinian resistance, Israel has both permitted itself, and obtained international permission, to wage regular war against the Palestinian Authority, which in the winter of 2001 had effectively ceased to exist. In the name of combating terrorism, the leader of the Palestinian Authority, Yassir

Arafat, was placed under house arrest, all the Authority's institutions, including the Palestinian's heliport, harbor and airport landing strip, were systematically destroyed and civilians' homes bombed. The reason given for this collective punishment was that the houses were used by terrorists. According to the Red Cross 90 families were made homeless. The Palestinians held responsible by Israel for the terrorist acts were executed without trial.

Following Sharon's accession to power we have seen a systematic dismantling of the Palestinian Authority, resulting in an all-out occupation of the Palestinian areas; yet the entire matter was still depicted by the press, politicians, and experts as if there were two parties capable of negotiating with each other. This view of the conflict was greatly facilitated by Israel's success in getting its conduct portrayed as a fight against Palestinian terrorism, which even a very superficial glance would reveal is far from the case, at least by the consensus definition of terrorism.

FROM CIVIL JUSTICE SYSTEM TO FOREIGN DEFENSE ACTION

The fact is that terrorism is a matter for police and civil legal systems. In other words, alleged terrorists should be prosecuted along the same lines as other criminals, and accordingly have the same rights as all other citizens. As global terrorism is on the rise, however, terrorism also becomes a matter of defense. This is already the case with regard to terror networks that, like the Taliban and al Qaeda, are organized across national boundaries and therefore compel states to work together in combating terrorism.

The agenda according to which a network like al Qaeda operates is not national but global, with defense therefore playing an increasingly important role in the fight against terror. The global aspect of terrorism is thus given as part of the reason why defense now, as opposed to previously, gives the fight against terror high priority. It is for this reason that in the aftermath of 11 September, the Danish Folketing significantly increased funding to the Defense Intelligence Service (the

FE). Yet the involvement of national defense in fighting terrorism ought to focus on international developments and not intervene in national ones, insofar as the fight against terror is to be kept within the limits set by a law-based society.

Despite great differences in national definitions of what constitutes terrorism, there has still been a broad consensus since 11 September that terrorism comes under the aegis of the civil legal system, which is why the Israeli use of military force and executions, for example, have nothing to do with fighting terror. It could be argued that the USA's fight against al Qaeda in Afghanistan by means of actual war is not a legitimate way to react after 11 September either. The facts of the matter, however, are different. For years the USA has tried through diplomacy, UN sanctions and direct negotiations with the Taliban, to have Osama bin Laden extradited; similarly, after the terror attacks against American embassies in East Africa (1998), a civil case was tried in the USA which proved that Osama bin Laden was involved in global terrorism. This did not prevent 11 September. Thus it can be argued that since the Taliban did not hand over Osama bin Laden after the attacks in Washington and New York, war was the only step possible – a step which both the UN Security Council and NATO sanctioned.

Israel can claim that, like the USA and without success, they have attempted to persuade the Palestinian Authority to extradite alleged terrorists, and that the lack of results justifies the use of the military to execute the persons in question as a preventive measure. Yet in doing so, Israel is clearly exceeding the limits of what can be defined as a fight against terror and should instead be defined as war, and, to cap it all, one that is being waged against the terms of the Geneva Convention.

In other words, if Israel is held to its claim that Hamas's attacks on civilians are to be defined as terrorism, Israel's response is illegitimate according to the current international consensus on the interpretation of terrorism. The point is that the definition of terrorism is not merely a tool that states can use to brand opposition groups with – provided that a court upholds their right to do so – but that, conversely, it ought also to give these very same groups legal rights, such as the right to appear before a court of law in which the prosecutor (the state) would have to prove that their involvement in terrorism.

Put more simply, either are Israel and the Palestinians at war, which means rules of war apply, or they are not, and Israel, in accordance with international consensus, ought to combat terrorism in the same way as other types of crime, such as politically motivated murder, by using the police and the judicial system.

In extension of this debate, the interesting question arises as to how the USA will continue its fight against terrorism. Although one can argue for the legitimacy of the USA's use of military force in Afghanistan, it is also obvious that military action is only the first step in a process that must be followed by political, diplomatic and economic measures: after the bombs, aid must follow. It can be feared, however, that the USA is using the war against global terrorism to impose a new world order which did not emerge after the Cold War, by dividing the nations of the world into those who are with them and those who are against them. For this reason, too, it is important that a definition be posted of what constitutes terrorism.

THE MESSAGE DROWNS IN APOCALYPTIC HORROR

Terrorism has become a European problem at least since the 1970s, and distinctions can be made between ethnic-nationalistic and ideological-political terrorism. Ethnic-nationalistic terrorism is usually based in an ethnic group's attempt to fight its way to sovereignty over certain territories. This is the case with the Irish Catholic group, IRA, for the Basque separatist movement, ETA, and previously for the Kurdistan Workers' Party. On the other hand, the 1970s also had such groups as the Rote Arme Fraktion in Germany and Brigate Rosse in Italy, which fought for the implementation of a Communist revolution, just as extreme right-wing groups in Italy made a name for themselves through acts of extreme violence intended to discriminate against left-wing groups. But what these had in common was that their terrorist activities had an ideological basis that was not bound to well-defined territories.

The 1990s saw groups with a religious platform asserting themselves: Christian groups in the USA, Jewish groups in Israel and Islamic groups with origins in the Middle East. Their activities and organizational structures caused several, mainly American, theoreticians and civil servants aided by new theories to argue that terrorism had changed character in the 1990s.[57]

The classic understanding of terrorism characterizes it as theater: the aim of terrorism is primarily to send a message, which is why it is a matter of "few killed, but in front of a large audience." This definition suggests a close link between the media and terrorism. Terrorism constitutes a proposal to negotiate and aims to ensure the attainment of a number of well-defined demands.[58]

By contrast, the new theories suggest that the aims of religious groups are abstract, and that the goal of terrorism is not the fulfillment of concrete attainable demands, but of a more apocalyptic or messianic nature. One example is the Japanese group Aum Shinrikyo ("the supreme truth"), which in 1995 released poison gas in the Tokyo underground apparently without any other motive than to kill as many people as possible. Another example is Osama bin Laden's international Islamic terror network consisting of veterans from the Afghan civil war, whose objective is to wage jihad against the "Jewish and Christian crusaders." New theories attribute groups such as these with motives that involve the killing of as many people as possible, without such massacre being accompanied by any concrete negotiable demands.

The terror attacks of 11 September are a good example of this new type of mass terrorism. It is increasingly feared that such groups or networks with international connections can come into possession of weapons of mass destruction (chemical, biological or nuclear weapons) and accordingly be capable of attacks of as yet unknown dimensions. This new type of terrorism is called super terrorism, catastrophic terrorism or postmodern terrorism in the USA.

Since the mid-1990s, the American State Department, the Department of Defense and the White House have pointed again and again to the new terrorism[59] as the greatest threat to American national security and the greatest challenge to security policy the country will face in the new millennium.[60] Thus in 1997 Secretary of Defense William Cohen said, with reference to new terrorism, that "the question is no longer if this will happen, but when".[61]

What is meant by new terrorism[62] is, as mentioned above, a terrorist attack that employs weapons of mass destruction with the aim of killing as many people as possible and creating maximum chaos and fear in society. Several of the USA's terrorism experts have depicted scenarios that describe the effects of an NBCR (nuclear, biological, chemical, radiological) attack in the middle of a large American city.[63] The consequences would be incalculable and not limited to an enormous number of deaths (from 100,000 to several millions), but could also include poisoning, anxiety and limitations on civil rights.

11 September confirmed that the consequences of reality exceed the imaginings of the mind: compared to the catastrophic scenes with which researchers had worked, the destruction and the number of dead were very limited, but the consequences nonetheless, not least in the areas of economics and civil rights, went far beyond what could be imagined. Who could have predicted that a terror attack in the USA would lead to a large Danish pension company teetering on the brink of bankruptcy? And who would have expected the European countries, including Denmark, to undertake a comprehensive revision of their legislation on combating terrorism as a direct result of the terror attacks?

A PRAGMATIC DEFINITION OF TERRORISM

It can be said that, with its focus on new terrorism, the USA had been preparing itself for years for a terrorist attack on American territory. One could almost say that 11 September had been foretold, since the USA had already been warned by the attack on the World Trade Center in 1993. At the time, the links to al Qaeda were unclear, but it became obvious during the investigation that those behind the attack came from circles in which Afghan veterans were prevalent.[64] Since 1993, the USA has been attacked several times, with the bombings of the embassies in East Africa in 1998 the worst until 11 September. Since then Osama bin Laden has topped the FBI's Most Wanted list, and funding for fighting global terrorism has steadily increased. After the bombing of the warship *USS Cole* in Aden in October 2000, a steady stream of threats of new acts of terror aimed at the USA came in, and the American military forces were constantly at the highest state of readiness until 11 September. The attack was sophisticated in its simplicity, which, along with some worrying failures in intelligence, was probably the reason for it not being stopped in time: rather than deploying sophisticated missiles or hi-tech weapons of mass destruction, the terrorists used old, well-known methods in such a way as to be terribly effective. Critics have since pointed to the fact that until 11 September, the USA was all too focused on high technology, and it is expected that there will be changes from now on in the gathering of intelligence data, as well as improved coordination between the different American intelligence services. Indeed, the terrorists did not use weapons of mass destruction on 11 September but conventional ones – to the extent, that is, that an airliner used as a missile can be called conventional. But that does not change the real risk that terror networks, potentially in cooperation with states, can obtain weapons of mass destruction. If this fact is taken together with the global character of the networks, then terrorism today has moved into a grey zone between the areas of civil legal systems and the military. This entails police and defense, to a much greater degree than before, working together to prevent terrorist attacks; this necessitates weighty consideration of the limits of their activities, which can only be resolved if we can reach political agreement on a pragmatic definition of terrorism, at the same time as having precise assessments of the threat at any given time.

It is, however, unrealistic to imagine that we will ever be able to arrive at an unequivocal definition of terrorism on which everyone, across political, national and religious affiliations, can agree. All things considered, there is nothing strange in this. As the German historian Reinhart Koselleck has pointed out, it is possible to distinguish between words and concepts: words can be defined, while the meanings of concepts will always be disputed.[65] We can therefore write history by writing the history of concepts, because by tracing which meanings have been dominant at different times, we understand what kinds of power relations have made themselves felt. Terrorism is closely linked with power, and, as we have discussed, legitimacy, which is why state definitions of terrorism will always be a kind of assertion of power. With respect to securing the rule of law, this is precisely why a pragmatic definition is necessary. When we [the authors of this book] speak of terrorism, we mean – quite imprecisely and pragmatically – planned violence targeting civilians or forces that are not in battle, carried out by individuals, groups or networks with the conscious aim of communicating a message of political, ideological or religious character.

3. GLOBALIZATION, NETWORKS AND CYBERWAR IN THE POSTMODERN WORLD

Terrorism changed during the 1990s, becoming more violent, more international and more diffuse. This chapter takes its point of departure in globalization after the Cold War and describes the period as an unstable and conflict-ridden time of transition, during which the USA, on the one side, increasingly focuses on a new form of terrorism as a new threat. On the other side, Arabs, Muslims and Asians increasingly see the USA's role in the Middle East as an expression of a policy of dominance that must be fought against. Against such a backrop, this chapter describes the USA's policy on the Afghan civil war. Finally, it focuses on the concept of networks, which, as forms of organization as well as communication, have become important for the superpower as well as for its adversaries.

In many ways the world was simpler during the Cold War. It was easier to keep under control because the two superpowers held each other in check by controlling their own areas of interest, whereas today, in principle, the USA controls everything alone. However, it is necessary to modify the concept of a unipolar order because, as it turns out, minor unruly centers of power emerged around the world and in cyberspace during the 1990s. These power centers are far from having the strength of a superpower but are nevertheless difficult to control and can have great impact on the international political situation. It is therefore more accurate to speak of a uni-multi polarity, and the problem with such a (dis)order is that it is particularly unstable, as countless regional conflicts and wars around the turn of the millennium clearly demonstrate.[66]

WEAPONS OF MASS DESTRUCTION ON THE BLACK MARKET

We can say that we find ourselves in a period of transition from a world order marked by rivalry between two superpowers to a new order that has not yet emerged as anything other than a new openness and globalization. Globalization means primarily greater economic integration in the world, supported by free trade agreements, economic liberalization and a general tendency towards privatization, all promoted by digital information technology. In Eastern Europe and former socialist countries in the south, this has meant that the economy is no longer controlled centrally by the state but that new private economic centers have been established. This is, of course, the whole idea behind liberalization but it has also created better opportunities for more shady types of economic activity, for instance the illegal sale of weapons and other forms of financial crime.

Both economic integration and criminal networks are supported by the other decisive characteristic of globalization, namely the revolution in communication in which the new information technology has resulted. In this connection the world has been called 'the global village', where communication and contact are not limited by distance or time zones. Economically this means that the world today is one big bazaar, where everything is up for sale.

Thus in Eastern Europe a large black market for all kinds of weapons and technology that can be used in terrorist activities has arisen. The terror attack by the Japanese group Aum Shinrikyo is an example of this. The group used the poison gas sarin, and it was only by a stroke of luck that total number of victims was limited to 12. But when the group's stockpile was found, weapons and modern helicopters bought for the purpose of spreading poison, possibly anthrax, over cities were discovered, in addition to large amounts of materials for the production of gas. This would have killed people in numbers incomprehensible to us. As it turned out, the leader of the group, the millionaire Shoko Asahara, had bought the entire arsenal on the black market in former USSR.[67]

At the same time, globalization has exerted great pressure on the nation-state and its borders: the supranational financial networks put pressure on states from the outside, while ethnic and religious communities challenge the nation-state's borders from within. Thus the flow of goods and money globally is at once simple to create and difficult to control. The same is true of arms, and the USA in particular has been anxious about the spread of weapons of mass destruction after the break-up of the Soviet Union.

At first, interest centered on the Soviets' nuclear weapons and their many poorly maintained nuclear power plants. Americans feared that the Russians did not have sufficient control over their nuclear warheads in connection with the destruction of their missiles armed with nuclear warheads. It was imagined that they could be just lying about, circulate as "loose nukes" to global terrorists or be sold on the black market and smuggled into what have been called the "rogue" states. The American Congress therefore passed the Nunn-Lugar-Domenici Program, named after the three senators who proposed it. The purpose of the program was to help the Russians both by financing the destruction and by granting fellowships to Russian scientists who had been employed in the weapons industry and were now, as a result of disarmament, unemployed and with no prospect of new work in the chaos that characterized Russia and the other new republics that arose from the ruins of the Communist empire.[68]

Attention increasingly turned, however, to biological weapons, and combating terrorism carried out with weapons of mass destruction was raised to top priority in the American Congress. First, it became clear in 1992 that the Soviet Union had a very comprehensive and well-developed program for the production of biological weapons, despite the fact that the state had committed itself to not producing them with the signing of international treaties.[69] Then came Aum Shinrikyo's chemical terror attack in Japan, the cult's attempt to obtain biological weapons and the fact that American extremists to the far right were discovered to have the same interests.

In particular a 1995 hearing on the spread of arms of mass destruction[70] made American policy-makers not only focus on new terrorism but also authorize the expenditure of ever greater sums for fighting it.

The American explanations for why government circles and Congress were convinced of the likelihood of an attack using on weapons of mass destruction can be summed up in the following points:[71]

- Access to components for the production of biological and chemical weapons of mass destruction is easy, and little more is required to produce such weapons than a basic education in science and access to bio-medical technology
- In the globalized world, the nation-state boundaries are under pressure and, in the former Soviet Union especially, there is relatively easy access to a large and well-assorted arms market, possibly including nuclear weapons as well as components for chemical and biological weapons
- Information technology has made it easy to spread knowledge about the production of weapons as well as recruit for terrorist organizations globally. In addition, a number of Russian scientists with expertise in the production of weapons of mass destruction have become available on the market and are feared to be willing to sell their knowledge to interested buyers
- There are a number of rogue states that do not observe international law, that sponsor international terrorism, produce weapons of mass destruction and would presumably cooperate with terror networks. The following states were in 2003 defined as rogue states: Iran, Iraq, Syria, Libya, Sudan, North Korea and Cuba. Depending on one's political orientation, point of view, reasons for and definition of terrorism, this list is very questionable, which shows that the concept of rogue states is just as debatable as the concept of terrorism.[72]

In the second half of the 1990s new terrorism became a theme for both the media and political circles in Washington. Some, however, were skeptical and criticized those who focused too much on high technology. They referred to the fact that with the exception of the Japanese cult's sarin attack, there was no knowledge of networks that had actually attempted to carry out mass terrorism with weapons of mass destruction; the major attacks were all carried out with conventional arms. The most obvious example of an organization or network that was believed to have the motives, the capability, the will, and the opportunity to obtain weapons of mass destruction was Osama bin Laden's al Qaeda network. At a trial in New York of four al Qaeda members charged with assisting in the terror attack on the American embassies in East Africa in 1998, it was established that al Qaeda had shown an interest in nuclear weapons.[73] Anyway, politicians focused on the new terrorism, also called postmodern, catastrophic or super terrorism, and it was increasingly used to explain and legitimize American policy in the Persian Gulf.

Under Bill Clinton a policy of double containment was carried out in Iran and Iraq, both of which were on USA's list of rogue states – or "states of concern," as Clinton preferred to call them. This meant that the USA maintained tough sanctions against Iran at a time when the UN was easing its treatment of Iraq with the oil-for-food agreement. The USA, on the other hand, insisted on sanctions and weapons control in Iraq and constantly had military bases in the Arab Gulf states and its navy patrolling the Gulf. These measures were intended to prevent the spread of weapons of mass destruction and reduce the threat of global terrorism. What is ironic and paradoxical about them, though, is that they significantly mobilized anti-American forces in the region, thus intensifying the motives for carrying out terrorism aimed at the USA.

The oil-for-food agreement

The oil-for-food agreement was signed by the UN and Iraq in 1996.

After the UN alliance under American leadership had defeated Iraq in 1991, a ceasefire was agreed upon by the UN and Iraq. Iraq committed itself to dismantling its production of weapons of mass destruction and to destroying any stockpiles of weapons. A special monitoring group from the UN was to supervise and ensure that Iraq lived up to its obligations, and until then Iraq was subjected to the most stringent economic sanctions a country had ever seen. They were intended to affect Saddam Hussein's regime but, needless to say, sanctions as comprehensive as these would inevitably affect Iraqi society as a whole. As early as 1991, therefore, the UN and the USA extended the offer of an agreement according to which Iraq, under close supervision, could sell oil and buy food and medicine for the money. The offer was rejected at that time and when it was presented again in 1995.

In 1996 the UN and Iraq finally signed the oil-for-food agreement. Initally it meant that Iraq could sell $2 billion worth of oil over a period of six months and use approximately two-thirds for food and medicine. The rest was to be used to pay for war damages and administration. In February 1998, the ceiling was raised to $5.265 billion and since then it was removed completely.

THE BACKGROUND TO ANTI-AMERICANISM

In the first half of the 1990s, the USA involved itself deeply in four problem areas, all of which were linked to the Middle East and aimed at bringing about greater stability. A major problem, however, was that the manner in which the USA conducted itself actually undermined its own objectives, motivating instead Islamic networks to intensify their armed fighting. The four problem areas were the developments in the Balkans, the Israeli-Palestinian peace process, the Gulf War and the civil war in Afghanistan.

With regard to developments in the Balkans and the Israeli-Palestinian peace process, many Muslims, namely in the Gulf and in South Asia, felt that the USA was playing two games at once, or at least had a double standard for its ethical assessment of the world's conflicts. While the USA had not hesitated to come to the aid of Kuwait when Iraq occupied the little desert nation, the superpower was much more hesitant in the Balkans, where years passed before the USA came to the aid of the Bosnian Muslims. With respect to Israel, the perception of many was that the USA automatically backed the Jewish state's illegitimate occupation of Palestinian territory. To many it seemed self-evident that the USA only reacted when its own interests or those of close allies were threatened, while other rules applied when Arabs, Muslims and Asians were involved. This assessment of American policy was seen to be confirmed by the Gulf War and by the USA's role in the civil war in Afghanistan.

For many Muslims, the Gulf War and its consequences are a clear manifestation of the USA's efforts to achieve dominance over Arabs and combat Islam, and the willingness of certain Arab regimes to assist them in the attempt. Many Islamists view the entire Iraq-Kuwait conflict as staged by the USA with the intention of acquiring a massive military presence in the Gulf, based on a desire both to ensure control over the area's energy resources and to fight Islam. When Saudi Arabia invited Americans in after Iraq's occupation of Kuwait, it was regarded as an unmistakable act of treason. The country, which bestowed upon itself the title of "guardian of the two shrines," compromised its religious convictions when fears arose in the regime that the monarchy was next in line as a victim of occupation.

All the consequences of the Gulf War, its conflicts over sanctions and weapons control, are interpreted by many Muslims as a mere confirmation of the American policy of domination, and the responsibility for the suffering of the Iraqi people is placed unequivocally on Washington D.C. and not on Saddam Hussein. The Iraq conflict is, as mentioned earlier, often compared with both the Balkans and the Israeli-Palestinian conflict: the question insists on being asked of how it can be that the Bosnian Muslims had to be subjected to the injustices of the Serbs for years without the West, the UN or the USA intervening; just as a glaring disparity is discerned between American willingness to liberate Kuwait and simultaneous support of the Israeli occupying power in Jerusalem, the West Bank, Gaza, Southern Lebanon (until May 2000) and the Golan Heights. In both cases there is clear evidence that the USA, the West and the UN behave according to a double standard and that Americans only act when their own, Christian and Western values and interests are at risk. The willingness of the Gulf states, Egypt, Jordan and, to a certain extent, Syria to cooperate with the USA is another sign that these countries prostitute themselves, betraying both the Islamic and the Arab cause simply to maintain their own power regimes. And this even though these states have expressed their reservations towards the USA's Iraq policy and attempted to persuade the superpower to exert greater pressure on Israel. For many Muslims in the region, however, the worst thing about the Gulf War was that the USA's military forces remained in the Gulf, where they established permanent bases.

Of the four events mentioned, the civil war in Afghanistan and its consequences in Central Asia and Pakistan are without doubt the most important. There are several reasons for this. For one thing, the victory of the Mujahideen over the Soviet superpower in 1989 became a strong mobilizing factor, and for another, the war meant the education of a large transnational network of well-trained soldiers who were highly motivated both to spread their ideology and to assist in the organization of armed fighting in the Caucasus, Philippines, Central Asia, Kashmir, the Balkans, Africa and the Middle East. Added to this is the fact that developments in Afghanistan have had a great destabilizing influence regionally. This is bound up with the dissolution of the Soviet Union and the subsequent establishment of a number of Muslim republics in Central Asia that are very politically unstable. First and foremost, though, it is tied to the global power game of where oil and gas lines are to pass through the region – that which has been called by some a new version of "The Great Game".[74] In this game, the USA, Russia, Turkey, Iran, Saudi Arabia, Pakistan, Afghanistan and the Central Asian republics all have major strategic interests, and in this regard Afghanistan, especially after the Taliban's takeover of power in 1996, has been able to use its connections in Pakistan to play the various agents against each other.

Pakistani intelligence in collusion with the USA

A single example of this success can be seen in the fact that, until 1998 at least, the USA was in dialogue with the Taliban with a view to establishing an oil pipeline that was to bypass Iran, where the USA had implemented a policy of containment. For this secret diplomacy the USA relied on information from the Pakistani military intelligence service, ISI, without being sufficiently aware of the fact that the ISI had become dependent on the Taliban regime for both money and power.[75]

The problem is that during the Afghan holy warriors' resistance against the Soviet Union, the ISI had the job of distributing the American and Saudi money and arms supplies, and were responsible for establishing training camps, recruiting and building networks. Thus ISI became a state within a state and sometimes, namely in the second half of the 1990s, had its own agenda that did not always coincide with that of the state of Pakistan. During the civil war, the ISI acquired enormous power and great economic influence, and in the effort to retain these privileges, has worked closely with the Taliban, sometimes in agreement with the government of Pakistan and sometimes in direct opposition to it. The problem grew after the USA put pressure on both Pakistan and Afghanistan to extradite Osama bin Laden and on Pakistan to curb terrorism in Kashmir, over which Pakistan was in conflict with India. President Clinton called this conflict the world's most dangerous after it had become clear that both Pakistan and India are in possession of atomic weapons. To get the conflict under control, the Americans, who are traditionally close allies of Pakistan, put pressure on the government in Islamabad to limit the fighting. By far the majority of those fighting in Kashmir are Afghans, Pakistanis and Arabs. At first they were trained and schooled primarily in camps in Pakistan, but following the pressure by Americans the camps were, in

> agreement with the Taliban, moved to Afghanistan, where al Qaeda was responsible for the training in its camps. This made Pakistan and the ISI dependent on the Taliban in the conflict with India over Kashmir, and the new question is how Pakistan will tackle the problem now that the al Qaeda camps in Afghanistan no longer function and the Taliban is gone. On the face of it, this should mean a fall-off of activities in Kashmir simply due to the lack of trained combatants. This would give the Pakistani government problems not only with the Islamic organizations in the region but with the large populations that have grown up with Islamic schooling as the only teaching they have received. On the other hand, one could imagine that Pakistan's President Musharrif would allow the camps to be reestablished, but along with internal problems, this would give rise to serious problems with both India and the USA.

It is not only ethnic and religious conflicts which destabilize the region, however: in Pakistan today there is no real political organization or party system, and economically the entire region is saturated by a black market and an extensive network of smugglers run by different local power figures and by the Taliban while it was in power. The ISI was involved in the smuggling network in an effort to retain its economic resources and power, which in turn means that its interests come into conflict with the official state of Pakistan. Who will run this smuggling network after the Taliban is not known, but the ISI will likely maintain its interests. For Pakistan, the price is extensive corruption and loss of large tax revenues, while the different smuggling networks, which work closely with Islamic networks, have won great influence in Pakistani society. Most people with intimate knowledge of Pakistan believe, however, that the greatest problem the country and the region are confronting is Islamization of the Pakistani society.[76] This bypasses the government in Islamabad, which, on the contrary, has attempted to contain it. It has its origin in the schools and social work on the streets, which is why we choose to call it "grassroots Islamization".

NETWORKS

The concept of networks has been used several times in connection with the organization of jihad. There is much that indicates that new organizational forms have developed along with the spread of new information technology – organizational forms that are best understood as networks, that is, virtual links which can shape ad-hoc groups under certain circumstances. The inspiration for this is the internet, where knowledge and information are organized in completely new and previously unknown forms: the organizational form is horizontal and flat, rather than vertical and managed from the top down. The principle of networks is not that of bureaucratic hierarchy but nexuses, which means possible (virtual) connections that can be established with a minimum of time and without having to go through hierarchical decision-making structures. The internet can be seen as an image of a completely new type of organizational form that is fast, effective and flexible. At the same time, the internet is the ideal form of communication for establishing contact between different groups across large distances in a short time. And the information stream is impossible to control because the amount of data is enormous and its suppliers can easily and with little effort change their location. It is possible to distinguish between cyberwar and netwar: cyberwar is an attack against a computer network, while netwar means, first, a new organizational form and second, utilization of new information technology.[77] Put another way: the internet is both an image of a new organizational form and a concrete opportunity for the rapid exchange of information.

Both can be said to have enormous consequences for new terrorism. If one looks at groups active in the Middle East, it is increasingly characteristic for many of them constantly to change their name. New groups appear all the time, while others apparently disappear. The reality is most likely that changes in networks occur continually, in the same way that home pages on the internet change character and appearance regularly. Changes occur with reference to specific nodal points, of which Osama bin Laden's headquarters in Afghanistan was just one that can probably be replaced by another; in principle the potential is unlimited as long as the structures on which a network like bin Laden's is sustained do not change.

Another aspect that confirms the internet-image is that of the ad hoc groups[78] such as the one behind the bombing of the World Trade Center in New York in 1993. This was a group that can best be characterized as a project group whose members were only together because they had a very specific common obejctive, that of leveling the Twin Towers. As we elaborate later in this book, everything indicates that those who were responsible for 11 September were also members of a project group that was founded with this one goal in mind. If one ad-hoc group is disclosed, another one can be established.

Another example of an ad-hoc network is the religious declarations that Islamic groups send out together. For example, the famous fatwa by Osama[79] that is signed by leaders of other networks: al-Jihad (Egypt), al-Jama'a al-Islamiya (Egypt), Jamiat Ulema-e (Pakistan) and Jihad-movement (Bangladesh). One can say that these groups have fused, forming a kind of united front against crusaders and Jews, but all things considered, it is more accurate to say that they are part of a well-structured network where the individual group keeps its identity and still has its own projects in the form of local jihad, at the same time as participating in global jihad. If the network structure is compared with the abstract – or simple – ideology based on a concept of "enemy" that characterizes fundamentalist movements, the possibility of creating cooperation is great – much greater than the forms of cooperation previously seen in the close relations between the Basque group ETA and Northern Irish IRA or in the case of the German Bader-Meinhof group, RAF, which received combat training for pay in Lebanon or Yemen organized by the Palestinian group PFLP.[80]

This second aspect, namely the use of the internet, is likewise apparent. For a long time now, the net has been used both for recruiting and for organizing the Afghan veterans. Today it is also used for the social work, da'wa, which Muslim movements perform on the streets in many Middle Eastern and Asian countries, for the spread of conspiracy theories, for PR, for presentations and for what one can call anti-information, which can take on the character of actual cyberwar. Everything suggests that many of the groups already known participate in such cyberspace-organized networks. These are groups such as GIA, Hamas, Hizballah, al-Jihad, Palestinian Islamic Jihad and al-Jama'a al-Islamiya.

Much indicates, however, that as a consequence of the developments outlined above, an unknown number of new groups has appeared, namely in Central Asia, Pakistan, Bangladesh and other places in Asia. These are groups such as Arafat al-Mujahideen (Kashmir), Islamic Movement of Uzbekistan and Jamaat ul-Fuqra (Pakistan). Yet new groups have also been established in the Middle East as offshoots of known groups or by changing name, in Egypt, Algiers, and in Lebanon, where a number of Sunni Muslim groups suddenly asserted themselves in 1999 and 2000 by attacking the Russian embassy in Beirut, very probably as a response to the Chechen conflict.

Throughout the 1990s several conditions have been present in the Middle East in South Asia for the growth of anti-Americanism based in a politicized interpretation of Islam: globalization, American dominance in the area and new forms of network. To these we will add in the next chapter the concept and spread of Islamic fundamentalism as the background to Islamist terrorism.

4. ISLAMIC FUNDAMENTALISM

This chapter begins by defining fundamentalism as a modern phenomenon that is both made possible by and a reaction to modernity and secularization. Next we argue that fundamentalism, including Islamic fundamentalism, takes on the character of a political ideology that gains ground particularly in the postmodern information society. Next, the discussion is made to relate to a critical interpretation of civilization and is then made concrete with the example of the growth of the Salafiya movement in Saudi Arabia. Finally we present a political interpretation of the Islamic mission work, da'wa.

It is common practice today to use the concept of fundamentalism to describe a religious consciousness that reflects a particularly literal reading and understanding of religious texts. The interpretation or understanding that emerges is absolute, that is, it does not accept other interpretations and it is totalizing, which means that it can explain everything of importance. The Islam scholar John O. Voll thus defines fundamentalist interpretation as "a self-conscious effort to avoid compromise, adaptation or critical reinterpretation of the basic texts and sources of belief."[81] A link is made between fundamentalism and religion, and the concept reflects a special belief in the religious precepts which give comprehensive instructions for how life is to be lived, society organized and states led. One can say that fundamentalist belief finds in the texts and sources of a given religious faith the answers to all the questions life and the world pose to human existence: religion provides the value base for how life in the world is to unfold.

A MODERN CONCEPT

Modernism and the modernization of society take place in parallel with the breakdown of traditional views of the world and value bases – Karl Marx and Friedrich Engels's formulation of these developments serves for posterity as a motto for the modern world: "all that is solid melts into air."[82] The concept of fundamentalism was grounded in a reaction against the dissolution of familiar and traditional value bases and against the idea that nothing – not even deeply rooted Christian concepts – has absolute meaning and significance. Such a reaction occurred in the USA, where from 1909 to 1915 a number of American theologians published a series of books with the name *The Fundamentals: A Testimony to the Truth*, in which they defined their notions of the fundamental truths of Christianity. Their conceptions build on a literal reading of the Bible, whereby the text is taken at its word and is not subjected to modernistic interpretations, such as attempts to reinterpret religious scripture as myth, story or metaphor, whereby the written word is not read literally but through new interpretations is made to conform to the ideas and sciences of the modern world. Theirs was a rejection of the text-critical methods that view the religious text as historical material, ask critical questions of the text or point out actual mistakes in it. Such modernistic interpretations that reconcile holy scripture with modern science were rejected by these American theologians. This group of Christian theologians was called fundamentalists.[83]

As a concept or term, "fundamentalism" is thus tied in its origin to Christianity and to a secular modernity against which it reacts and from which it dissociates itself. Although it has later become common to use the term fundamentalism indiscriminately in connection with religions other than Christianity, the use of the term in connection with Islam has, however, been strongly criticized. There are several reasons for this. First, many, namely Muslims, hear a derogatory tone in the concept, with a connotation in the direction of simple-minded reaction. Second, it has been pointed out that the concept does not even exist in the Arabic language and that it therefore has nothing to do with the Muslim faith. The way the concept has been linked with modernity, thereby defining Islamic fundamentalism as a singularly modern phenomenon, is a third aspect that has been criticized by prominent scholars of Islam. Accordingly, John O. Voll, among others, argues that the phenomenon can be found far back in the history of Islam.

INEQUALITY AND THE LACK OF POLITICAL INFLUENCE

One point in our argument is that Islamic fundamentalism is a (post)modern concept closely tied to the processes and problems that global political integration – or the lack of same – involves. The political background to Islamist ideology is the lack of political influence and institutions through which the critique of regimes can be expressed; the sociological background is the growing social need and polarization where lack of basic conditions for life, such as work, income and decent housing, is striking and constantly increasing – a development that is occurring at the same time that the gap between the world's rich and poor is growing steadily. The media images, for instance, of Israel's military operations in the occupied areas and the USA's military presence in the Gulf are today accessible on television screens all over the Middle East and South Asia, even in the most remote and smallest of villages, making it seem as if the West and the USA, in collusion with Israel, are only out to subject Arabs and Muslims to the Western order with a view to exploiting their resources. That which years ago was interpreted in Marxist terms as imperialism has, for many Muslims in fundamentalist groups today, assumed the character of a clash of civilizations in which the Judeo-Christian civilization is fighting the Muslim world. As many have rightly pointed out, one can speak today of a post-materialistic critique, where the ideological basis of the criticism of the rich West is more value than materially-oriented now than ever before.[84] This does not mean that the poor no longer desire material well-being, but that the terminology in which critique and ideology are formulated refers more to religion than to society, which is also reflected in the fact that the leaders who speak on behalf of the masses are often well-educated and well-off themselves. Thus the USA is criticized not only for economic exploitation but also, and just as importantly, for seeking to spread an individualistic, consumption-based and ultimately highly decadent view of the world.

As such, the critique by scholars and ideologues such as Sheik al-Hawali, about whom we will hear more in Chapter 5, Osama bin Laden and Ayman al-Zawahiri resembles the critique of civilization[85] prevalent in the 1960s and 1970s as advanced by left-wing intellectuals like Herbert Marcuse and Theodor Adorno, but now with references to a fundamentalistic conception of Islam instead of to orthodox Marxism.[86] The difference in ideological bases does not disguise the fact that freedom must originate in the third world. Thus it is not far from the glorification of violence verbalized by the French philosopher and critic of civilization Jean-Paul Sartre in the introduction to Frantz Fanon's famous book *Wretched of the Earth*, to Osama bin Laden's justification of the murder of Americans. Sartre wrote: "They would do well to read Fanon; for he shows clearly that this irrepressible violence is neither sound and fury, nor the resurrection of savage instincts, nor even the effect of resentment: it is man re-creating himself. I think we understood this truth at one time, but we have forgotten it – that no gentleness can efface the marks of violence; only violence itself can destroy them. The native cures himself of colonial neurosis by thrusting out the settler through force of arms."[87]

While the targets of Sartre's and Fanon's critique were the European colonizing powers, Osama bin Laden and his like-minded cohorts aim their critique at the USA because globalization is seen as the proliferation of an entirely American World Order dominated by excessive consumption, decadence and oppression of all civilizations other than the Judeo-Christian. Thus the thinking of those who are behind the Islamist critique of the USA closely resembles paradoxically some of the ideas asserted in Samuel Huntington's controversial book *The Clash of Civilizations*.[88]

In the book, the author argued that the conflicts and wars of the future would be played out among the major civilizations, of which he identified seven, pointing out that a future conflict would involve the Judeo-Christian civilization against the Islamic one, which would have interests in common with the Confucianism of the East. Ironically, Huntington gains sympathy for his ideas from Islamists such as Osama bin Laden, who argue precisely for a close link between the critique of America and the critique of globalization, interpreted as a form of cultural imperialism which must be fought.

Although many have attempted to find other designations for recent political Islamic groups, such as Islamism, political Islam, Islamic radicalism or, in French contexts, integrism, the phrase "Islamic fundamentalism" actually seems to describe the phenomenon well – precisely because its modern context is thus reflected. Apart from this, John O. Voll points out in his article on Islamic fundamentalism that the term is also increasingly used in Arabic contexts (usuliya). In the following, we employ the terms "Islamism" and "Islamic fundamentalism" interchangeably to designate a politicized interpretation and use of Islam which thereby assumes the character more of political ideology than of religion. The fact that Islamic fundamentalism is identified as a modern phenomenon means that it develops as a protest against the forces that undermine Islam, regardless of whether they are Arab regimes that stray from orthodoxy or the USA which with its money, arms, and global dominance represses the Islamic foundation in the Middle East.

As an ideological alternative, Islamic fundamentalism easily lends itself to communication through effective slogans that play on familiar ideas and traditions and which at the same time offer a cultural identity that is Muslim. It is worth noting that the Islamic movements have gained popularity since their emergence at the end of the 1920s, during periods when other ideologies have foundered or have had lesser status. The military defeat to Israel in 1967 was also a farewell to Egyptian President Nasser's pan-Arab socialist project and was followed by a tremendous flourishing of Islamic fundamentalism. Another example is the Palestinian freedom fight. For a long time it was fuelled ideologically by communist anti-imperialist theory, with nationalist freedom fights in Cuba, Algeria and Vietnam as ideological frames of reference. The developments in the communist world at the end of the 1980s, culminating with the fall of the Berlin Wall, led to the Palestinian freedom fighters in large numbers turning away from socialist ideology and joining instead the Islamic groups Hamas and Islamic Jihad. Large groups in Algeria, Egypt and the Israeli occupied areas, for example, are now finding that neither Western capitalism and liberalism nor the socialism that had failed in so many places holds serious political bids for a better future. It is therefore relevant to turn towards an alternative Islamic fundamentalism which both is comprehensible and offers a cultural identity that is neither Eastern nor Western, but, precisely, Middle Eastern.

FUNDAMENTALISM
– A PRODUCT OF SECULARIZATION

Seeing Islamic fundamentalism as a modern project acknowledges its unique relationship to Islamic tradition. The fundamentalists are highly critical of institutionalized Islam as it is found, for instance, in the Sunni Muslim stronghold and state-run al-Azhar University in Cairo. First, traditionalists are criticized for having merely to function as religious justification for the regime's policies, a role which becomes evident with the state's taking over the mosques in 1961. Second, fundamentalists insist on a new reading of the Koran with a view to bringing to light the text's statements on state, society and the like.

One can object that the term "fundamentalism" seems misleading if the radical Islamic groups must undertake such a new reading and explanation of the Koran: on the face of it, such a strategy can seem irreconcilable with the idea behind a literal reading, which is to let the truth appear at once. Heated debates have also taken place over the applicability of the interpretation of Islamic law (shari'a) to the Islamic tradition, where those who are more radical, for example, Shukri Ahmad Mustafa, the leader of the group Jama'at al-Muslimin (The Muslim Society, which is probably better known by the name given to them by the Egyptian press, Jama'at al-Takfir wa-Hijrah, or the Group for Excommunication and Emigration) has very provocatively called the history of Islam "a series of stories of doubtful authenticity." The more moderate the Muslim fundamentalists are, the more they can build on history and tradition. The more radical they are, the more they consider tradition, that which is established and realized, a veil that hides the real truth and which must therefore be torn away, which can only happen through a revolutionary overthrow of the entire society. Yet it is namely in this radicalized new reading of the holy scriptures that Muslim fundamentalists reveal their modernity: clearing away history in order to pave the way for something new – even if this something new is formulated as a return to an original foundation – is precisely a modern project.[89]

Modernity is, however, more than the critique of tradition and value relativism to which the fundamentalists' project has been put in relation here. For the German sociologist Max Weber modernity is synonymous with reason and characterizes the way Western nation-states have developed.[90] Decisive features are that the legal system and morals as well as technology and science are based on rational principles and that religion is limited to the private, individual sphere. Politics, science and law are thus explained not with reference to religion, but in accordance with a principle of reason. The separation of politics and religion is, in other words, characteristic of modernity, and it is precisely for this reason that many will claim that Islamic fundamentalism is not a modern phenomenon, since the link between religion and politics always has been a distinctive feature of Islam.

It is certainly also correct that a main issue for Muslim fundamentalists is the recreation of the link between religion and politics in the formation of an Islamic state. Their critique is that Islamic societies today are not subject to Islamic forms of government. They are completely right in this critique: most of the policies laid down by the governments in Alger, Cairo, Damascus, Khartoum and Riyadh are implemented independent of Islam. On the other hand, this also means that Muslim fundamentalists are obliged to position themselves, plan strategies and act in relation to a society which, if not modern in Max Weber's sense of the term, is nonetheless marked by modernity. There are several examples of the fact that one does not necessarily have to celebrate modernity in order to think modern. It is typical of the critics of modernity that in their style and mode of address, in their interpretation of texts and tradition and in their political strategies they exhibit features of the very modernity they criticize, including its separation of religion and politics – and this applies to Muslim fundamentalists as well.[91]

A unique feature of modernity is thus that critique is primarily justified and expressed secularly, that is, without religious references and ties. This means that in principle everything can be made an object of critique, even religious texts. Such a concept of critique is, as has already been mentioned, completely unacceptable to Muslim fundamentalists.[92] Despite the fact that they must voice their political critique of and fight against secularization in a context in which the political scene is dominated by the practice of separating religion and politics, there is no doubt that their own self-conceptions are based entirely on religion – on interpretations of Islam and the Islamic tradition. There is no doubt, either, that different fundamentalists read and interpret Islam very differently and that this difference is of great importance for the interpretation of their own situations and the political picture to which they must relate. There are major differences, for instance, between the Islam to which the Shia-based Hizballah group in Lebanon relates and the interpretation which is professed by al Qaeda, Abu Sayyaf in the Philippines, Harakat al-Mujahidin and the GIA in Algeria. Yet common to them all is a strongly politicized understanding and use of Islam.

ECONOMIC AND CULTURAL GLOBALIZATION

When the Danish author, the late Hans Jørgen Nielsen had to explain the concept of postmodernism in the Danish newspaper *Dagbladet Information*, he took as his point of departure a soccer game between France and England. The time was the mid-1980s, the place was the Parc des Princes stadium in Paris, and France won the game, as far as we remember 3-0. With the French player no. 10, Michel Platini, who at the time was considered the best soccer player in the world, France introduced a whole new playing style, in which playfulness and weightlessness were crucial, in contrast to the physical strength and mechanical logic that characterized the English national team's kick-and-rush system. For the English it was a question of the defense players wresting the ball from their opponent, then kicking it far up the field in the hope that it would fall on the head of a forward, who could then drum into the goal. This system required physical strength and no imagination or creativity, unlike the French playing style, which was performed by light and elegant players who practically danced around the field.

France's way of playing soccer was for Hans-Jørgen Nielsen a metaphor of what some calls the postmodern world and others refer to as the information society: a world based on streams of information and computers in contrast to a modern world whose image is dominated by smoking factory chimneys and powerful machines. The transition from industrial society to information society has made itself felt on many levels. Much indicates that international terrorism has also utilized the opportunities provided by the postmodern world. Our identification of Islamic fundamentalism as a modern project is related to the fact that the politicization of Islam as a protest movement begins at the same time that modernity seriously begins to leave its mark on the Middle East after the First World War. The proliferation of Islamic fundamentalism, which interprets jihad as part of a global conflict, first begins to occur for real in connection with globalization following the Cold War.

When people first began to speak of globalization, they did not think only in economic terms but also in terms of a form of cultural globalization, whereby the world generally would become Americanized. What would be seen, according to many, was that the cultural features that were prevalent in the USA would spread to the entire world. Although Coca Cola is now drunk and burgers eaten everywhere, there is not much to indicate that a cultural Americanization has taken place. On the contrary, economic integration seems to run parallel to increased cultural diversity. Nations based on new forms of ethnic and religious identity are seen to appear everywhere. Pressure is put on the former nation-states and their borders both from above, in the form of supra-national economies and from below, in the form of small ethnic or religious-based cultural units.

The emergence of new forms of cultural identity can be explained partly as a result of the new openness in the postmodern world but also as a protest against American domination. This is the case, for example, with the Islamic based terrorist groups, where an abstract political message about unity in the Islamic world is always accompanied by vehement critique of the USA and American/Western culture. It is, however, worthy of note that other terrorist groups with reference to other religions also combine an abstract message with a dismissive critique of Western and American culture. Regardless of whether terrorist groups are based in Japan, the USA, the Middle East or Europe, one finds that they usually combine an abstract religious message with some kind of conspiracy theory like the one that maintains that the USA, in collusion with the Jews, intends to achieve absolute global domination and exploitation. This cocktail of religion, politics, and fanaticism is shared by the new terrorist groups, whether they refer to Islam, Judaism, Hinduism or Christianity. Cultural identity has become a distinctive feature of terrorist groups in the 1990's. Often it is not the traditional political ideologies, communism or fascism which constitute their message, but religion.

NEW RELIGIOUS MOVEMENTS

References to culture and religion do not, however, disguise the fact that the message is abstract and its aims distinct and undefined. Accordingly, they merely reflect a situation which is generally characteristic of many people in the postmodern world, namely that the end of communism in Eastern Europe, the impotence of scientific Marxism as ideology and strategy, paves the way for disillusionment or emptiness, which some people have replaced with all manner of irrational doomsday theories. Many of those who turn their backs on neo-liberalism and capitalism and who feel the world to be in moral decay with increasing social inequality, or who for other reasons are searching for the meaning of life, find the truth in new religions.

This is the case for Hollywood actors like Richard Gere, for performers like Madonna and for people who are tired of regimes in the Middle East and other places – regimes which cannot reconcile rhetoric with reality. Some people react by making nature and ecology religion. Others react by cultivating a new kind of Puritanism or by being saved by a neo-romantic cultivation of individualism. Still others become religious fundamentalists. Some of them become terrorists. The difference in ideology and existential interpretations of life between the eco-feminist in Manhattan and the Muslim fundamentalist in Kabul is not great. But while the eco-feminist can write an op-ed on her PC for one of the major newspapers, the fundamentalist in Kabul finds it easier because of his socio-economic conditions to gain a sense self-worth and pride by grabbing his Kalashnikov, donning his battle uniform and taking part in jihad.

The progression from frustrated citizen to holy warrior does not, however, occur in a social vacuum, but is motivated both by concrete events in the region and by the spread of new ideological and political interpretations of Islam which gain increasingly greater ground in countries like Algeria, Egypt, Saudi Arabia, Pakistan, Afghanistan and more generally in the areas in which Afghan veterans take up residence. Thus, the emergence of the Salafiya movement, an Islamic reform movement that has been revived in renewed form as the new grand narrative and frame of reference for the marginalized Muslims who have ended up on the dump heap of globalization. Out of the ruins of modernity's breakdown of the classic tales of peace and the future, there has arisen a powerfully active and politicized conception of Islam, which on the one hand believes in purity and on the other gives the concept of jihad a whole new meaning.

SALAFIYA AND GLOBAL JIHAD

In an edition of the Danish television news magazine *Horisont* on Saudi Arabia,[93] representatives of the Saudi regime described Osama bin Laden as a madman who had nothing to do with Islam, especially not that conception of Islam, Wahhabism, which the Saudis profess. It is common both in the Middle East and among Islam scholars in the Western world to dismiss Islamists' religion as interpretations that belong within Islamic tradition. It is said that those from the GIA in Algeria, the Afghan Veterans in the al Qaeda network and the militant activists in Egypt's most violent group, Al-Jama'a al-Islamiya, profess a perverted, and at best mistaken understanding of Islam, and that their ideology therefore has nothing to do with Islam, just as the Islamic reason for the terrorist attack 11 September does not hold water theologically. It is understandable that Muslims and scholars of Islam want to distance themselves from Islamism – the politicized conception of Islam behind, for instance, 11 September – in this way, and it is also extremely important to stress that there is no natural link between Islam and terrorism whatsoever.

The problem with excluding Islamism from Islam, however, is that one thereby excises something from the tradition that in fact has its own history in the grand narrative of Islam. In the exact same way that the Christian fundamentalists in the USA – who today do not refrain from using violence and who can certainly be thought to at least toy with the idea of attempting something similar to 11 September– refer to a concept of Christianity that in one way or another is at least remotely related to established Christianity,[94] Islamism, Islamic fundamentalism in all its forms, is of course a part of Islam.

Evidence can be found for rejecting Osama bin Laden and those with like mind as philosophers of Islam in the fact that they are rarely theologically educated but must be regarded laymen with regard to religious issues. Nevertheless, Islamists themselves claim that not only do they tread safely on Islamic ground, but they do so, on the basis of a correct reading and understanding of the original scriptures in contrast to established Islam, in which history and tradition have gradually veiled the original truth. In this context, an increasing number of Muslims look to the Salafiya movement.

In the beginning of the 1990s Salafiya followers received a great deal of popular support and were able to recruit people for militant activities around the world. An important reason for this was that the concept of jihad had to be revised in connection with the recruitment of volunteers for the war against the Soviet Union in Afghanistan, which was encouraged by Pakistan, Saudi Arabia and the USA. The Afghan war had to be defined as a just war, in which it the duty of Muslims to defend the country against the infidels. This provided the religious guarantee that martyrdom was assured in the event of death on the battlefields of Afghanistan. In other words, it was the need for volunteers for the war in Afghanistan that paved the way for a more militant conception of jihad in Saudi Arabia. With this view in mind, the Arab volunteer fighters could go to war in Afghanistan certain that they were fighting a holy war; yet at the same time, there was increasing focus on a more militant conception of jihad, and this of course did not change when the Afghan veterans, from 1989 and in greater numbers from 1992, began to return home to their Arab countries after a job well done.

With the success in Afghanistan, and the Salafiya critique of regimes, in mind, jihad was now reinterpreted to include combating the un-Islamic – fallen – regimes in Saudi Arabia and elsewhere, and not least defending Islamic society against penetration by the USA: after Afghanistan, Osama bin Laden can, to a certain extent and with backing from parts of the young generation of Islamologists in Saudi Arabia, spread the message that it is a sacred duty of Muslims to fight the un-Islamic regimes and the USA. The Afghan veterans' interpretation of jihad was reminiscent of the one at which Sayyid Qutb and other politicians from the Islamic fundamentalistic circles had arrived 20 years earlier. This made the fight against the regime in Cairo precisely as just a cause as Osama's fight against the royal family in Riyadh.

Osama bin Laden's announcement that al Qaeda would not renounce its jihad against the USA before the Palestinian conflict was solved[95] was thus a clear and logical extension of the very basis according to which the Islamists had for a long time interpreted the new world (dis)order. With the Salafiya movement's critique of established Islam and the radicalized and militant interpretation of jihad, the ideological basis for armed struggle and – it was to be seen – terrorism, was present. The motive for converting theory to practice was provided by the political developments in the Middle East after the Cold War.

The Salafiya movement

The Islamic reform movement Salafiya was founded by Jamal al-Din al-Afghani (1838-1897) and Muhammad Abdu (1848-1905), who reject the entire Islamic tradition as a great deception and corruption of true Islam, which can only be deduced from the Koran and the prophet's Sunna.[96] By Sunna is meant the acts of the prophet, that is, his doings, as they are handed down through the written accounts, the hadith, which were collected for centuries after his death and achieved canonical status.

Historically, the role of Islamic clerics has included adapting conceptions of Islam to the changes and demands posed by developments in society, yet in doing this, they have moved away from the true foundation. Thus, it is now a question of purging and removing all that is false in the tradition and arriving at – or rather, perhaps, returning to – the pure and fundamental Islam.

It is not only Islamists and lay people who argue this case. In Saudi Arabia, as we will discuss later in this book, a new generation of Islamic scholars openly professes to the Salafiya movement. This is the case, for example, with sheik Safar al-Hawali, whose writings and lectures have been studied carefully and referred to often by Osama bin Laden.[97] If one reads Osama bin Laden's fatwas closely, one finds that he takes great care constantly to make reference to the Koran and well-known Salafiya sheiks like, namely, al-Hawali – a mode and method (minhaj) of writing, which according to the Islamologist Quintan Wiktorowicz is typical of the Salafiya movement.

DA'WA

The Islamization of societies in Central Asia is organized by da'wa movements, which have flourished as a result of the networks built by Afghans, Pakistanis and Arab Afghan veterans with economic backing from Saudi Arabia and the USA in particular during the resistance against the Soviet Union. After the Soviet withdrawal and during the Afghan civil war, support from the Saudi state and from wealthy private funds and rich businessmen on the Arabian Peninsula continued.[98] The USA, which stopped its support in 1989, at first backed the Saudis' and others' channeling of funds to Islamic schools, but grew more critical of Saudi and Pakistani policy as politicians in Washington realized that militant anti-Americanism originated from the Peninsula and South Asia.

Da'wa can be translated as a call, an appeal, a prayer or a mission. The concept appears in the Koran and has its place in Islamic tradition[99] but it is not until the twentieth century that its activities are in a more social sense becoming institutionalized. This is occurring along with the development of an Islamic reformism taking place, for example, within the Muslim Brotherhood in Egypt and similar movements in Pakistan, India, the Far East, Afghanistan and elsewhere. In the 1970s states such as Libya[100] and Saudi Arabia[101] began establishing and supporting the da'wa movements, which especially aimed to disseminate their interpretations of Islam to young people. Saudi Arabia's efforts to preach Wahhabism, the official Saudi orthodox and highly puritanical interpretation of Islam, have been made for a long time through support for da'wa movements both in the Middle East, Pakistan and Central Asia and in Islamic immigrant communities in the West. At the same time, in frustration over the lack of results of state initiatives, a number of more radical Islamic movements have underscored time and time again the need for da'wa, and everything indicates that they have been successful in Pakistan and Central Asia and that they are also attempting to establish da'wa in Europe, where they have had some impact, especially in London. Since the 1970s da'wa has thus been institutionalized both under state auspices in several countries, where the International Da'wah Academy in Islamabad from 1985 is one example, and in non-state networks.

The objective is to train imams, local leaders and others with influence in da'wa in the sense of missionary activity, and to develop teaching materials, arrange seminars and conferences and publish literature, directing their activities towards military personnel, journalists, teachers and other opinion-makers in the communities from which these come and in which they are to pass the message on to the young. Missionary activity, the spread of Islam, is obviously the primary work of da'wa, but in order that this not be seen as a new kind of colonialism, da'wa is conceived as being closely connected with social work. Thus in 1981 one could read in the *Islamic Herald*, published in Kuala Lumpur, an article which viewed the Islamic world from an economic angle: "Da'wah work must be supplemented with the social, cultural, and economic development of the country. A substantial amount of funds should be allocated to be spent in these countries for health, education, and better living conditions for the people living there in the form of grants, aids or loans [...]. The spirit of service and brotherhood should inculcate and permeate all the activities of development, so that people may appreciate the difference between this work [da'wa, ed.] and colonialism"[102] The building of schools, health clinics and the like thus basically serves a higher purpose, that of carrying out missionary activities, which in and of itself there is nothing strange or wrong with. If, however, the Islam preached in schools draws significantly on the Salafiya movement's new interpretations of the enemies of Islam and jihad, it not only a matter of missionary activity but of the systematic and extensive proliferation of a politically militant message.

On the whole, da'wa can be seen to be a religious effort to spread knowledge of Islam: yet regardless of this, the mission has been taken over to a great extent by politicized Islamic groups who have thereby had the opportunity to spread their very action-oriented conception of Islam and to create environments which have fostered young men, some of whom have been motivated to join al Qaeda or other militant networks. This was of course the background to the fact that the Taliban, which is in fact a product of da'wa, al Qaeda, and other militant Islamic networks were – and according to some no doubt still are – very active in the da'wa movements in Pakistan, Central Asia and the Far East. In principle, this activity can be seen as a pious desire to spread knowledge of true Islam and along with this, of redemption. This is how many in the movements seem to see it. But it is natural to assume that in the da'wa milieus, including in the madrasas (Koran schools), young people are recruited and later receive actual military training for conflicts in Central Asia, the Caucasus and Kashmir or in terrorism directed against the Arab regimes, the state of Israel or the USA and American representatives around the world.[103]

It is difficult to obtain a precise view of the problem, because there is no consistent registration of the madrasas. In Pakistan attempts have been made to register the schools in pace with the attempts of the Pakistani government, that is, with Musharrif's coming to power in 1999, to tackle the problem. But the schools have done everything they can to avoid this, because they do not want to be put under state control. Whereas the state is not capable of providing a normal primary school education to the population, the madrasas offer not only free teaching but also free food, clothing and shelter. As long as the state has nothing better to offer the poor rural population, it is clear that they will send their children to the madrasas, which intensifies the already massive grass roots Islamization which is already taking place. As long as these are controlled by radical and fundamentalistic networks, there will be

Mujahideen, who in addition to posing a threat to Pakistan itself perhaps will appear in other conflict zones around the world. Grassroots Isamization can to a certain extent be seen as a result of Saudi Arabia's export of its internal conflicts. This is so, because it is namely Saudi Arabia that finances the activities its dissatisfied young men leave home to participate in. More on this in the next chapter, which goes behind the Saudi Arabia's role in global jihad.

5. SAUDI ARABIA'S GLOBALIZED DILEMMA

This chapter shows how the USA and the West turned a blind eye to Saudi Arabia's extensive suppression of human rights because the country is a guarantor of oil for the Western world. The role of Saudi Arabia in Pakistan and Afghanistan is defined as an exporter of jihad and is examined in this chapter in relation to the country's own Islamic opposition, which criticizes the royal family for leaving the true path of Islam.

Two weeks before the terror attacks in Washington and New York the powerful Prince Turk al-Faysal retired from his post as chief of Saudi Arabia's intelligence service.[104] Prince Turk, who had held the post since 1977, had a free hand with an annual budget of $4 billion, part of which he used to nurture his contacts in the Pakistani military intelligence service, ISI, thereby looking after Saudi Arabia's major interests in Central and South Asia. In addition to taking care of the monarchy's contacts with foreign intelligence services such as the CIA, the MI6 (UK) and MIT (Turkey), Prince Turk was responsible for Saudi Arabia's interests in Pakistan, Afghanistan and for relations with the Taliban, Osama bin Laden, the militant Islamic networks and their training camps in South Asia, Yemen and North Africa. In this connection, Prince Turk met with Osama bin Laden on several occasions and probably also visited him in Kandahar.[105] It was also Turk who persuaded Saudi Arabia's King Fahd to open a Saudi office in Riyadh for communicating with the Taliban, which could be used in connection with the extradition of Osama to the USA. It was this task in particular that the USA, not least the Bush administration, wanted Saudi Arabia's intelligence service increasingly to give top priority.

POWER STRUGGLES IN SAUDI ARABIA

Yet American frustration with its closest Arab ally grew steadily and surely. Prince Turk did, it is true, have several activities and large networks in the region to attend to, and Saudi Arabia assured the USA that the country was doing everything it could to combat the militant Islamists both internally and throughout the region; but no results were forthcoming and there was growing doubt in Washington about the Saudis' real intentions. Turk's dismissal followed intense American pressure, exerted, as it happens, at the same time that the State Department and Department of Defense were negotiating with representatives of Taliban with the clear intention of persuading the Afghan regime to extradite Osama bin Laden.[106]

The retirement of Prince Turk and the transfer of real responsibility for the intelligence service to Abd al-Malik al-Sheikh of the influential Sheikh family is seen as a consolidation of Crown Prince Abdallah's power in Riyadh and as such can be interpreted as the result of an internal Saudi power struggle. The very intense negotiations between the Saudis and the Americans which immediately followed 11 September seem, however, clearly to confirm the interpretation of growing American dissatisfaction with its Arab ally. There was indeed considerable speculation in the American press about a cooling off of relations between the two countries, and attention was also given to the fact that Saudi Arabian newspapers circulated conspiracy theories that 11 September was staged by the Israeli intelligence service Mossad with a view to provoking American aggression against Islam. More concretely, in the period from the 15 to 28 September, intense diplomatic activity between the two countries was seen.[107] In Washington long-standing Saudi ambassador Prince Bandar and the Foreign Minister Saud al-Faysal and above-mentioned Malik al-Shaikh were called to meetings; in Riyadh there was a hectic schedule of meetings among Pakistani, American and Saudi Arabian diplomats, as well as representatives of the intelligence services, and on a tour of the region, Secretary of Defense Donald Rumsfeld paid an official visit.

The aim of American pressure on Saudi Arabia was to obtain permission to use the American bases in the country for the air strikes against the Taliban and al Qaeda that began 7 October. But it was also necessary in order to facilitate the close cooperation of intelligence services in the intense efforts to track down Osama bin Laden and his closest associates. Saudi Arabia had formally to break off diplomatic relations with the Taliban – a step that was not actually taken until 25 September, the day after Bush had praised the cooperation of the Saudis at a press conference – and finally had to stop the flow of funds to individuals and organizations affiliated with al Qaeda. A list of these was first made public on 24 September and caused something of a stir by including the names of numerous Saudis.[108] Finally there can be no doubt that the American authorities, led by the FBI, asked Saudi Arabia to investigate 15 Saudis whom the USA claimed had been directly involved in the attacks in 11 September. Naturally, it was embarrassing for Saudi Arabia that 15 of the 19 suicide activists allegedly came from the kingdom, and the country was particularly reserved in its comments on the case, stating only that they were waiting for further documentation from the Americans. As thanks for Saudi permission to use American bases, the American government officially kept a low profile on the Saudi Arabian leads.

BUSH'S TURNAROUND ON THE PALESTINE CONFLICT

Despite Saudi Arabia's questionable role in combating Islamic networks, their lack of pressure on the Taliban and their unofficial support of al Qaeda and other militant Islamic organizations, it seemed at first that the Bush government was prepared to tread softly around its Arab allies. There were even indications that the USA would put pressure on Israel in the Palestine conflict as payment for Arab support of the "war against terror." Consequently the Bush administration did not include Hamas and Palestinian Islamic Jihad on the list of terrorist organizations that were to have their economic assets frozen or confiscated, on the grounds that they were not a part of global terror. This view aroused indignation in Israel, where government leader Ariel Sharon came close to a hysterical fit of rage. It did not help Sharon that in the beginning of October Bush gave his full support to the idea that the Palestinians were to have an independent state. Apart from Clinton's practically private speech to an Israeli interest organization in Washington[109] on December 2000, this was the first time an American president had clearly and unambiguously supported the idea of a Palestinian state.

After only a week's time, however, Bush was seen to do an abrupt turnaround when he outspokenly declared that there was no link between the war in South Asia and the Palestine conflict. The fact of the matter is that his support of the idea of a Palestinian state and his reluctance to focus attention on Hamas and Palestinian Islamic Jihad had met with harsh critique in the American Congress, where a largely unanimous Senate demanded that Bush change his wording, which was found to be ambiguous in terms of American support of Israel.[110] For Bush, domestic support of the war in South Asia was much more important than Arab participation, which is why he clearly chose to follow the Senate's call for undivided and unambiguous support of Israel; and it was a visibly satisfied Ariel Sharon who, after a bloody weekend in Israel, could return to Jerusalem from Washington on December 3 and use language aimed at Palestinians that was identical in every respect to Bush's rhetoric towards Osama bin Laden.[111]

THE USA TURNS A DEAF EAR

Saudi Arabia is the USA's most important ally in the Persian Gulf. First, with what is referred to as its policy of dual containment with regard to Iraq and Iran[112] Saudi Arabia is the only one of three regional major powers in the Gulf with which the USA is on good footing. Second, with regard to security policy, the USA needs Saudi Arabian territory for its American military bases, which have become even more necessary with the military escalation after September 11th. Third, Saudi Arabia has over 25% of the world's known oil resources at its disposal, and the country plays a key role in OPEC, especially when prices are rising; it is Saudi Arabia that the USA is able to pressure every time to keep prices at a level that is reasonable for the West. Finally, Saudi Arabia has played an important role in American interests in Central and South

Asia – where, for example, a large portion of the financial support for the Afghan Mujahideen was channeled through the kingdom – and in the Israeli-Palestinian peace process (the Oslo process), in which Saudi Arabia backed the American course both politically and economically, while at the same time sending large sums of money to Hamas, which opposed the Oslo process.

It is particularly since the Gulf War in 1991, when Saudi Arabia asked the USA for military aid for defense against Iraq, that the country has conducted itself like the pet of the Western world in matters of security policy, and has been rewarded for it by both the European countries and the USA refraining from critiquing too loudly the country's notorious and extensive violations of human rights, which caused Amnesty International to carry out a campaign against the country in 2000.[113]

Saudi Arabia did indeed get a kind of parliamentary council in 1992. This occurred as an offshoot of the Gulf War and in the wake of domestic political pressure. The council has later been expanded by 30 seats to comprise 90 people in all today. The members are not elected but are hand-picked by the king, and their opinions are tolerated only as advice which the king and his ministers, that is, his brothers and half-brothers, can either follow or not. Although one of the best Arab newspapers, *al-Hayat*, which is known for its relatively liberal editorial pages, is financed by Saudi Arabian money and can be bought in the country, basic human rights such as freedom of speech and religion, the right to assemble, the right to vote, the right to form associations and the right to be put before an independent court of law after arrest are completely lacking in the daily life of Saudi Arabia. It is particularly bad for women, who must cover themselves up completely, may not go about alone, must use special entrances to restaurants, are prohibited entrance, for example, to record shops, and are not allowed to drive. Foreigners, not least the many guest workers from Asia, obviously have no rights at all, and violations of Saudi law are punished with a mixture of incarceration, whipping, amputations, and in more serious cases such as possession of narcotics, public executions by beheading, which occur every week of the year in a central square in one of the towns. This extensive social control extends to sports clubs, schools and work places, where professional informers watch people's goings on, and in the streets it is the religious police (mutawwa'in) who zealously make sure that prayer is said five times a day, reprimand those with indecent clothing and improper behavior and drag those who do not conduct themselves according to precept to the nearest office for questioning.

THE EXPORT OF JIHAD

Saudi Arabia is, in other words, a state whose form of government approaches totalitarianism. Yet, because of its importance regarding both security issues and supplies of oil to Western countries, the country has largely been allowed to manage its domestic affairs with little more than superficial or purely ceremonial Western critique. The West and the USA have simply turned a blind eye to the gross violations of human rights in the Saudi Arabian kingdom. The problem with this policy, however, is that the conflict within the country between the authoritarian and dictatorial government on the one hand and a scattered but growing opposition on the other threatens to destroy from within, thereby creating a power vacuum in the entire region. Another, and just as significant, problem is that for the last 20 years the country's conflicts have more or less been exported both to the region and to the West, particularly to the USA.

Taking an extreme view, one could regard the conflict between the USA and Osama bin Laden's al Qaeda network as a globalization of the conflicts surrounding Saudi domestic policies. As Mamoun Fandy, among others, has pointed out in his important book *Saudi Arabia and the Politics of Dissent*[114], both the state of Saudi Arabia and its opposition have become globalized in the 1990s, which in this context means simply that as a political entity the country constantly finds itself in the crossfire between local and global forces. With its strategic location and the conflicts between traditional and modern political forces that mark the country's political climate, this precarious position is particularly important and visible in the case of a country like Saudi Arabia.

Saudi Arabia's highly problematic role has been clear for a long time. A striking example of this is the country's official support for the Oslo process whilst, at the same time, openly allowing wealthy businessmen, princes with close links with the government, and Islamic funds managed by the country's religious elite, to support Hamas and Palestinian Islamic Jihad. This occurred even though it was well known that the money went not only to Islamic opposition to Arafat's Palestinian Authority or to charity, but also to what is referred to by some as Hamas's military strategies – that is, suicide bombings in Israel.

Likewise, the country has both permitted, and itself extensively supported, the spread of Islam in Central and South Asia, that is, through Islamic universities, schools and missionary activities which have then passed the funds on, for example to militant groups in Kashmir, the Philippines, Indonesia, Malaysia, Pakistan, Afghanistan, Uzbekistan, Tadzhikistan and further into Central Asia and the Caucasus. Saudi Arabia has dismissed American demands to control, much less stopped, these activities by claiming that that the donations are usually – but far from always – made by private organisation, and that the money only goes to charitable causes. EU member states and the USA have both turned a blind eye to this traffic. In doing so, the West has effectively condoned the financial support of the development of the anti-American militant Islamic movement that has fueled al Qaeda's fire up to today. Many have seen the irony in the fact that the Mujahideen, who formed al Qaeda and thus made the terror attacks of 11 September, were only created thanks to American support in the 1980s. Although to all appearances this view seems to exaggerate the USA's role in the Mujahideen's fight against the Soviet occupying power in Afghanistan[115], what is worse is that it disguises the real problem, namely that the USA and the Western world did not go into the region constructively after the Soviets' withdrawal from Afghanistan in 1989. The USA and the West had had ample opportunity to help establish a new and better security order in the region, but chose instead to leave the scene to questionable Saudi Arabian policy interests and an unpleasant war by proxy in Afghanistan between Pakistan and Iran, in which Saudi Arabia backed Pakistan's support of the Taliban. Instead of entering the region with long-term development projects and cool-headed security policy, the USA left the scene after the defeat of the Soviet Union to regional and local warlords and bandits who, instead of instituting security and order, aided the development of a mire of conflicts, poverty and hopelessness that formed the perfect seedbed for global terror networks.

There are probably two reasons for this short-sighted policy with no view to the future. First of all, it is much easier to obtain political support for the military combat of threats to American interests than for long-term development projects. Second, Washington has regarded Saudi Arabia as a dilemma with a choice between Scylla and Charybdis – that is, either to permit a Saudi Arabian policy of power involving the violation of human rights in the country and exporting domestic conflicts out of the country, or running the risk of destabilizing an important ally in the Persian Gulf. Faced with such a choice, any American government would choose the first and hope that things would not turn out as badly as the Arabists in the State Department always predict.[116] It is to be feared that when the smoke has cleared after the defeat of the Taliban and al Qaeda's camps in Afghanistan, the USA and Europe will again choose to forget the region and leave the long-term resolution of conflicts to local lords and countries such as Pakistan, India and, namely, Saudi Arabia.

That this scenario arouses concern is due not only to the lessons of the past ten years but also to the fact that the conflict in Saudi Arabia is far from a closed chapter; on the contrary, it is deeply rooted in the country's political structure and will therefore characterize the situation for a long time to come. The problem is that only a thoroughgoing reform of the Saudi Arabian system can resolve this globalized conflict and that, until then, the country will continue to export Islamism as a political ideology to the same extent as before. So the situation could last for years, as it is very difficult to imagine the royal family voluntarily relinquishing power. Conversely, nothing indicates that the opposition should be successful in either pushing the reform process through or carrying out a revolution that would depose the Saudis. Looking round the Middle East, it is striking that states which at first glance seem to be under intense pressure both internally and externally actually demonstrate a surprising stability: this was the case with a country like Iraq, which for over 10 years was subject to the toughest international sanctions ever imposed on a state, and was challenged internally by two opposition groups that represented the majority of the population, namely the Kurds in the north and the Shiites in the south. Still, Saddam Hussein seemed to be firm in the saddle. Similarly, the Algerian state is still intact, despite the fact that for over a decade the country has found itself in a civil-war-like conflict between Islamists and the military.

THE YOUNG EXERT PRESSURE

The greatest short-term threat to Saudi Arabian stability appears to come neither from outside the country nor from the opposition, but from the royal family itself. King Fahd's stroke in 1995, which completely incapacitated him, threw the royal family into an internal power struggle about who will take over when the ailing king dies. It is true that a crown prince has been selected, namely the half-brother Abdallah is the de facto leader of the country and has capably consolidated his position since taking power, but who still cannot be completely certain of succeeding to the throne after Fahd. In other words, the coming years will find the country suffering from internal power struggles over succession and the regime's handling of opposition. So Saudi Arabia will probably still be the main supplier of dissatisfied young people who go out into the world to join jihad, wherever it may take place.

This prospect seems relatively certain because the country's internal problems are structural. First, a number of social factors come into play, making it of great significance for the political process, the population on has grown steadily and become increasingly younger, so that over half today are under 15 years of age, at the same time as becoming better educated, so that the vast majority today can read and write. Together, these factors place heavy demands on the state to improve the now worn-out infrastructure, to build schools, hospitals, and – a seemingly impossible task today – to create jobs. This development is taking place at the same time that young people are becoming well-educated and well-informed about what is happening both inside the country and around the world. There is no definitive causal relation between level of education and political affiliation, but as several researchers have pointed out, a general incidence of reading and writing skills means that any political opposition has far better chances of spreading its message than if it is solely dependent on communication by cassette and video tapes.

At the same time that the young are standing in line to enter an increasingly crowded job market – not considering all the manual work done by cheap Asian labor – and that demands for welfare improvements are growing, Saudi Arabia has had major problems in balancing the national budget. Consequently it has accumulated foreign debts and, since the Gulf War, has shown a deficit on the state budget after emptying its currency reserves to pay for the War. In this connection, it makes sense for the opposition to call for a transparent financial policy and demand a reasonable expenditure policy. The government has responded by attempting to implement privatization in a number of areas and Crown Prince Abdallah has pushed to limit the widespread corruption. The following quote from a television interview illustrates the prevalence of the phenomenon, in that Prince Bandar heatedly reacted to an interviewer's question about corruption by pointing out that the royal family had used almost $400 billion to develop the country, and continued: "If you tell me that we, when we built up the entire country ... misused or were corrupt with $50 million, I say "Yes ... what about it?"".[117]

But there is still a long way to go, and the royal family is still extremely vulnerable to criticism because of its extravagance and private consumption. Thus there is a widespread perception in the population, among dissidents in the country as well as critics outside it, that the princes use enormous sums on luxury items, alcohol and prostitutes, despite the fact that these are strictly prohibited in the country.[118]

Rebellion by cassette tape

Cassette tapes are still a very common medium for spreading political messages in the Middle East. One of the critical sheiks from the Islamic opposition in Saudi Arabia, Salman al-Awda, estimates that a shop that sells tapes on Islamic topics can

> have up to 9,500 titles and sell approximately 60,000 copies a month, and that popular tapes are typically reproduced in 30,000 copies.[119] In spite of this, researchers like Fandy, Eickelmann and Gauss agree that printed material such as books and pamphlets plays a still more important role today. As in Iran, where printed matter that is critical of the system can be bought on almost any street corner, religiously based social critique literature is widespread in Saudi Arabia, without the government being able to do much to prevent it. The most forceful opposition groups outside the country have namely used printed material, distributed with the help of fax machines, extensively in order to spread their messages.[120]

THE ALLIANCE BETWEEN AL-SHEIKH AND AL-SAUD

It is precisely the critique of corruption that is one of the most pervasive themes in Middle East Islam-based opposition criticism of its leaders, whether in Algeria, in Hamas's critique of Arafat's leadership, in Iran or in Saudi Arabia, where it is a constant and high-priority issue for the entire opposition. Although there is secular opposition to the royal family that focuses mainly on economic policy, the most comprehensive, best organized and most well-known critique of the regime comes from Islamic based groups and individuals in and outside the country. That there is Islamic opposition in a country like Saudi Arabia, which appears to be one of the most absolutely conservative and religiously orthodox states in the world, may seem something of a paradox. Nevertheless, since the beginning of the last century the royal family has had to secure its power base by on the one hand insisting on its legitimacy on the grounds that it is based on a true Islamic foundation, and on the other keeping the all-too Islamic forces at bay.[121] The Saudi Arabian state is a result of the alliance between the sword, represented by the Saud family, and the Koran, represented by the al-Sheikh family.

Outwardly it appears that the alliance between the Saud family and the Sheikh family creates stability in the country, but there are a number of sources of conflict in Saudi Arabian society: conflicts between genders, conflicts between the Sunni Muslim majority and the Shia Muslim minority and conflicts between the royal family and all those excluded from political influence, and not least Islamic opposition to the government itself. When Ibd Saud formed an alliance with the al-Sheikh family and incorporated leading members into power, a critical Islamic opposition was established – which for the most part saw the new religious elite, the ulama, as a claque for the sitting king and had the job of granting legitimacy to the reigning power. Ibn Saud's incorporation of religion into power structures was rather a reflection of the attempt to contain critics and gain maximal control over them, at the same time that the ulama officially – both inside the country and outwardly – sanctions the Saud family's power by giving it religious legitimacy.

The opposition, many members of which profess the Salafiya movement, opposes the nationalization of Islam – the state being subject to Islam – insisting instead on Islamization of the nation– on Islamic scholars themselves choosing their leaders and thereby taking responsibility for the management of the state. In other words, they are fierce opponents of the secularization, the separation of politics and religion, that they increasingly criticize the royal family for leading the country toward. The closest anyone has recently come to their Sunni-Islamic ideal of Islamization of the state is the Taliban in Afghanistan.

Because Muhammad's descendants were elected and not determined by succession, the royal family's legitimacy is contested from the start. This problem worsens if the actual leadership of the country comes into conflict with fundamental Islamic principles and ethics. This means that as early as the beginning of the establishment of Saudi Arabia as an independent state, a number of religious schisms were seen: both with the oppositions between Sunni and Shia and between official Islam with its state-recognized leaders and a marginalized opposition which perceived the whole structure as so deeply problematic as to border on blasphemy.

With Wahhabism as a building block

The al-Sheikh family traces its roots back to Sheik Muhammad bin Abd al-Wahhab, who became known as an Islamic philosopher of reform in the 18th century. Wahhab's alliance with the Saud family formed the basis of the first Saudi state (1744-1811), and his interpretation of Islam is still current in Saudi Arabia today and is preached throughout Central and South Asia.

Put somewhat strongly, it can be said that Wahhabism today has spread in pace with the movement of Afghan Veterans around the world. But in fact the ideology has been in effect in Afghanistan since as far back as 1824, when the Wahhabi Sheik Sayyid Ahmad declared jihad against the English in the Punjab province. In 1830 the Wahhabis occupied Peshawar and established a state there. The Wahhabis became known for their resistance against the British in India (1857-59). Beyond Saudi Arabia, Wahhabism is prevalent today in Qatar, parts of the United Arab Emirates, parts of Africa, South Asia, Central Asia and the Caucasus.

It was the founder of the modern Saudi Arabian state, Ibn Saud, who made Wahhabism the state religion in 1930, but that happened, typically enough, after a violent clash with those who were most orthodox within the tradition, second only to the Abd al-Wahhab Brotherhood (Ikhwan). While for Ibn Saud, who practiced *realpolitik*, it was a question of uniting the country into those areas that more or less constitute Saudi Arabia today, Ikhwan wanted to spread Wahhabism to neighboring Jordan and Iraq as well as to the British protectorates in the Gulf, through a radical interpretation of the concept of da'wa. This project could have completely destroyed all chances of forming a Saudi Arabian state, which Ibn Saud, who was cunning in *realpolitik*, could clearly see. Instead, he clamped down on Ikhwan, ousted its most radical members, and invited the rest along as ideological leaders of the new state, which officially achieved independence in 1932.

ISLAMIC FUNDAMENTALISM AND THE GULF WAR

With the social improvements that came with the enormous earnings from the sale of oil, and that brought real benefits to the population in the form of increased affluence, the critical voices of the opposition did not receive much attention from the people. Although loosely organized opposition groups had been formed as early as the 1950s, little was heard from them, and they had no popular support worth mentioning. As Saudi Arabian society was modernized, it became increasingly necessary for leaders to ensure Islamic sanctioning of the increasingly visible difference between the leaders of state and society's religiously based social spaces. This happened formally in 1971, when Saudi Arabia's third King Faisal bin Abd al-Aziz established a number of councils through what was known as Faisal's decree.

The task of the councils was to build a bridge between the state and society. The idea was that the councils – with the most important one, the Council of Senior Ulama (Majlis Hay'at Kibar al-Ulama) comprising the most competent Islamic scholars and led by Abd al-Aziz Bin Baz – would supplement the traditional interpretation of Islamic law (shari'a), with the aim of adapting the needs of modern society to traditional Islam.[122] On the surface it looked as if the regime was opening itself more to the advice of Islamic scholars, but in fact their agenda was greater control and containment of Islamic institutions. This had two contradictory consequences: on the one hand control was increased; but on the other, the entire question of who was to define true Islam became even more politicized, with the result that the opposition became more self-assured.

The first time the royal family was seriously challenged was in November 1979, when two Islamic rebels, Juhayman bin Muhammad al Utaybi and Muhammad bin Abdallah al Qahtani, occupied the Grand Mosque in Mecca, Islam's most holy site, where along with several hundred sympathizers, they initiated a revolt against the regime. The rebels did not succeed in mobilizing the necessary popular support, probably because they had chosen an Islamic institution rather than a palace or government building for their action, and the rebels were removed by force. The result was closer monitoring of the population and more power to the Mutawwa'in, the religious police.[123] Yet the action had demonstrated that the regime was vulnerable.

Throughout the 1980s, a politicization of Islamic studies was seen at universities, for instance, that resulted in the education of a new generation of young sheiks and professors who, along with new students, were much more openly critical of established Islam than had previously been seen. A number of young Saudis, probably numbering around 15,000, went to Afghanistan to take part in the holy war against the Soviet Union; the very mobilization of this jihad – along with a generally growing awareness of conditions in the Middle East and the signs of bad leadership of the country – helped to spread the opposition's message.

The major turning point, however, was the crisis in the Middle East occasioned by Iraq's occupation of Kuwait in 1990. It was feared both in the USA and in Saudi Arabia that Iraq had plans to continue its military advance into the country, and the regime's reaction to the Iraqi threat was to ask Americans for military aid. Because the Saudi-Arabian government had obtained support for this reguest from the Senior Ulama, who issued a fatwa, or religious sentence, the government was further discredited in the eyes of the opposition. The UN Security Council condemned Iraq's invasion of Kuwait and demanded Iraqi withdrawal; if this did not occur the UN, under the leadership of the USA, would force Iraq out of the little desert country. The result was that over a half million American soldiers came to Saudi Arabia. This was met with criticism by the opposition on two counts. First, considering the billions of dollars in oil money that the government had invested in arms, it was deeply humiliating that Saudi Arabia was still not able to defend itself; this revealed the incompetence of the country's leaders as well as the lack of credibility of the images the princes had created of themselves as heroic warriors. Second – and of much greater importance in the long term – it was problematic to invite ungodly soldiers, some of whom were even women who covered themselves only if forced to, to defend the holy ground of Islam. The royal family swore that the American soldiers would leave Saudi Arabia immediately after the liberation of Kuwait, but this did not happen.

Ever since, the USA has had at least 20,000 soldiers in the Middle East, a number of whom are located at bases in the Arab Gulf states, including Saudi Arabia. The bases were used – discreetly, as agreed upon with royal family, so as not to challenge the opposition unnecessarily – for weekly bombing missions into Iraq, which the USA claimed were necessary after Saddam Hussein pressed the UN's weapons inspectors out of the country in 1998. The USA's policy in Iraq was also the object of growing critique in the Middle East, because the sanctions and bombings affected only the Iraqi population, while Saddam remained in power, by all appearances producing whatever weapons suited him. In the eyes of many Muslims, the fact that the USA, backed by the UK, continued to bomb and stubbornly insists on upholding the sanctions, is a sign that Americans intend only to repress Islam and Arabs and exploit the region's resources. Finally, most Arabs see the USA's role in the Israeli-Palestinian conflict as one-sided American support for Israel, or at least, as the USA's giving Israel a greater amount of leeway than the Palestinians.[124] From this perspective, the fact that Saudi Arabia formed a close alliance with the USA is therefore a clear sign that the royal family left the true path of Islam long ago and is prepared to sell out on all values, with the objective of staying in power.

THE OPPOSITION SOUNDS OFF

The Senior Ulama's fatwa that supported the royal family's plea for American military aid was the crucial piece of evidence for the opposition that things were totally amiss in the country. In the attempt to oblige the opposition, King Fahd promised reforms, including the formation of a kind of parliament, but this did not prevent some sheiks, mainly younger ones, from voicing their criticism of the reigning elite through pamphlets and cassette tapes. In the spring of 1991 some of the most prominent sheiks, Sheik Salman al-Awda and Sheik Safar bin Abd al-Rahman al-Hawali, wrote a letter that circulated in various religious circles. The regime put an end to this, but the rebellious sheiks continued their efforts and during the summer of 1992 were able to present to the country's top religious leader, Sheikh bin Baz, a declaration recommending thorough reforms and attacked the established institutions' monopoly on interpretations of Islam. The king reacted by demanding that the Senior Ulama displayed their disapproval of the declaration by issuing a fatwa, but several of the council's members refrained from participating in the proceedings against the young sheiks, a clear sign that the opposition had now gained broad support.[125] After this, there was open conflict between the groups seeking reform and the regime (and the established interpretation of Islam). The following year six sheiks founded the Committee for the Defense of Legitimate Rights (CDLR) with Muhammad al-Mas'ari as spokesman. Al-Mas'ari was forced into exile and in 1994 settled in London, from where his criticism of the Saudi Arabian regime was distributed via fax machines. In London, which is a Mecca for all sorts of Islamic opposition movements, al-Ma'sari came into contact with still more radical groups, such as Hizb al-Tahrir, which has its headquarters there, giving rise to internal tensions in CDLR, which ended up declaring bankruptcy in 1996. Still more Saudi Arabian opposition groups, like the Movement for Islamic reform in Arabia (MIRA), led by Sa'd al-Faqih, and Osama bin Laden's Council and Reform Committee (ARC), which was an umbrella organization for more radical and militant groups, had their headquarters in London.

Most of the opposition faced by Saudi Arabia's royal family in the 1990s had prioritized a strategy of non-violence. Yet there have been examples of unrest in connection with demonstrations,[126] which are prohibited, and actual terror attacks have twice taken place in the country, on both occasions aimed directly at American forces in the country. The first time was in Riyadh in 1995, when five American soldiers were killed; the second time was the following year in al-Khobar on the Gulf coast, where several hundred people, mostly locals, were wounded, with 19 Americans losing their lives. No official investigation of either of these actions has been completed, although in May 1996 Saudi Arabia executed four Saudi Arabians in connection with the Riyadh attack. Three of these were Afghan veterans and all of them had announced on Saudi Arabian TV that they were affiliated with CDLR and thus the Islamic opposition. They were beheaded before the FBI, according to their own account, had had the opportunity to interview them, and a great deal of doubt has therefore been raised about whether their confessions are reliable or whether they were made under duress. Saudi Arabia chose to present them and thereby officially confirm that the terrorist attacks against the USA were entirely rooted in internal Saudi affairs, which is both extremely embarrassing and an unusual move for the country, and therefore suggests that the four at least had something to do with the bombings.

The al-Khobar bombing has also been linked with the Afghan veterans, and increasingly to another internal Saudi Arabian conflict, namely that between Sunni and Shia Muslims, which is felt most strongly on the east coast. There are thus persistent rumors and accusations that Iran had been fishing in troubled waters and that a Saudi Arabian counterpart of Hizballah was to have been behind the attack. This accusation was made among others by Louis Freeh, the head of the FBI under Clinton, in an interview for the *New Yorker* magazine in the spring of 2001.[127]

So far the government in Riyadh has been successful in limiting the conflict to scattered demonstrations, the two terrorist attacks mentioned, and the political activities of the exiled groups in London and of lobbies in Washington, which up to now have had only limited impact on American policy. This has been possible because the government has successfully maintained officious control of the population and strictly limited the young ulama's opportunities for speaking up at all in Saudi society. Sheik al-Auda and Sheik al-Hawali were thus imprisoned for five years from 1994 to 1999, which has not kept them from voicing their criticism of both the established power elite in Saudi Arabia and of the USA and the West. Saudi Arabia has also been able to put a lid on the conflict by simply exporting it to Central and South Asia, for example, and indirectly at least to the USA and the West. It is in this connection that Osama bin Laden comes into the picture, namely as one of Saudi Arabia's most visionary exporters of jihad.

The opposition in Saudi Arabia is not only Islamic. Critique of the royal family's mismanagement is also heard from other parts, such as young Western-oriented and Western-educated businesspeople who are indignant over the princes' excessive consumption and the regime's refusal to provide the Saudi public with more basic information about the economy that might facilitate greater transparency in economic policy. What has been characteristic up through the 1990s, however, is that the critique from such secular groups has approached that of the Islamists, which in turn has something in common with that of the shia muslims; taken together, this means that, despite their clear differences, the opposition groups are increasingly joining forces to oppose the royal family[128] – a situation not unlike the one in Iran prior to the revolution in 1979. And as was the case in Iran, the political critique comes to expression in and around Islamic institutions, schools, universities, mosques, Islamic charity organizations and funds, because these areas still have the greatest degree of autonomy in spite of the state's efforts to control them. There are limits to how hard the regime can clamp down on these organizations if it is to avoid collapsing in the vulnerable alliance between the sword and the book; and after 11 September, new and narrower limits have been set for the degree to which domestic policy conflicts can be exported as jihad to other regions and countries. The Saudi dilemma has, in other words, grown significantly after 11 September.

So far, Saudi Arabia has avoided major visible problems with Islamic based terrorism at home, through its systematic control of the opposition and by exporting its domestic policy problems. This has been possible largely because of the country's strategic location and strong position among oil exporting countries. Like Saudi Arabia, Egypt has been a major supplier of Islamic fundamentalistic ideology and volunteers for the war in Afghanistan. The next chapter examines more closely the background for Islamic fundamentalism in Egypt.

6. EGYPT: A HISTORICAL SETTING FOR MILITANT ISLAM

Islamic fundamentalism and militant Islamic groups are not new phenomena in Egypt but part of a political tradition that harks back to the beginning of the 20th century, when the Muslim Brotherhood was founded and formulated its critique of the established Egyptian society's lack of emphasis on Islam and Islamic values. But it was not until the appearance of the Islamic ideologue Sayyid Qutb's analysis of Egyptian society as being in a condition of jahiliya – referring to the ignorance, or unknowingness that characterized human existence before the revelation of the Koran – and the Egyptian leaders as apostates and infidels, that there was a decisive break with the tradition of Islamic opposition as it had been up to then. This was also the case with the concept of jihad, which was reformulated, interpreted as having a more offensive connotation, and expounded as the duty of the individual, making it an ideological and action-oriented starting point for generations of militant Muslims who directed violent attacks against the Egyptian state and its leaders.

The Muslim Brotherhood was established in Egypt in 1928 by Hassan al-Banna, who agitated for social, economic and political reforms based on an Islamic foundation. The Brotherhood's activities comprised the founding of various associations, the building of mosques and schools, the establishment of hospitals and health clinics, and the publishing of books and tracts. In this period the foundations and tradition of social work undertaken by the Muslim Brotherhood and other later Islamic groups were laid.

Their activities were not, however, limited to social and political work but also included terrorism, targeting British installations around the Suez Canal and the Egyptian Prime Minister, who was assassinated in 1948. The Brotherhood was also active in the popular uprising that paved the way for the Free Officer's coup in Egypt in 1952, and the Brotherhood's broad popular support was, from the very beginning, a threat to the power of the military. General Gamal Abdel Nasser, who was one of the leaders of the coup and Egypt's President from 1956, therefore introduced early on a hard-line and repressive policy against the Muslim Brotherhood, which included mass arrests and executions. This policy was followed for the most until Nasser's death in 1970.

MODERATE AND MILITANT WINGS

The Muslim Brotherhood criticized Nasser's introduction of Arab socialism, which they characterized as atheistic and as a foreign element imported into Islamic tradition. Nasser was thus regarded a traitor. In 1965 the conflicts between Nasser and the Muslim Brotherhood deepened, and in 1966 several of the movements leaders, including the forceful ideologue Sayyid Qutb (1906 – 66), were hanged. After this the Muslim Brotherhood lived in obscurity until Sadat came to power in 1970 and gave greater leeway to the Islamic forces in Egyptian society, though first and foremost within universities. The idea was that the Islamic movement was to counterbalance the strong influence of the Nasserists and the socialists. Many Muslim brothers were released from prison, where they had been put as a consequence of their Islamic activities under Nasser.[129]

This divided, and changed the contours of, the Islamic movement in Egypt, which since the early 1970s has generally been divided according to two tendencies: the moderate and the militant. The moderate wing employed peaceful means in attempts to advance its aim: the establishment of an Islamic state in Egypt. This tendency was represented most clearly by a reoriented Muslim Brotherhood, which has worked within the framework of Egyptian society since the early 1970s. The militant wing comprises those Islamic groups who used violence in their attempts to destabilize the Egyptian regime and take power in Egyptian society in order to further its aim of the immediate establishment of an Islamic state in Egypt.

SAYYID QUTB AND THE STATE OF JAHILIYA

The militant Islamic groups who have asserted themselves in and outside Egypt since the 1970s have found much of their ideological foundation and inspiration in Sayyid Qutb's ideas and social analyses.

The basis for Qutb's radicalism was partly a series of personal experiences and partly a number of social factors. Qutb was educated as a teacher and in the 1940s was employed in the Egyptian Ministry of Education, where one of his responsibilities was to draft proposals for reform of the education system; yet his numerous proposals were rejected. Qutb was also a writer of fiction and a social critic, and on several occasions this put him at odds with the royal Egyptian leadership, who wanted him imprisoned. Instead, he was sent to the USA in 1948 for the official purpose of studying the American education system, although the Egyptian government also hoped that the visit to the USA could make Qutb more pro-American. What happened, however, was the opposite. Qutb received a very negative impression of American society, which he found completely lacking in values and morals, and he rejected American materialism. Qutb also experienced strong anti-Arab sentiment in American society, which came to expression, for instance, with the founding of the state of Israel in 1948. The personal consequences for Qutb of his time spent in the USA were his condemnation of Western culture and his turn towards Islam instead. In 1951, he returned to Egypt, where he voiced his anti-Americanism so loudly that he was forced to leave the Ministry of Education, after which he became an active member of the Muslim Brotherhood. In 1954 Qutb was imprisoned – along with a number of leading Muslim brothers – and his time in jail, which lasted until 1964, was a major contributory factor to the radicalization of his thinking.

The social factors harked back to the end of the 1950s, when the new Egyptian leadership under Nasser had led to no significant changes in an Islamic direction. On the contrary, as mentioned above, conditions became more difficult for the Muslim Brotherhood. This meant that Qutb, unlike al-Banna, put more focus on the Islamic tradition within Egypt. For Qutb, the country's difficult foreign relations after the Free Officers' coup were not a sufficient explanation for the lack of social changes in Egypt. The work that became the most important source of inspiration for militant Islamic activism since the 1970s was Qutb's *Milestones*, written between 1962 and 1964, while Qutb was imprisoned.[130] *Milestones*, which achieved great popularity, contains by way of introduction an analysis of the current society, which Qutb regarded as a false Islamic one. The book propounds various recommendations for how society was to be changed and replaced by a true Islamic society – that is, a society based on the Islamic values that were present under Muhammad and the four well-guided caliphs.

Qutb rejects Western and secular ideologies, capitalism, socialism and Marxism as man-made ideologies and systems that, in his view, cannot satisfy the needs of human beings; he finds in the secular mentality of the West an explanation for the decay of the Western world. "The period of the Western system has come to an end primarily because it is deprived of those life-giving values which enabled it to be the leader of mankind".[131] God-made Islam is Qutb's weapon in the showdown against man-made ideologies.[132] His point was precisely that it is not God-made Islam that characterized the Muslim societies of his time. He therefore found it necessary for mankind to have new leadership and a true Islamic system and society.[133]

In his book he concludes that the entire world is in a state of jahiliya, the ignorance in which human beings lived before the Koran was revealed to the prophet Muhammad. Jahiliya is a key concept in Qutb's social analysis and ideology.

In a true Islamic society, according to Qutb, God is sovereign and the Koran is the only object of worship. In a society in the state of jahiliya, divine sovereignty and worship are granted to or usurped by people or parties who have elevated themselves to this level. Here, Qutb is taking aim not only at Nasser but also at leaders of the other Arab countries that are designated jahiliya societies: "all existing so-called Muslim societies (are) also jahiliya societies [...] not because they believe in other gods than God, or because they worship anyone other than God, but because their lifestyle is not exclusively based on submitting oneself to God".[134] Qutb, then, regards the Middle Eastern societies as un-Islamic and illegitimate, and he stresses that compromise is unacceptable to Islam. A society is either jahiliya or it is Islamic.

After this analysis of the state of jahiliya, Qutb emphasizes the duty that rests upon the enlightened, namely taking the cause into one's own hands and establishing an Islamic order. Qutb names jihad as the means by which to combat jahiliya[135] and denies that jihad must only be interpreted in a defensive sense, which is the usual interpretation or tradition generally emphasized by cleric.[136] The aim of jihad is naturally to establish God's sovereignty on earth. Qutb's interpretation therefore breaks with tradition and constitutes a new starting point in the fight against governments and leaders who limit a Muslim's opportunities to live in a free and Islamic society.

In *Milestones* he discusses martyrdom and underscores that it is achieved only by those who fight God's fight. The criterion for fulfilling the aim of establishing a true Islamic society is the formation of a vanguard of enlightened individuals: "It is necessary that there should be a vanguard which sets out with this determination and then keeps walking on the path, marching through the vast ocean of Jahiliya […]. This vanguard should know the landmarks and the milestones of the road toward this goal so that they may recognize the starting place, the nature, the responsibilities and the ultimate purpose of this long journey."[137] "I have written Milestones for this vanguard, which I consider to be a waiting reality about to be materialized."[138]

Qutb's analyses and interpretations represent a radicalization of what had been the main currents for the Muslim Brotherhood, whose methods and strategy he rejects. His final showdown with society, rulers and the moderate part of the Muslim Brotherhood was characterized by the view that human beings are not Muslims as long as they life life in a state of jahiliya.[139]

Full freedom of speech was not a right existing in Egypt, and Qutb was imprisoned again in 1965 and executed in 1966 for conspiring to overthrow the Egyptian regime. Thus he did not get the chance to witness attempts to realize his ideas. But with Qutb and *Milestones* the concepts of jahiliya and jihad took on great significance for later militant Islamic activism. As pointed out by the renowned Islam researcher Kepel, the book was a major source for those who wanted to replace an ungodly society with an Islamic state, and "Qutb's *Milestones* marked out the starting point of the road along which the militants of the Islamicist movement would travel".[140] As Kepel concludes, "If this logic is taken to its conclusion, Qutb's thought must lead to a violent takeover of power".[141]

THE IDEOLOGY IS REALIZED

One of the most spectacular Islamic fundamentalistic movements in Egypt was the Muslim Society (Jama'at al-Muslimin), which was in reality two different groups whose histories were closely interwoven. The one group was established in 1971 under the leadership of Salah Sariya and is most known for an unsuccessful coup in 1974, the purpose of which had been to establish Egypt as an Islamic state by a regular takeover of power. Ideologically, the group condemned the political system but not Egyptian society as a whole, which was regarded as a conscienceless and ungodly victim of the political system's leadership.[142] Inspired by Qutb, Sariya regarded Egypt as a profane state and Sadat as a blasphemer who had to be got rid of. The plan was as simple as it was naive. First the military academy in Cairo was to be taken over and governmental power seized. The coup attempt took place 18 April 1974, with plans to drug guards and then secretly take over the academy, don uniforms and use the military vehicles the following day to drive to the parliament building where Sadat was to give a speech. The rest of the plan was to murder Sadat, take the other leaders hostage and then declare live on television the establishment of the Islamic Republic of Egypt.

The plan failed in its very first phase. The attempt to drug the guards failed and the activists, including Sariya, were arrested and the leaders executed the following fall. The Egyptian authorities officially accused Libya of being behind the coup attempt, which was probably an effort to suggest the episode had taken place under external influences and thereby deflect attention from the circumstance that the authorities themselves had to a great extent advanced and motivated the Islamic movement.

The coup attempt and the subsequent executions meant the end of the movement, though some of its members joined other groups.

The group within the movement, the Muslim Society, was founded in 1972 by Shukri Mustafa, who had previously been a member of the Muslim Brotherhood and spent six years in prison from 1965 to 1971, and was then released when Sadat attempted to ally himself with Islamic forces. The Muslim Society did not distinguish between the political system and society but regarded them as closely linked, like two sides of the same coin. If the political system was diseased so was society, and vice versa.[143]

While in prison, Shukri had studied Qutb's works, and immediately following his release he broke with the Muslim Brotherhood and the moderate branch and began recruiting members for his own group. In practice Shukri wanted to isolate his group from the surrounding jahiliya society, which is why the members of the group refused to participate in Friday prayers in the state-owned mosques and to serve their military duty in the Egyptian army, and did not want to take jobs in the public sector.

In July 1977 the group kidnapped a former minister of religious affairs who was later murdered, which led to the arrest of several hundred of the group's members; at the subsequent military trial five people, including Shukri Mustafa, were sentenced to death and executed in March 1978.

In addition to the Muslim Brotherhood, the militant Islamic groups of the 1970s stemmed from the Muslim student movement Jama'at, the dominant student movement at universities in the 1970s; it took over several of the existing student movements and underwent a radicalization that was completely underestimated by Sadat.

Part of the success of the Muslim movement was due largely to the way the student movement identified the students' concrete and practical problems of migration, modernity and gender roles. The movement became an important psychological factor as a kind of shelter against modern life in larger cities.[144] The student movement built camps, terra islamica, where Koran reading was a central element, and the students were part of a number of social contexts which Kepel designates "microcosmic experiments in an Islamic utopia – past and present [...] the camps were to be models of coming/emerging Islamic societies, which the young Islamists planned to build on the ruins of the jahiliya society".[145]

THE ASSASSINATION OF SADAT

In September 1981, some 1,500 Islamists were arrested, partly as a result of unrest that broke out between militant Muslims and Christian Copts in a district of Cairo in the summer of 1981, and partly as a result of the increasing tension between the Islamic groups and the Egyptian regime, which culminated in the murder of Sadat at a military parade in Cairo on 6 October 1981.

The assassination was carried out by a group named al-Jihad, which probably stemmed from the Islamic student movement. Several of the student leaders, who came from the Nile city of Assiut, became emirs in al-Jihad[146] "Emir" is an Arabic expression that means "lord", but in the political Islam brought about by the militant movements, the expression has taken on a new meaning and today can be compared with the expression "operative leader", just as the Arabic word "shura", which means "deliberation", has almost come to mean "executive committee". This kind of Shura committee, consisting of several emirs, coordinated the general strategy for al-Jihad. One emir for al-Jihad was the ideologue Muhammad Faraj, who wrote the ideological justification for the murder of Sadat – another was Tal'at Fuad Qasim,[147] who later became part of the leadership of al Jama'at al-Islamiya and resided in Denmark from 1992-95, as we relate later in Chapter 9.

The group had contact with Omar Abdel Rahman, who was a professor at the university in Assiut and who became the group's mufti in the spring of 1981. "Mufti" is the designation for the person who has the authority to issue fatwas. The group had probably not been in contact with Rahman, since as early as the late 1970s he had already issued a fatwa that could be interpreted as a legitimization of the killing of Sadat for not ruling in accordance with what was recommended by God.[148]

Rahman also issued fatwas legitimizing al-Jihad's actions in Assiut, where militant Muslims were promised admittance to Paradise when they joined the armed fight or when they killed and robbed Coptic jewelers to raise money for financing the militant Islamic movement. Among those arrested in September 1981 was one of the student leaders at the university in Assiut, Mohammed Shawki al-Islambuli, brother of

Khalid al-Islambuli, who was one of the culprits behind the assassination of Sadat. Mohammed's arrest and harsh treatment by the authorities of was an important personal motive for Khalid to participate in the assassination.[149] The arrests also had great significance for the radicalization of several youths at the universities, who were frustrated and disillusioned over the student movement's lack of ability to take action; thus they joined al-Jihad, which was known for more direct and violent actions.

The ideological point of departure for al-Jihad is contained in the pamphlet *The Neglected Duty*, drawn up by the ideologue Muhammad Faraj (1954-82). The title refers to a Muslim's "neglected" obligation to wage jihad against an infidel.[150] The pamphlet's 140 paragraphs give the reader insight into the ideological thought and the strategies that provide the basis for the group's assassination of Sadat. The pamphlet both marks a shift in the ideology and strategy of militant Islamic movements since Qutb's *Milestones* and serves partly as a justification for the killing of Sadat.

Faraj wanted to reverse what he regarded as the futile developments for the Islamic movement in relation to the political system in Egypt in the 1970s.[151] But the crucial issue for Faraj and al-Jihad is not the potential for progress within the framework of the Egyptian society nor grassroots Islamization, but the very exercise of power by the regime and its leaders in relation to an Islamic society. Faraj gives higher priority to the concept of jihad, which therefore assumes a more central significance in the pamphlet and in the group's ideology, which, simplified, consists of direct insurrection against the regime and killing of the head of state. Faraj expresses it thus: "Jihad (struggle) for God's cause, in spite of its extreme importance and its great significance for the future of this religion, has been neglected."[152]

In the pamphlet Faraj argues that insofar as an Islamic state cannot be established without a fight, this fight then becomes a duty. On the question of whether Egypt is an Islamic state, Faraj not surprisingly arrives at a "no". So the leader of such a non-Islamic state cannot be called a Muslim either. Thus, although Sadat was born a Muslim and called himself a Muslim, he was to be regarded as an apostate, and his fate, Faraj clearly states, on the basis of Islamic law, is death.

Faraj underscores that jihad is an individual and personal duty if the enemy is among Muslims and especially so if the enemy directly constitutes the leadership: "We must concentrate on our own Islamic situation: we must establish the rules of God's religion in our own country first [...] there is no doubt that the first strike for jihad is the destruction of the infidel leaders, so they can be replaced by a complete Islamic order. From here we can begin."[153] Which is exactly what they did.

On 6 October 1981 President Sadat, together with his Vice President Hosni Mubarak, much of the political establishment and a number of foreign representatives, participated in a military parade on the eighth anniversary of the Egyptian – and Syrian – armies' attack on Israel. Sadat had positioned the majority of his bodyguards behind the stands in case of an attack "from outside," that is, from groups in Egyptian civil society who constituted a threat. The assumption behind this decision was probably that Sadat did not imagine that the threat could come from units within the Egyptian army upon whose loyalty and control his power rested – like most other leaders in the Middle East. Sadat was not surprised, either, when one of the participating military vehicles suddenly stopped in front of the stands. It was not unusual for old Soviet military vehicles to have engine failure. But the stands were suddenly transformed into a bloodbath when four people from the military truck aimed their automatic weapons and hand grenades at the sitting crowd and killed a large number of people, including the Egyptian president.

The spectacular assassination ended with Sergeant Khalid's legendary remark: "I am Khalid al-Islambuli. I have killed the Pharaoh, and I do not fear death."[154]

Tal'at Fuad Qasim has described how he, as emir for Khalid al-Islambuli, took part in planning the assassination of Sadat, and how Khalid was very enthusiastic. "He asked me several times for permission to bomb Sadat's palace [...] I reassured him and hinted that a large action was being prepared, and that he had to wait. Later I incorporated Khalid in the unity that was behind the coup attempt."[155]

There is no doubt that the aim of the assassination of Sadat was the establishment of an Islamic state in Egypt, but whether Faraj and al-Jihad had considered the concrete situation following the assassination is unknown. Apparently the group had no plans for the practical execution of the coup d'etat. The group's self-image presumably included a strong belief that the assassination of Sadat and the consequent removal of the "fallen tyrant" would trigger spontaneous popular support, as was the case in Iran in connection with the fall of the Shah two years earlier.

A rebellion in Assiut on 8 October 1981 was quickly suppressed by security forces from Cairo.

Faraj's strategy was mistaken. Society did not change, even though the head of state had been murdered. Many of the al-Jihad group's members were arrested and charged, and Faraj, along with Khalid, was sentenced to death and executed in April 1982.

NEW TENSIONS BETWEEN THE GOVERNMENT AND OPPOSITION

After the assassination of Sadat, Mubarak and the Egyptian regime markedly altered their strategy with regard to the Islamic movement, which temporarily neutralized the militant Islamic groups, who did not begin to challenge the Egyptian regime again until the end of the 1980s.

Incipient confrontations between the regime and militant Muslims at universities in particular culminated in the election year of 1987, when more than 500 members of militant Islamic groups were arrested after an assassination attempt on a former minister of the interior and two American diplomats.[156] Tensions between militant Muslims and the regime continued in 1988 and 1989, when several thousand students were arrested for "anti-national activities." In 1990 parliamentary elections were held, with a campaign that was marked extensively by violent opposition to and anger over Egypt's pro-Western position toward Iraq's invasion of Kuwait in August 1990. The critique was put forward by Islamic activists in particular, and tension was further increased with the assassination of the chairman of the Egyptian parliament in Cairo in October. In the most comprehensive security operation since the murder of Sadat, security forces made a number of arrests of Muslim activists in the suburbs of Cairo and in Assiut, and members of al-Jihad were later held responsible for the assassination of the Parliament chairman.[157]

However, it was not only in Egyptian university circles that Muslim activists had the opportunity to establish networks. The growing number of private mosques also contributed to contacts made between a large number of youths and people affiliated with the militant groups. The poor socio-economic conditions in slum areas in and around the large Egyptian cities has, to a great extent, advanced Islamic activism, and the many private mosques in these areas have become pivotal sites for the spread of militant ideology. In the mid-1990s there were 70,000 mosques in Egypt, and the number is increasing – from 1961 to 1984 alone, the total number of mosques grew from 17,000 to 50,000. More than half of the 70,000 mosques are private and therefore outside the control of authorities, which the regime considers a serious problem, since the private mosques constitute a form of logistical support and important recruitment base for the militant Islamic groups.[158] The Egyptian authorities have therefore given high priority to the fight against and control of the private mosques in the effort to combat Islamic fundamentalism and its recruitment opportunities.

The mosques owned and controlled by the state are linked to the established form of Islam represented by the ulama, the council of learned clerics, which in many Muslim countries has a virtual monopoly on theological and intellectual activity and teaching, and many of whom hold positions as teachers, judges or imams in mosques. First and foremost, the ulama lays claim to interpretations of shari'a without attacking or challenging the nature of the political system. The council of clerics thus has an indirect legitimizing effect on the regime, which, in return, is charged with the duty of defending the Muslim social community.[159] The ulama concerned was attacked by the Islamists on two counts. First, for its submissiveness and loyalty to those in power, by which it went far in legitimizing Nasser's socialism and Sadat's liberalism and generally accepting a secular regime and its laws that conflicted with shari'a. Second, Islamists attacked the ulama's compromise with Western modernity on the central issue of the separation of religion and politics.[160]

Politicization of the Islamic concepts of jahiliya and jihad thus became an important point of departure for generations of militant Muslims who challenged the non-Islamic state and its leaders from within the framework set by these two highly motivating and emotional concepts. It was, however, not only within Egypt that militant groups attempted to make jahiliya and jihad matters for direct action. This was also the case outside the Middle East, namely in Afghanistan, as we shall see in the next chapter.

7. THE SOVIET INVASION OF AFGHANISTAN

One of the reasons for the Middle East's turbulent recent history is the rivalry between the superpowers that, for half a century, was played out between the USA and the Soviet Union. In the Middle Eastern region, Iran and then Afghanistan became pivotal pawns in the geopolitical game between the Soviet Union and the USA. In this chapter we look more closely at the background for the Soviet occupation of Afghanistan and at the USA-led anti-Soviet alliance, which was a crucial prerequisite for the creation of the resistance against the Soviet occupying power in Afghanistan.

Dramatic developments in key countries in the Middle East have always increased the tension in the region and almost always have global significance. The Iranian revolution in 1979, which completely and radically altered Iran's international relations, also had very great consequences in and outside the region. Iran had served two purposes as one of the USA's certain and important allies: the country had played a role in the global containment of the Soviet Union, which had been the USA's military-political strategy since World War II, and at the same time functioned as a stabilizing state for the promotion of Western interests in the Middle East.

The Arab Gulf states and Iraq reacted to the Islamic revolution in Iran by regarding the new Shia-Islamic state as an unmistakable threat to their existence. Khomeini stressed that the Islamic revolution did not recognize national boundaries but ought to be a model for the formation of states everywhere around the world. It was on this basis that the idea of exporting the Islamic revolution was formulated. The idea was that the Iranian Islamic civilization was to spread to the rest of the world, though especially to the Gulf States and other Arab countries that accused Iran of supporting rebel movements. The most obvious example was Iran's establishment and control of Hizballah in Lebanon.

The Iranian revolution

Following extensive unrest the Shah left Iran 15 January 1979 never to return; two weeks later, on 1 February, the Ayatollah Khomeini flew to Teheran from Paris. In one fell swoop the USA's best and most reliable ally in the Middle East became its worst enemy. In spite of disagreement among members of the Iranian power elite, relations with the USA – which shortly before the revolution had, in the words of President Jimmy Carter, regarded Iran "an island of stability" in a region marked by conflict – were effectively ended. On 4 November 1979, the American embassy in Teheran was occupied and over 50 American employees were held hostage by a group of radical students who wanted to force the USA to hand over the Shah, who was in New York at the time.

The occupation and the hostage crisis came to last 444 days and was a bad humiliation for the American superpower. It was made no less so by an unsuccessful liberation attempt that cost the lives of several American soldiers whose helicopters collided as they took off from the Saudi Arabian desert.

THE CARTER DOCTRINE

The Islamic revolution in Iran in 1979 occurred at the same time as another important event in the region that still has international political significance today, namely the Soviet invasion of Afghanistan in December 1979. The Soviet Union was only 400 kilometers from the Gulf, and the USA reacted by establishing what was called the Rapid Deployment Force (RDF), which involved a permanent American presence in the Gulf and bases in countries such as Turkey, Kenya, Morocco and Egypt, as well as military armament of the coral island of Diego Carcia in the Indian Ocean. The great strategic importance of the Middle East and the Gulf region for the USA was emphasized in January 1980 by the American President in what has later come to be called the Carter Doctrine: "An attempt by any outside force to gain control of the Persian Gulf region will be regarded as an assault on the vital interests of the United States of America, and such an assault will be repelled by any means necessary, including military force".[161]

With that, the Islamic revolution in Iran and the Soviet invasion of Afghanistan caused the strategic weight in the USA's containment policy to be transferred to Afghanistan, which became the site for the writing of the final chapter in the Cold War superpower rivalry between the USA and the Soviet Union.

COUP IN AFGHANISTAN

Prime Minister Mohammad Daoud's coup in 1973 put an end to the ten-year period of democratization of Afghanistan's political system that had created a constitution with a bipartite division of power into a Senate and a people's chamber, free press, increased equality between the sexes and more. Strong political interests opposed developments along the lines of Western-oriented democracy. There were those who were known as "traditionalists", who wanted to preserve an Afghan culture under the strong dominance of Islam, and there were Marxist-Leninists, who desired a revolutionary upheaval of the Afghan society. The political oppositions resulted in a number of strikes and, from 1968, student unrest in many places throughout the country. The end of Afghan democracy came in July 1973, when Daoud carried out his coup and abolished both Afghan democracy and monarchy and founded a republic with himself as President. Daoud's coup was welcomed in broad circles in Afghanistan. The army and the intellectual elite had lost influence with the democratic reforms, and there was widespread dissatisfaction with increasing nepotism and corruption in the Afghan state machinery. In his previous term in office, Daoud had cooperated closely with the Soviet Union, which expressed satisfaction with the new political situation in its neighbor to the south.[162] But Daoud had no plans to further Soviet influence in Afghanistan. On the contrary, several left-wing members of the government were replaced, and army leadership was likewise gradually replaced with more Daoud-faithful officers. Yet a large proportion of the influential officer corps was sympathetic towards the Soviet Union, especially those who had received military training there.[163] Through them, the Soviet Union maintained a certain degree of control over developments in the Afghan army, and in the event that Daoud should fall, by a coup from either the right or the left, the Soviet Union could continue to influence developments in a pro-Soviet direction[164] and thereby ensure Soviet control of Afghan domestic and foreign policy, with the strategic objective of Afghanistan becoming a Soviet satellite state.

THE QUESTION OF PASHTUN

Several of the Soviet motives for wanting Daoud to remain in power, however, gradually disappeared during his term in office. Daoud improved Afghanistan's relations with Pakistan, and in particular resolved what was known as the "Pashtun question" for the time being.

The problem originates from the establishment of the state of Pakistan. The boundary between Afghanistan and British India ran through an area which divided the Pashtun clans without taking their ethnic community into consideration. The Afghans wanted this boundary, which has never really been acknowledged in Afghan consciousness, moved eastward, so that all Pashtuns would become citizens of Afghanistan. India, which was against the establishment of a Pakistani state, backed the Afghans on the question of the drawing of boundaries, based on their desire to weaken the newly founded state of Pakistan.[165] The English did not have this kind of solution in mind and people in the border area, the North-West Frontier Province, were instead asked whether they wanted to join Afghanistan or Pakistan. An overwhelming majority wanted to join Pakistan. Afghanistan maintained that the clans had more in common with the Afghans than the Pakistanis. The tone between Afghanistan and Pakistan was appalling in 1947, and along with a propaganda war between the countries, mutual harassment began. On the Pakistani side, Afghan transport of goods passing through Pakistan was delayed, and Afghanistan was the only country to refuse to vote for Pakistan's membership in the UN in 1947.[166]

With regard to the Pashtun problem, the Afghans also requested American support – in the form of both political backing and military equipment. The Americans did not, however, fall for the Afghan threats to become more pro-Soviet if the support did not materialize. Afghanistan was forced to realize then that it did not play any special geopolitical role for the USA, and could not expect the USA to protect it against the Soviet Union, which the Afghan King Shah Mahmud was told while on a visit to Washington in 1951[167] The USA's unwillingness to grant Afghanistan military aid and the Pakistani blockade policy gradually pushed Afghanistan into the arms of the Soviet Union[168] and in 1959 the two countries signed a trade agreement, after which Afghanistan became more and more dependent on the Soviet Union.[169]

Attempts to reduce dependence on Soviet aid were made during Daoud's time in office, with Afghanistan establishing contacts with Saudi Arabia, Kuwait, India and China with the aim of obtaining economic aid.[170] Daoud also began sending soldiers to India, Egypt and the USA to receive training, but most were still sent to the Soviet Union and the country's aid to Afghanistan was substantially greater than all the others' put together[171] Still, the relationship between Moscow and Kabul cooled markedly, and in 1977 the Soviet leader Brezhnev demanded that Daoud get rid of Western advisors and install the Afghan Communist Party, PDPA, in the government. Daoud replied that when Afghanistan no longer needed foreign advisors, they would all be asked to leave, including the Soviets.[172]

THE COMMUNIST PARTY

The Communist Party, PDPA, was founded in Kabul in 1965, but as early as 1967 it was split into two factions, mainly because of personal oppositions between the party's front figures Babrak Karmal and Muhammad Taraki, each of whom became leader of his own faction. In 1977 and 1978, the factions moved closer together, which was clearly in the interests of the Soviet Union.[173] Both factions had suffered under Daoud's persecution, and the planning of a new coup, with or without Soviet help, was begun. In 1977, a number of political murders were committed – one in particular was heatedly discussed. A pilot from the national association of airlines was shot outside his home, giving rise to much speculation as he resembled Karmal and was indeed his neighbor. The Minister of Planning, Khoram, was killed by a person who confessed that he belonged to a group comprising 54 people, all of whom were involved in a plan to murder Daoud and his ministers. The government claimed that the killer was trained outside the country's borders, but gave no further details.[174]

On 17 April 1978 another murder was committed, however, which, regardless of motive, was to have political consequences. A well-known member of the communist opposition was murdered by people unknown. Two days later, the PDPA held a large demonstration at which the American Intelligence Agency, the CIA, was accused of being behind the killing. The funeral procession numbered between 10,000 and 15,000, which alarmed Daoud, who gave orders to arrest a number of leading Communists – and with that, the starting signal for revolution was given.[175]

On 27 April 1978, the PDPA took power through a coup. Its rebel forces were better coordinated than the government's, and several PDPA officers still held key posts in the army[176] and were thus able to control events, either because they were in command or because they had killed their superiors. Muhammed Taraki became both Prime Minister and President, while Karmal and Hafizullah Amin, who were also among the founders of PDPA, became Deputy Prime Ministers. Moreover, Karmal became Vice President.[177]

The new political leaders stressed that in spite of their Communist ideology, they were not controlled by the Soviet Union but took as their starting point Afghan nationalism, Islamic justice and a neutral and alliance-free foreign policy.[178] Yet in December 1978, the leaders signed a treaty with the Soviets that clearly stated that the Soviet Union regarded Afghanistan as a socialist country, thus belonging to the Socialist bloc. The treaty included, for example, a paragraph on Soviet military aid to Afghanistan that practically committed the Soviet Union to military intervention if the Communist government fell. With this, the treaty formed the basis for the invasion a year later.[179]

POPULAR UPRISING

With regard to domestic policy, too, the new government showed their true colors, and PDPA presented a traditional Communist reform program that among other thing involved an extensive program for land reform. The land reforms constituted a break with traditional economic and social structures in a society strictly divided into clan and tribal affiliations. Throughout the summer of 1978, protests became more and more vocal and in the course of the fall of 1978 and spring of 1979, there was extensive unrest and anarchy in a number of towns and provinces in Afghanistan. In at least 24 of the country's 28 provinces violent uprisings took place.[180] In March 1979 a large uprising broke out in the western province of Herat, which borders Iran. The government in Kabul was shocked. When the fighting was over and the uprising crushed, between five thousand and twenty-five thousand people had been killed.[181] Soviet and Afghan authorities accused forces from outside the country of backing the uprising with the goal of starting a counter-revolution. The accusations were directed at the newly established Islamic regime in Iran. According to Olivier Roy, scholar of Afghanistan and Islam, some militant Muslims had resided in Iran for a period prior to the uprising, and had worked out a plan for the rebellion.[182] It is, however, unclear whether Iran was involved.

Within the PDPA there was also unrest and continuing rivalry among the leaders. Several replacements took place, and the new government leader was Foreign Minister Amin, whose forces attacked the Presidential palace and took Taraki hostage until he was murdered on orders from Amin.[183] Amin now had complete power over the government but increasingly expressed distrust of the Soviet Union, which he suspected of being involved in a number of attempts to have him deposed. The situation in the fall of 1979 was chaotic. The Afghan army was nearly falling apart and parts of the country were controlled by local tribe leaders and the Afghan resistance movement, which had been established already before the revolution in 1798 in the Pakistani border town Peshawar. It was clear to the Soviet Union that the Communist regime would fall if the Soviets did not actively intervene.[184] The relationship between Amin and the Soviet Union remained very tense and, in the fall of 1979, the Soviet Union improved relations with Vice President Babrak Karmal. Amin was an Afghan nationalist first and a Communist second, so the Soviet Union banked on his political rival, Karmal, who could not be put in power until Amin was deposed and Soviet military units, had reestablished law and order until a rebuilt Afghan army could take over these functions itself. In mid-fall of 1979 the Soviet Union began preparations for the invasion of Afghanistan,[185] which was initiated on Christmas night 1979. With this, the Soviet Union made the last move in its strategy in Afghanistan, which since World War II in particular had been aimed at bringing Afghanistan under Soviet supremacy.

THE RUSSIANS ARRIVE

On Christmas night of 1979, the Soviet invasion of Afghanistan began. Sections of the Soviet Union's 105th Guard's parachute division, reinforced with sections of the 103rd Guard's parachute division and a special unit from the Special Purpose force, SPF, landed in Kabul; and on 27 December, after three days of flying reinforcements in, with 75-120 flights per day, an SPF special unit of 100-200 men advanced on the Darulaman Palace outside Kabul, defeated the palace guard and their eight tanks, and killed President Amin who had been in the palace since 20 December. On the night of 27 December, Soviet troops blew up Kabul's telephone exchange, captured Radio Kabul and took over most of the government facilities in Kabul. By dawn the following day, the Red Army had the situation under control.[186]

At that time Karmal was staying in the Soviet Republic of Tadzhikistan, from which he declared on 27 December, that as the leader of a new government in Afghanistan, he had requested political, moral and economic aid, including military aid, from the Soviet Union, and that the Soviet Union had accepted the Afghan government's request. Later it was officially announced that Amin, whom the Soviet Union suspected of being a CIA agent, was found guilty of crimes against the state and executed.[187]

The official Soviet explanation for the invasion was that the Soviet Union was acting in accordance with the Soviet-Afghan peace treaty, and that three different Afghan governments had requested assistance in the defense of Afghanistan against intervention by outside counter-revolutionary forces. The Soviet motives for the invasion are to be found in what was called the Brezhnev Doctrine, which was formulated by the then Soviet leader in connection with the uprising in Czechoslovakia in 1968 and the subsequent Soviet-led military defeat of the forces for democratic reform. The Soviet Union claimed that they had been requested to intervene against counter-revolutionary forces threatening the Communist government in Prague. Brezhnev explained that the Soviet Union would no longer accept socialist states being in danger of counter-revolution. Yet the Brezhnev Doctrine is a reflection of more than ideological considerations. Geopolitically, it was about the Soviet Union's need for security. The Soviets have always attempted to ensure that their territory had extended buffer zones of loyal or neutral states around its borders. If a state was to fall away and go over to the enemy, that is, the USA and the West, it could result in a weakening of the Soviet Union's defense and could trigger a domino effect that would have serious consequences for the Soviet Union. This security requirement has been one of the most important reasons for the Soviet invasion of socialist countries like the DDR in 1953, Hungary in 1956, Czechoslovakia in 1968 and Afghanistan in 1979.

THE PERSIAN GULF AND IRAN

In addition to the security aspect, the Soviet Union also had strategic and offensive objectives with the invasion of Afghanistan: control over the Persian Gulf and the Indian Ocean, a new balance of power in relation to China, and the growth of Islamic fundamentalism in Central Asia.

The desire for control in the Persian Gulf is closely linked with the area's oil resources. At the end of the 1970s over half the oil in international trade came from the Gulf and to a great extent supplied Japan, Europe and the USA. Soviet control over the passage to and from the Persian Gulf through the Strait of Hormuz could give the Soviet Union an important geopolitical foothold in that part of the Middle East and thereby make the West vulnerable to various forms of economic, political and military extortion. If the Soviet Union ever wanted to enforce control over the oil traffic in the Persian Gulf using military might, its forces could use a geographically defined corridor running from the Afghan-Soviet border to the Afghan-Pakistani border in Afghan territory, and in the southern part of Iran to the Iranian harbor city Bandar Abbas, that lies by the narrow Strait of Hormuz.

Whether the aim of the Soviet invasion in Afghanistan was access to and control of the Persian Gulf or whether its presence there merely gave an improved strategic position in the area in and around the Persian Gulf is open to discussion. A Soviet invasion of Iran could have resulted in war with the USA and possibly also Western Europe, which the Carter Doctrine was meant to emphasize.

Excerpt from the magazine of the Soviet Army

"The hundred-year-old dream of our people has become reality. Soviet warships are now seen on all oceans and in all harbors.... They are seen in Aden at the southern tip of the Arabian Peninsula and on the island of Sokotra outside it. They are seen in Ethiopian Massawa, and from here the supply route can be controlled. Here is the one blade of the Russian pincers that are about to close around oil fields and oil routes. The second one can be created by advancing through Afghanistan's Baluchistan province toward the Indian Ocean and the Strait of Hormuz or an occupation of Iran's southeastern corner."[188]

THE INDIAN OCEAN AND PAKISTAN

Another reason for the Soviet invasion of Afghanistan might have been access to the Indian Ocean and its ice-free ports, which had been an aim of Russian expansion ever since Peter the Great. The Afghanistan invasion might have been part of this plan. The Soviet Union and the USA have fought over dominance of the Indian Ocean since World War II, and in 1979 the USA was the strongest. The Soviet desire for access to the Indian Ocean necessarily meant that the Soviet Union had to continue advancing on and occupying Afghanistan's neighbor to the southeast, Pakistan. Soviet naval bases in Pakistan's southern port city Karachi, for instance, would weaken American dominance in the area. At the same time, the Soviet Union had strengthened its strategic position in relation to the Persian Gulf. However, it is doubtful whether the Indian Ocean was a short-term goal subsequent to the Soviet invasion of Afghanistan; it is more likely that an added bonus of the invasion was consolidation of the Soviets' position with regard to Pakistan and support of forces in Pakistan that, in the long run, could pave the way for the strategic goal – ice-free ports in the Indian Ocean. It was more expedient to create the conditions necessary for the Pakistani government to fall for domestic policy reasons, than it was for a foreign invading power to occupy the country.

Since its establishment in 1947, Pakistan has been in conflict with the militarily superior India, and three wars have been fought between the two countries. So it was a highly superior force that Pakistan would face in the beginning of the 1980s, if the country were to be attacked by India at the same time that Soviet troops advanced in Afghanistan. Pakistan had serious economic problems in 1979, and the Pakistani government wanted immediate aid from both the USA and the Arab countries, especially the rich Gulf States. It was clear to Pakistan that the USA would probably not involve itself militarily should the Soviet Union and India both attack Pakistan. Such a situation would be fatal for Pakistan and hopeless for the USA, despite the intention of the Carter Doctrine, since the USA would lack important military operative prerequisites, namely logistical support in the form of bases and other supply facilities in friendly neighboring countries.

The fall of the Shah in Iran, Khomeini's anti-American policy and a Communist government in Kabul gave the Soviet Union room for maneuvering, which could change the balance of power in the Persian Gulf and the Indian Ocean. The Soviet invasion of Afghanistan could thus create a breathing space in American containment policy, which had been the USA's geopolitical doctrine in relation to the rival superpower since the beginning of the Cold War.

REGIONAL AMBITIONS AND CHINA

The relations between the two rivaling regional powers, the Soviet Union and China, might also have played a role in the Soviets' decision. China had just normalized relations with Japan in 1978, and China and Pakistan were both involved in the construction and completion of the strategically important Karakorum Highway that connects the two countries through very difficult and mountainous terrain. In April 1978, China had furthermore informed the Soviet Union that without new negotiations there was no interest in renewing the Chinese-Soviet friendship treaty, which expired in 1980. Concurrent Chinese-American talks contributed further to increasing the Soviet security consciousness, and in mid-July of 1979 border clashes between the Soviet Union and China took place. The Soviet invasion of Afghanistan could also have created a breathing space with regard to China that made the regional containment and rivalry less threatening. But with that, the regional balance between China and the Soviet Union was disturbed. As a superpower, China has historically had the same need to ensure breathing spaces in a containment policy that comprised Vietnam, Mongolia, the Soviet Union and India. Chinese efforts to achieve security as a consequence of the Soviet invasion of Afghanistan were just as psychologically motivated as they were militarily determined. Afghanistan shares a border with China in the Wakhan corridor, a narrow area that forms the corner between the Soviet Union, Afghanistan, Pakistan and China, but the area does not have any real military significance in itself. On the other hand, China has deployed a number of its nuclear isles in the western and Muslim Xinjiang province, and there is no doubt that the

Soviet engagement in Afghanistan made the Chinese nervous. This was underscored later by the Chinese support of the Afghan resistance, and China played an important, though less obvious, role in this new version of "The Great Game," which was the expression used about the two great colonial powers, England and Russia, in their battle over control of Afghanistan in the regional geopolitical game in the 1800s.

Finally, one of the reasons for the invasion might have been a Soviet fear that Islamic fundamentalism would spread from Afghanistan and Iran into the Central Asian Soviet republics, where Muslims constituted by far the majority of the populations of Uzbekistan, Tadzhikistan and Turkmenistan. In the Muslim republics there was a fertile basis for Islamic fundamentalism throughout the 1970s, not least as an alternative to state-directed Communism. But in the Central Asian republics there has not been an organized Islamic movement to the same extent as in Afghanistan, and the growth of Islamic fundamentalism in the Central Asian republics should be seen rather as a consequence of the Soviet invasion of Afghanistan than the other way round.

THE ANTI-SOVIET ALLIANCE

In the days around Christmas 1979, President Carter and the American government ascertained that the country needed important and powerful allies in the fight against the Soviet presence in Afghanistan. This need was underscored further by the ongoing hostage situation at the American embassy in Teheran. Three countries soon assumed central importance for the USA in the fight against the Soviet occupation of Afghanistan – Saudi Arabia, Egypt and Pakistan.[189]

Saudi Arabia was the USA's chief oil supplying country and an important trade partner, and the royal family had carefully considered the risk of the Soviet Union having the Persian Gulf as its strategic goal for the invasion of Afghanistan. Saudi Arabia's location on the Persian Gulf also gives the country great geopolitical significance for the USA and possible bases for American military action in the Afghan theatre.

The traditional regional superpower in the Middle East, Egypt, had been completely isolated in the Arab and Muslim world after signing the

Camp David agreement in March 1979. Egypt was accused of selling out on Islamic values in favor of Western interests in the Middle East, and the country eyed a chance to break its isolation by joining an alliance that was to the advantage of the Muslim country of Afghanistan. And a large American financial contribution did nothing to weaken their motivation.

As mentioned earlier, Pakistan had obvious military and political interests in joining the alliance against the Soviet occupation of Afghanistan, and because of its location, became a key player in the military and political alliance against the Soviet Union. But one of the absolutely central preconditions for the success of the American plan and the protection of Pakistani, Egyptian, Saudi Arabian and Chinese regional interests, was the Afghan resistance, the Mujahideen. It had been established as early as 1978 in the Afghan-Pakistani border town of Peshawar by much of the Islamic opposition. The presence of members of the Afghan resistance in Pakistan and the foreign financial, logistical and material aid had not only regional importance in terms of the Soviet occupation, but also equal global significance, as we shall see in the following chapters.

8. THE MUJAHIDEEN AND THE ARAB BRIGADE

The Afghan resistance movement in Pakistan was base camp for Afghan opposition and the several thousand Muslims who traveled to the border area between Afghanistan and Pakistan to receive military training from foreign instructors. This extensive jihad operation was financed largely by the USA and the rich Gulf states, whose interest in Afghanistan changed in pace with the Soviet withdrawal, after which Saudi Arabia and Pakistan in particular continued to exert influence, while the USA quickly lost interest. However the Soviet withdrawal did not result in a peaceful and stable Afghanistan, but threw the country into a long civil war in which Pakistan, with the backing of Saudi Arabia, grasped the opportunity to create and use the Taliban movement to further its own regional interests.

The Mujahideen movement consisted of an assortment of different Afghan political parties, groups and movements with different religious, political and ethnic affiliations. Yet common to them all was the resistance to the Soviet occupying powers in Afghanistan and the Communist government in Kabul. Seven Sunni Muslim parties formed the resistance movement that was established in the Afghan-Pakistani border town of Peshawar immediately following the Communist coup in 1978. Basically the resistance movement comprised two wings: a fundamentalistic wing, was led by Burhaneddin Rabbani and his party Jamiat-e Islami, and a radical fundamentalistic wing, of which the key parties were Hizb-e Islami, led by Gulbuddin Hekmatyar, and the Ittihad Party, led by the Afghan professor Abdul Rasul Sayyaf, whose group later moved from Peshawar to the Philippines, where they carried out a number of attacks and kidnappings during the 1990s from their bases on the island of Mindanao.

The four other Sunni Muslim parties in the Afghan resistance comprised moderate and traditional Muslim parties whose leaders came from the ulama, that is, the Islamic clerics.

HEKMATYAR AND RABBANI — TWO KEY FIGURES

Hekmatyar and Rabbani were by no means new to the political scene in Afghanistan. Both had a past in the Muslim Youth Movement, which was active in university circles in Kabul during the 1960s and '70s. There, the movement led debates and confrontations with the Marxist student movements that dominated student milieus at universities, just as in other places in the Middle East and in the West for that matter. Hekmatyar, Rabbani and the Islamic Youth Movement in Afghanistan were strongly inspired by Sayyid Qutb and the Muslim Brotherhood in Egypt, with which Rabbani and Professor Sayyaf in particular became acquainted during a lengthy period of study at al-Azhar University in Cairo.[190] There was even a cooperation agreement between al-Azhar University and the theological faculty in Kabul, where, at the beginning of the 1970s, half of the teachers had degrees from Al-Azhar.[191]

Hekmatyar, an engineering student, was imprisoned in 1972, partly for "anti-national" activities and partly for ordering the killing of a Maoist student.[192] Rabbani, who comes from the Tadzhik minority in Afghanistan, was professor at the national Islamic faculty in Kabul. Both Hekmatyar and Rabbani had left Afghanistan with the coming to power of the Communists, and both were in Peshawar. That busy, dusty city on the Silk Road near the notorious Khyber Pass, was the center of the Afghan resistance from the start and thus played a very key role for militant Islamic activism, whose holy warriors have been a force to reckon with in the Middle East, Asia and the West since the beginning of the 1990s.

PAKISTAN'S INVOLVEMENT

Both Hekmatyar and Rabbani spoke at a general assembly of the student movement at the University of Peshawar in the summer of 1979. Both attacked the Communist government in Kabul for its malicious treatment of religious institutions and Muslims in Afghanistan.[193] For Hekmatyar and Rabbani this was not merely empty rhetoric or the usual political declarations of intention, but a strong appeal for active resistance against the occupying power in Afghanistan and the Communist puppet regime. Hekmatyar's and Rabbani's speeches and verbal attacks on the Afghan government were also heard outside the University of Peshawar, namely in the USA and in the Pakistani intelligence service, ISI. ISI already had intimate knowledge of Hekmatyar, with whom they had previously worked closely, as, according to some sources, he had worked as an agent for Pakistan as early as the 1960s.[194] Hekmatyar, Rabbani and the Afghan resistance movement in Peshawar became an important base for the establishment of a strategic alliance between the USA, the front-line state of Pakistan and other regional participants in their common fight against the Soviet occupation of Afghanistan and the accompanying Soviet influence in the region.

Hekmatyar had a very strained relationship with the USA from the beginning, however, and despite great diplomatic pressure, refused to meet with the American president, Ronald Reagan, when Hekmatyar took part in the UN's General Assembly in New York in 1985. At the General Assembly the following year, Reagan was visited by the more moderate Rabbani, who attended as leader of a Mujahideen delegation.[195]

Along with ISI, the USA, including the CIA, formed the backbone of the fateful foreign support of the Mujahideen movement.[196] In January 1980, President Carter's Security Advisor Brzezinski met with Pakistan's President Zia-ul-Haq, reaching agreement on guidelines for international support: all types of arms support, financing and training of the Afghan resistance movement were to be provided with Pakistani supervision and direction and not directly by the CIA. This gave Pakistan and ISI a key role from the beginning in the implementation of the large-scale operation.[197] This role was also important to Pakistan for political reasons. According to Olivier Roy, Pakistan's greatest fear was that the Afghan resistance movement would develop into a refugee problem like that of the Palestinians in the states around Israel, since there were several million Afghan refugees in the Pakistani border area. A certain amount of internal division was considered by ISI to be the best insurance against the Afghan resistance movement and the many Afghan refugees taking control of the political and military might in the area.[198]

EGYPT'S ROLE

Yet before his meetings with Pakistan's President Zia-ul-Haq, Brzezinski had been to Cairo in order to persuade President Sadat to participate in the anti-Soviet alliance.

In addition to political support from Sadat, the USA also had a more concrete goal. The plan was to use the Islamic fundamentalists in Egypt as ideological exponents of the fight against the atheistic occupying power in the Muslim country of Afghanistan. Leaders of the powerful and active Islamic movements in Egypt could be talent scouts on the lookout for young Egyptians who would go to Pakistan and join the Afghan Mujahideen movement.[199] Of course, there was already a shared ideology and personal connections among several of the leaders of the resistance movement and key individuals from the Islamic movements in Egypt. Al-Azhar University in Cairo was often the scene of meetings, contacts and friendships among people from the entire Muslim world. Dreams and ideas were exchanged, and Islamic ideologues among the teaching staff and among students inspired each other to spread knowledge of the more political interpretation of Islam within and outside of the Middle East.

A number of the Islamic movements and their leaders in Egypt, whom Sadat himself had supported throughout the 1970s, were increasingly critical of the the President. Particularly following the Camp David Agreement, the Islamic movements and their leaders directed violent attacks against Sadat, whom they accused of betraying Islam and the Palestinian cause.

Sadat, and not least the USA, had probably hoped that Egyptian support of the Afghan resistance movement could placate the critical Islamic fundamentalists.

Already at the end of the 1980s, American military personnel were instructing the Egyptian supervisors who would be training the volunteer Egyptians prior to their joining the Afghan Mujahideen movement in Peshawar.[200] Towards the end of 1980, the American Congress, which had authorized $1.5 billion to Egypt as a result of the Camp David Accords, approved another $2 billion over a four-year period to Sadat as thanks for his loyalty and support in favor of the Afghan

Mujahideen movement.[201] At the same time that Sadat was traveling in Southeast Asia, seeking support for the Afghan resistance movement, the old Soviet-made military hardware was being flown in American transport aircraft from Egypt to Pakistan, where it was transported further by the Pakistani defense and middlemen to Mujahideen training camps in the Pakistani border area.

Yet, as mentioned earlier, relations between the Islamic movements in Egypt and Sadat worsened. The critical Islamic fundamentalists had by no means softened. On the contrary: Sadat attempted a balance between a hard line with regard to Islamic movements in Egypt and continued urgings and support to young Egyptians to go to Pakistan and join the Afghan Mujahideen movement in its training camps in and around Peshawar, from where jihad, holy war, was being waged against the Soviet occupying power. But he could not maintain that balance. His support of the fighting Muslim brothers in Afghanistan was not enough to ensure forgiveness for the Camp David Accords, and 6 October 1981 Sadat was killed in Cairo. The intolerable conditions for the Islamic movements in Egypt after the assassination of Sadat meant, ironically enough, that many young Egyptians with or without affiliation to the Islamic movements fled from the Egyptian authorities, with Peshawar as their destination.

CHINA AND IRAN AS PLAYERS

Another important player in the American-Pakistani plan, and thus for the Mujahideen movement, was China. Although relations between the USA and China had improved after President Nixon's visit in Beijing in 1972, they had not expanded to the extent that an American-Chinese alliance in the question of the Afghan resistance movement had become official foreign policy for the two countries. Their cooperation therefore had to be handled with the utmost discretion, and it was possible to keep Chinese participation secret for several years. As mentioned, China has strategic motivations in its regional rivalry with the Soviet Union, and participated from the beginning of 1980 with extensive arms support to the Mujahideen movement in Peshawar. Later, Chinese support also included military training of volunteers from the Muslim Xinjiang Province, which wished to participate in jihad in Afghanistan.[202] Just how many of these were local Muslims and how many were Muslims from the surrounding countries in Central Asia is unclear.[203] Military training and support for foreign militant movements was nothing new for the Chinese, who were experienced in providing support to a number of Maoist and left-wing movements in South America and Africa in the 1960s.

At the beginning of 1980, the situation was different. The USA and China were on speaking terms and the country quickly profited by the established USA-Pakistan-China axis, when the American Congress, in late January 1980, approved China as a "most-favored nation" in trade.

Iran and the new Islamic regime in Teheran also attempted to gain influence at the beginning of the Soviet occupation of Afghanistan by uniting a number of different parties and tribes representing the Shia Muslim minority in Afghanistan. Almost all the Shiites, who constitute about 15% of the Afghan population, belong to the ethnic group Hazara and live primarily in the capital city of Kabul in the central Afghan mountain region and in the western part of Afghanistan. The Shiite minority has been politically, economically and religiously oppressed for long periods, and until 1963 excluded from careers in the Afghan army and from political participation.[204] There have always been strong connections between the Iranian clergy and the Shiite clergy in Afghanistan, and the Iranian revolution inspired many young Afghan Shiites.[205] Eight Shia Muslim parties that expressed their support for Khomeini formed a coalition in the Iranian city of Qom and tried to join the Sunni Muslim seven-party group in Peshawar. This did not work, chiefly because of Pakistani, Saudi Arabian and American influence on the party group in Peshawar. These countries had no intention of furthering Iranian interests in Afghanistan. On the contrary, Iranian influence in Afghanistan and on the resistance movement was limited from the start.[206]

RECRUITMENT

Pakistan was responsible for local recruitment for the Afghan jihad from among the Afghan tribes and clans and the approximately three million people who had fled to Pakistan during the Soviet occupation. It was especially up to religious institutions and Islamic charity organizations to recruit the foreign Muslims who went to Pakistan and joined the resistance movement. In North Africa, and to some extent in Europe, the Pakistani da'wa movement, Tabligh Jamaat, play a particularly key role. For years, the Tabligh movement has established and run what are known as the madrasas, Islamic schools, in Pakistan. In pace with the arrival of more and more young people from the Arab countries and a number of Muslims from Europe to training camps in and around Peshawar, the Tabligh movement began to operate more actively in North Africa and Europe.

From the mid-1980s, the Tabligh movement was also active in several European countries, where it had elaborate recruiting networks in France and Germany for the benefit of the Afghan Mujahideen movement. This came to have great importance in the 1990s, as Muslims from Europe continued to travel to training camps in Pakistan and Afghanistan and formed networks that Osama bin Laden could use in connection with terror.

Missionary work and recruitment were two sides of the same coin. The Tabligh movement founded what were known as "cultural centers", from which they offered trips to Pakistan and free studies in the Pakistani religious schools to young people from the major North African cities of Algiers and Tunis. The visitors were not offered military training at the beginning of the six to eight week stay, and the link between Afghan jihad and the visit was not apparent until the end of the course, when individuals affiliated with ISI showed up and presented opportunities for weapons training.[207] Those who were interested were then transported to training camps in and around Peshawar, where along with other Muslims from the international brigade of holy warriors they received the necessary training to be able to move into Afghanistan and fight against the Red Army.

Both the Tunisian and Algerian governments were skeptical about the grass-roots Islamization and missionary activity practiced by the Tabligh movement. The authorities in Morocco and Libya were worried about their lack of control of the work of the Tabligh movement. Like a number of other countries in the Middle East, both countries have a long tradition of attempts to link religious leaders with religious movements and subject them to the country's political power. In doing so, the countries' political leaders try to allow political needs and interests to rule over religious interpretations.

The USA was also an important recruiting base. Recruitment took place in mosque milieus and via a number of Muslim charity organizations around the country. The Afghan refugee center al-Kifah in Brooklyn, also known as the jihad center, became a pivotal point for recruitment, political and religious inspiration, and not least, collection of money for the benefit of the Mujahideen movement.[208] One of the key persons in the recruitment of Muslims from the USA was Omar Abdel Rahman, another important person in the Muslim milieu in the USA was Abdallah Azzam[209], a Jordanian Palestinian and in 1988 founder of Hamas, the Islamic resistance movement in Gaza and on the West Bank.

Hamas

Hamas has roots in the Muslim Brotherhood, yet its leaders had strong reservations about the young fundamentalists' strongly publicized and aggressive anti-Israeli image and policy. The Muslim Brotherhood would fall into disrepute with authorities if it openly and actively propagandized for radical, politicized Islamic theology. The head organization in Egypt officially takes exception to terrorism and would not like to see its name mentioned in connection with terrorist activities, not even if they were to take place outside Egypt's borders.

At the end of the 1980s and after more than 20 years' occupation, very large groups within the Palestinian population were prepared for a renewed fight against Israel, and since the Marxist-oriented nationalists were unable to do anything, a large number of Palestinians were motivated to rally round Hamas. In addition to its official political and missionary work, Hamas has an intelligence service with many branches, which serves both to enlist agents and guerrilla soldiers and to gather information about collaborators. The latter are harassed, if not killed outright or persuaded to return to the pure path of Islam; this they can convince the clergy of by fighting or recruiting candidates for suicide bombings, which are referred to as martyrdom.

The militant branch of Hamas goes by the name of the Izz-din al-qassam Brigade, which comprises over 100 activists organized into smaller operative cells. The activists are young Palestinians who, with a view to martyrdom or hero status, put their lives on the line and make it impossible for the Palestinian police and the Israeli military to prevent terrorism. For what security system can guarantee that a person with a bomb around his or her waist cannot cross the border between the Palestinian Authority and Israel, or the borders of an open Europe? On the face of it, to blow oneself up seems to be a fanaticism that borders on madness. The reality is, however, that the psychological step from being a fearless fighter to sacrificing one's life to serve a cause is a lot smaller than one would think. The young Muslims who are selected for the job are drawn into a milieu where their leaders coach them about the cause and the great importance that precisely they have to fight for a Palestinian nation or the Islamic cause. They are flattered with arguments about the great opportunity they have to become one of the few chosen by fate for the great honor of sacrificing themselves for their people or for Islam and thus achieving martyrdom in the next life and becoming an immortal hero in this one.[210]

FINANCING

An important prerequisite for the Afghan resistance was financing – of everything from logistics in Pakistan and travel activity to propaganda and Stinger missiles.

The logistics were financed by Osama bin Laden among others, via a number of relief organizations in Peshawar: the Saudi Arabian Islamic World League, the World Assembly of Muslim Youth, Saudi Red Crescent Society, Kuwaiti Red Crescent Society and other organizations that took part in solving many of the practical and logistical problems of getting to Peshawar. The organizations were also an important link to the Mujahideen movement.[211] Abdallah Azzam founded the "Services Office" in Peshawar, known by the name MAK, the Arabic abbreviation for Maktab al-Khidmat, which played a very central role in the recruitment and organization of young Arab Muslims who traveled to and from Pakistan. MAK also sent out reports on the resistance movement and the Afghan war.[212] The operation of MAK was financed by Osama bin Laden, who also established the Islamic Salvation Foundation, which coordinated all support, but primarily that from Saudi Arabia.[213]

Travel was financed, among others, by the Saudi Arabian intelligence service. Arab Mujahideen defectors have thus related how they travelled to Pakistan and Afghanistan via Saudi Arabia. The Saudis paid for 75 % of the ticket and arranged for the necessary visas and along the way, the volunteers and coming holy warriors stayed in the kingdom for two months and met others, including Egyptians, Sudanese, Syrians and people of other nationalities who all belonged to Islamic groups and who were able to tell of how they had received financial aid from Saudi charity organizations.[214]

The principal financier, however, was the USA. The CIA's former director of operations in Islamabad estimates that the total American support to the Mujahideen from 1979 to 1989 was about $2 billion,[215] with the greatest amount given during the period 1986-89, when support reached $400-600 million per year.[216]

The USA channeled money to the Mujahideen through the CIA and a number of Arab countries headed by the rich Gulf States and Saudi Arabia. Muslim charity organizations and fund raisers around the world also contributed to the financing of the Mujahideen movement's activities.

Another source of income was the sale of opium. The Mujahideen and their local allies were behind the building and control of a large international smuggling network. Afghanistan produced large amounts of opium, which could not be sold via the usual channels because of the war, and as the Mujahideen and the Pakistani border authorities took part in arms transports from East to West, opium was transported the other way.[217]

An active Mujahideen could earn between $100 and $350 a month, depending on the type of job he had and the kind of skills he had acquired. This was a large amount of money, which the many Afghan and foreign Mujahideen would have had difficulty earning in more traditional jobs in Afghanistan or in the Arab countries from which most of them came.[218]

Abdallah Azzam

Abdallah Azzam, Jordanian Palestinian, was an important person in the Muslim milieu in the USA.

In 1988 he was co-founder of Hamas, the Islamic resistance movement in Gaza and on the West Bank, but was not given the opportunity himself to follow Hamas in its political struggle for an independent Palestine. The end of Azzam's life was just as violent as the activities for which he recruited others. He was killed by a car bomb in Peshawar in 1989. Just who was responsible has never been determined but several people wanted to take Azzam's life, including rival groups in Peshawar. Before 1989 he had resided both in the USA, where he visited more than 25 American states and inspired, recruited, and collected raised money for the benefit of the Mujahideen, and in Peshawar, where as the leader of the Muslim Brotherhood's local office, he organized activities for the many arriving volunteers.[219]

> Throughout the 1980s, Azzam had close connections to Hekmatyar and Sayyaf. During the war he and Osama bin Laden met. The acquaintance may go further back, namely to Saudi Arabia, where Azzam was teaching at King Abdul Aziz University at the time Osama bin Laden was a student.[220] After Azzam's death, Osama bin Laden took over his logistical activities and networks in Peshawar.
>
> Azzam's son-in-law, the Algerian Afghan Veteran Abdallah Anis, worked for the Algerian terror organization the Armed Islamic Group, GIA, and was also the editor of the news magazine Jihad News, which contained articles about and photographs of the Mujahideen movement's battles and regularly issued calls to young Muslims to join the holy warriors in Afghanistan.[221]

FROM TRAINING TO COMBAT

The USA, England and Pakistan were all actively involved in training the Mujahideen.

In the USA, instructors were trained in weapons use, sabotage, various techniques for killing, the use of modern communications equipment, and more. These skills were then passed on in the military training camps in the Pakistani border area to tens of thousands of Mujahideen, who thereby formed the foundation for military combat against the Soviet occupying power. In the camps, members of American special units and of the British elite force, Special Air Service (SAS), participated in training.[222] The majority of these American and British soldiers were officially on leave during the first years of the war and thus exempted from service so that formal connections to the USA and Great Britain were severed.[223]

From the mid-1980s, the British army participated directly in the education of the Mujahideen, several of whom were flown to England and installed in secret camps in the Scottish Highlands.[224] There, they took lengthy courses in the use of various kinds of weapons systems which could be effective against the Soviet air force, especially against the low-flying Soviet military helicopters.

After their stay in England the course participants were flown back to the camps in Pakistan, and from there into Afghanistan, where their newly acquired military skills were put to the test in real combat.

In the Pakistani training camps, the Mujahideen acquired a very important skill – the use of explosives in the production of bombs. There was both theoretical and practical teaching in the production of fuses, timers, explosives, remote-controlled bombs, rockets and more. One person who was later in charge of teaching the chemistry and electronics of bomb production was the Kuwaiti-born Ramzi Yusef, who was sentenced in the USA in 1997 for having made the bomb that exploded at the World Trade Center in New York on 26 February 1993. The training camp east of Peshawar where Yusef taught, "Jihad University", was an important site for the education of a number of Islamic terrorists who put their acquired skills into practice around the world in the 1990s.[225]

The foreign support of the Afghan Mujahideen movement meant that as early as a few months after the Soviet invasion the movement was already in possession of a number of arms, from Egyptian-donated Soviet Kalashnikovs and mortars to air force missiles.[226] Experience with the production and use of explosives increased in pace with the concrete actions and combat against the Soviet occupying power. Supply lines, bridges, buildings, airports and electricity installations were typical targets for the Mujahideen actions, and they acquired detailed knowledge of different kinds of explosives, how to get the greatest possible effect and where best to place them in relation to selected targets.

The use of helicopters was an important part of the Soviet anti-guerrilla effort because of their high degree of mobility, often combined with heavy fire power. The Russian Hind helicopter in particular was almost invulnerable in Afghanistan[227] until the Mujahideen began using the Stinger missile. This was in 1986, when use of the missile was introduced into the course offerings in the Scottish highlands. Until then, the Mujahideen had had limited success in military battles. The Stinger missile limited the Hind helicopter's operations in partially open terrain such as mountains, where the Mujahideen could move more freely and undetected. From 1986 to 1987 the Mujahideen received about 900 Stinger missiles, which resulted in the shooting down of about 270 Soviet military helicopters.[228] Access to Stinger missiles was both an important psychological and military reason for the tide of war turning for the Mujahideen, and many of them obtained both theoretical and practical experience with such weapons for their personal baggage.[229]

The Stinger missile also meant a break with the official American policy that until 1986 consisted of what was diplomatically termed "plausible deniability" with regard to American involvement in the Afghan conflict, and therewith support for the Afghan resistance movement. Such blatant support from the beginning of the war would doubtlessly have entered into Soviet propaganda and legitimizations of the Soviet presence in Afghanistan.[230]

The foreign Muslims participated in combat chiefly at Khost, Jalalabad, Kunduz and Kandahar, where there was intense fighting near the end of the Soviet occupation. In the course of the summer of 1988, about half of the approximately 115,000 Soviet soldiers were pulled out of Afghanistan, and in February 1989 the rest of the troops. The plan was that Afghan government soldiers were to fill the military vacuum, but expectant Mujahideen found the time was ripe for initiating final battles around the strategically significant cities in Afghanistan, and in August 1988 they took the city of Kanduz, which also became very important 13 years later as one of the Taliban strongholds where foreign fighters by the hundreds stayed. The same significance was attached to the city of Kandahar, at which the Mujahideen movement aimed violent attacks in 1988 in the same way that American special units and soldiers from the Afghan North Alliance did at the end of 2001.

Estimated American military aid to the Afghan resistance movement

Year	Amount (millions US dollars)[231]
1980	30
1981	35
1982	35-50
1983	80
1984	122
1985	280
1986	470-550
1987	600
1988	400
1989	400-500

THE ARAB BRIGADE IN NUMBERS

Throughout the 1980s there were between 80,000 and 150,000 full-time Mujahideen in the Afghan resistance movement, and from 1983 to 1987 there were approximately 80,000 in the Pakistani camps[232], both Afghans and foreign volunteers. Naturally, there are no official statistics of the total number of foreign participants in the Mujahideen movement, and the numbers and nationalities are likewise uncertain. It can, however, be ascertained with reasonable certainty that volunteers from more than twenty Muslim countries took part, and that by far the majority were Arabs from the Middle East, Muslims from Asia, the USA and Western European countries, who were issued visas through Pakistani embassies to facilitate legal arrival in Pakistan, participated in fewer numbers. In 1992, the Pakistani embassy in Algeria, for instance, issued 2,800 visas to Muslims who allegedly took part in the Afghan resistance.[233]

One of the busiest countries of transit was Yemen, which was used by between 5,000 and 7,000 people as a starting point or as a transit country on the journey to Pakistan.[234]

Around 1992 there were between 4,000 and 5,000 foreign fighters in Afghanistan and Pakistan,[235] and in 1994 the Egyptian authorities signed an agreement with Pakistan on the extradition of militant Egyptian Muslims who continued to operate in Pakistan.[236] On that occasion, the Pakistani Minister of Justice stated that about 3,000 Arabs, including 500 Egyptians had already been deported from Pakistan in 1993 and an additional 150 Arabs were awaiting deportation.[237]

The total number of foreign Mujahideen in Pakistan and Afghanistan from the time of the Soviet invasion until the fall of the Communist regime in April 1992 was probably between 20,000 and 30,000 Muslims, of which the great majority, as mentioned, were Arabs from Egypt, Algeria, Saudi Arabia and Yemen. The CIA's station director at the American embassy in Pakistan from 1986 to 1989, Milton Beardon,[238] estimates that the total number of Arab Mujahideen in Afghanistan and Pakistan from 1979 to 1989 was 25,000.[239] In all fairness, however, it must be noted that there were also foreigners in Peshawar who were not involved in military training and combat but who performed all kinds of much-needed relief work, just as it cannot automatically be deduced that individuals who have participated in the war in Afghanistan are terrorists.

OUTSIDE THE SUPERPOWERS' SEARCHLIGHT

With the Soviet withdrawal in 1989, and especially after the dissolution of the Soviet Union in 1991, support for the Communist regime in Afghanistan waned. The American mission was therefore brought to an end, and Afghanistan's geopolitical significance for the victorious superpower USA changed. With that, support of the Afghan resistance also waned.[240]

However, the resistance movement continued its fight against the Communist regime, which did not fall until April 1992 – when Mohammad Najibullah, Afghanistan's president since 1986 and former head of the Afghan intelligence service, KHAD – was deposed. Najibullah attempted to flee to India by way of Kabul airport and seek political asylum there. The attempt was unsuccessful, and he remained in the custody and protection of the UN until Taliban forces took Kabul in September 1995 and, as one of their first deeds, officially hung Najibullah from a lamppost in front of the presidential palace in Kabul.[241] Beside him hung his brother Shahpur, who had been head of security until April 1992. The fall of President Najibullah and the Communist regime created neither peace nor an Islamic state in Afghanistan. More than three million people were killed or seriously wounded after the Soviets invaded, and some six million sought refuge in Iran or Pakistan.

The reconstruction of an Afghanistan devastated by war had to wait because of political differences between the seven key political parties in the resistance movement, and after victory in April 1992 the schisms soon flared up. The common enemy had been defeated, and now it was time to claim the political prize. This game of realpolitik over power in Afghanistan soon resulted in the two dominating members of the resistance movement, Gulbuddin Hekmatyar and Burhaneddin Rabbani, turning their weapons against each other and thereby continuing the military struggle for power in Afghanistan.

Their intentions were good enough. Immediately after Najibullah's fall a Mujahideen council – influenced by Pakistan – was set up, with Professor Sibghatullah Mujaddidi as chairman and interim president. Mujaddidi came from an influential family and was affiliated with the moderate wing of the traditional Islamic leadership in the country. The Mujahideen council comprised 30 Mujahideen commandants, ten religious leaders and ten civilians.

The ethnic differences that have always played a role in Afghan politics and that attempts had been made to balance under Pashtun domination became visible again in the vacuum of power that followed the hanging of Najibullah. Concretely it meant that for the first time in 300 years, Kabul was not under Pashtun control.[242]

After two months, the commission was to hand over power to a provisional government under the leadership of Rabbani, who was part of the Tadzhik minority. Rabbani's ally, Ahmad Shah Mas'ud, a Tadzhik and Mujahideen leader, was appointed Minister of Defense, and the Pashtun Hekmatyar was offered post of Prime Minister but refused it.[243] The capture of Kabul on 25 April 1992 had further deepened conflicts between Mas'ud and Hekmatyar, because the head of Kabul's defense had surrendered to Mas'ud,[244] which meant a significant loss of prestige for Hekmatyar and worsened his military and political negotiating position in the end game over power in Afghanistan.

In March 1992, General Abdurrashid Dostum, a North Afghan commandant of Uzbek origin and to this very day the wild card in Afghan power politics, defected from Najibullah and the Communist regime to the resistance movement and ordered his troops to occupy Kabul's airport. Dostum remained loyal to Rabbani and his decision to change sides contributed to the fall of the Communist regime.

On 30 December 1992, Rabbani was declared President for a two-year term, but much of the political opposition did not recognize his mandate, and new negotiations in March 1992 led to the reduction of Rabbani's presidential term to 18 months and to Hekmatyar taking office as Prime Minister, with his rival, Ma'sud, stepping down. Alongside the political negotiations, Rabbani-loyal and Hekmatyar-loyal soldiers were fighting against each other, and Afghanistan was marked by anarchy and political unrest.[245] Fighting between the Iran-backed Shia party Hezb-e Wahdat and the Saudi-supported Sunni party, Ittihad-e Islam, also marked Kabul in the summer and fall of 1993.[246]

In 1994 General Dostum formed an alliance with Hekmatyar, and intense fighting over Kabul lasted the entire year without any of the warring parties decisively defeating any other. In 1994 Afghanistan was split into a number of autonomous political units. President Rabbani controlled Kabul and parts of the northeastern region of the country, while three provinces in the western part of the country, with the city of Herat in the center, were controlled by the commandant Ismail Khan, who was a former member of Rabbani's Jamiat-e Islami. In the eastern part of the country three Pashtun provinces were under the leadership of the Mujahideen commission, and Hekmatyar controlled areas south and east of Kabul.[247] The southern part of Afghanistan and the city of Kandahar were divided among a number of former Mujahideen commandants and more or less criminal groups who made life even more difficult for the already sorely tried Afghan people.[248]

THE TALIBAN

At the same time that Rabbani and Hekmatyar, the two former allies from the resistance movement against the Soviet Union, threw the country into civil war and brutal clashes over the country's political power, another political and military group sprouted up, namely the Taliban. The civil war was not only a domestic Afghan problem but just as great a problem for the regional power, Pakistan, which was prevented from gaining the geopolitical advantage made possible by the dissolution of the Soviet Union. Pakistan desired a peaceful, and better still a Pakistan-controlled, Afghanistan, which could provide access to transit to the new independent Central Asian republics that were opened for Pakistani trade and political influence by the breakdown of the Soviet Union. Saudi Arabia had similar political ambitions in Central Asia, which is why Saudi Arabia and, in particular, Pakistan had an interest in establishing and backing the Taliban movement, which originally consisted of Afghan refugees and veterans of the Afghan war who came from the many religious schools in Pakistan.[249] The Pakistani connection has been clear from the start, although Pakistan has never officially confirmed it. As soon as it appeared in 1994, however, the Taliban movement was already heavily armed and capable of using modern weapons. The religious students had apparently spent their time in the Pakistani madrasas in other pursuits than merely studying the Koran.

Pakistan and Saudi Arabia were thus successful in minimizing Iranian influence in Afghanistan, and Saudi Arabia again secured itself a foothold in the regional rivalry with Iran that has characterized relations between the countries since the Iranian revolution in 1979.

The Taliban took the southern city of Kandahar in the fall of 1994[250] and in 1995 Herat came under its control. A truce between Rabbani and Hekmatyar in June 1996 did not change the political and military means for fighting the Taliban movement, and with the Taliban's capture of Kabul in September 1996, the two were forced to flee to the northern part of Afghanistan along with the former Minister of Defense, Mas'ud.[251] There, an unholy alliance of Taliban opponents was formed, and when the Taliban movement attempted to conquer the entire country, intense battles broke out several times in and around the northern Afghan city Mazar-e Sharif, which Taliban forces finally seized in 1998. These were not merely random encounters between the Taliban movement and its opponents. Northern Afghanistan is namely an important area, both in terms of military strategy and of its natural resources, which is why the question of who controls and utilizes that part of the country is not insignificant. So occupation of the northern part of the country is of great strategic importance, because it can ensure control over access roads via the corridor at the Salang Pass between Kabul and Afghanistan's northern border, which is otherwise cut off by the impassable mountain areas that divide Afghanistan.[252] Rabbani and Hekmatyar were formally recognized by the UN as President and Prime Minister respectively until the formation of a new government in Afghanistan could take place after the fall of the Taliban in the fall of 2001. Rabbani lived in the northernmost part of the country until then, and Hekmatyar had resided in Iran for a long period, while Mas'ud, who was one of the key military leaders in the Northern Alliance, was assassinated just before 11 September.

UNEMPLOYED AFGHAN VETERANS

In 1992, Afghanistan was thus country devastated by civil war, with some 5,000 highly trained foreign Muslim fundamentalists experienced in war, known as the Afghanistan veterans or Afghan Arabs.[253] These foreign fighters from the Mujahideen movement probably found it difficult to identify with the domestic Afghan power struggle, and at first glance, there were three possible ways for them to put their acquired special skills to use. They could return to their homelands, among them Algeria, Egypt, and the Philippines, or they could travel to new battle zones in the Balkans and in the Caucasus, or they could go to the West and the USA.

What all the Afghan Veterans had in common was that they had met Muslims from other countries in the training camps in Pakistan, and had exchanged ideas and experiences there while building networks that cut across nationalities and affiliations to specific national Islamic movements and groups. They strengthened their sense of community and faith in the physical, religious, political and ideological fight for Islam – the holy war.

In the Afghan Veterans' self-image, they had defeated the ungodly Soviet Union thanks to a strong faith in Islam. The military success was achieved through armed combat combined with a strong religious and ideological focus on jihad. The fighting Muslims, both Afghans and foreigners, were prepared to fight and die for their religious convictions, which, with their emphasis on an offensive and politicized jihad, were formulated within a revolutionary and ideological context. The fact that they had learned what it was like to defeat a superpower had great psychological significance: if it were possible to defeat the Soviet Union in Afghanistan, it was natural for many of the Afghan Veterans to ask whether it might also be possible to fight unwanted regimes elsewhere. The Pakistani training camps and combat in Afghanistan enabled them to acquire military skills including the production of explosives and bombs, the operation of sophisticated weapons and the use of modern communications equipment; and their military know-how and operational capabilities qualified many Afghan Veterans to join or rejoin the militant Islamic groups that were active in the Middle East in different battle zones or that had networks in the West.

Common to several of the Afghan veterans was the fact that after their time spent in Pakistani training camps and on the Afghan battlefield, they had the motives, capabilities and will to continue the holy war. Whether these Afghan veterans were also able to use their skills in the places to which they traveled after their stay in Pakistan and Afghanistan was an open question. The answers are to be found in the next chapter, as we follow the Afghan Veterans back to some of their homelands, mainly in the Middle East, to new battle zones and to the West.

9. THE AFGHAN VETERANS, NATIONAL TERRORISM AND INTERNATIONAL NETWORKS

A number of countries in the Middle East saw an increase in political violence and terrorism in the early 1990s. A number of new battle zones outside the Middle East also saw attempts by militant Islamic groups to fight their way to power or independence. The character of terrorism quite simply changed at the beginning of the 1990s. The basis for this shift was laid in the training camps in Pakistan and in the encounter with the Red Army on the battlefields of in Afghanistan. There, the Afghan veterans acquired the necessary military know-how and quickly became the core of the militant Islamic groups inside and outside the Middle East.[254]

Confrontations between police forces and military on the one hand and militant Muslim groups on the other were a daily occurrence in several Middle Eastern countries for periods of time during the 1990s. Assassinations of politicians, journalists and intellectuals, massacres of civilians and the killing of foreign tourists were also recurring episodes in several Middle Eastern countries in that decade; Egypt and Algeria in particular were thrown into a long and bloody strife between national authorities and militant Muslim groups. Yet other Middle Eastern countries were also challenged, though perhaps to a lesser degree, by militant Muslim groups who attempted, with the use of armed force, to destabilize the countries and assume political leadership.

EGYPTIAN AFGHAN VETERANS ON NEW MISSIONS

During the 1990s Egypt, with its pro-Western policy, appeared on the one hand to be a kind of guarantor for processes of reconciliation and peace-making in the Middle East. This was manifested clearly by the Camp David agreement in 1978 and by the Gulf War, in which Egypt sided with the USA and the UN in the fight against Iraq. Added to this was Egypt's important role in attempts to mediate between the Israelis and Palestinians in the difficult implementation of the Oslo process. But on the other, Muslim fundamentalists were successful in using terrorism and armed attacks against the Christian Coptic minority, intellectuals, authorities, police and politicians, including a number of assassination attempts on President Hosni Mubarak, to create an image of Egypt as a country from which unrest and violence could be spread to the rest of the region, with instability and armed conflicts in the Southern Mediterranean as a result.

From 1992 to 1995 political violence escalated, with 1993 as the worst year with over 1,100 people killed or injured as a result of terrorism in the country. This was three times the total number of casualties in 1992 and twice the number in 1994 and 1995.[255]

By all accounts, the reason for this increase in terrorism was the Afghan veterans' return to Egypt, where the skills they had acquired in the war against the Soviet Union strengthened the operational capacity of already existing groups. From 1992, in other words, the military capability of Islamists was greatly enhanced.[256]

The militant groups themselves, however, were not responsible for the crisis and the problems with which Egypt had to contend. Terrorism and social problems were not new phenomena in Egypt, either. Egypt's is a complex history; in addition to the Islamic groups' revolutionary struggle and rivalry between the official Islam surrounding al-Azhar University and its opposition, the Muslim Brotherhood, there is also the issue of the state's lack of legitimacy and backing among the population beyond the ranks of Muslim fundamentalists. Added to this was a weak economy, an explosive growth in population, high unemployment, a huge but inefficient public administration and problems with corruption and nepotism.²⁵⁷ Nevertheless, it can be ascertained that the Islamists became more advanced and brutal in their militant strategy after the Afghan veterans' homecoming. In this respect, al-Jama'a al-Islamiya was the most forceful group. Knowledge about both its founding and its leadership is veiled in uncertainty, but both Omar Abdel Rahman and Tal'at Fuad Qasim have assumed key positions as the leaders of the movement. Rahman is regarded as the spiritual leader and inspirer,²⁵⁸ while Qasim probably functioned as operative leader and second in command from the end of the 1980s.²⁵⁹ In 1995 Rahman was sentenced to life imprisonment in the USA for being the ideological source of inspiration behind a number of planned bombings, including the UN building, FBI headquarters and some central bridges and tunnels in New York. Both Rahman and Qasim had connections to Denmark: Qasim had, as mentioned earlier, asylum there from 1992 until he disappeared in 1995 during a study trip to the Balkans, and Rahman visited Denmark at least twice at the beginning of the 1990s.²⁶⁰

In an interview with the Middle East periodical *Middle East Report*, Qasim related that Sayyid Qutb was his ideological basis and emphasized that "Qutb has influenced all those interested in jihad (holy struggle) throughout the Islamic world".²⁶¹ In the mid-1980s the leaders of al-Jama'a al-Islamiya established themselves in Peshawar, where Qasim states the group had central importance and large presence on the Afghan battlefield. Many young Islamists were sent to Afghanistan, partly for protection against arrests and other forms of persecution in Egypt, and partly to receive military training, which could be used in Egypt later.²⁶²

As a consequence of charges of complicity in the assassination of Sadat, Qasim spent eight years in Egyptian prisons until he was able to flee the country via Sudan to Peshawar, where he became the leader of the Arab Press Association and Managing Editor of the periodical *al-Murabitun*.²⁶³ Immediately following the fall of Najibullah in April 1992, he arrived in Denmark, where he applied for and was granted political asylum on the basis of the death sentence imposed on him in absentia by the Egyptian authorities for a coup d'etat and for assisting in the murder of policy makers.²⁶⁴ In an interview with the Danish newspaper *Dagbladet Information*, he described his role as high-ranking member of al'Jama'a al-Islamiya and ideological inspirer as such: "I have had no physical contact with al-Gama'a [al-Jama'a] in Egypt since I left the country. The connection is on a spiritual level. Maybe people read my publications or hear my talks,"[265] yet he emphasized that his "knowledge of the organization makes [him] completely able to speak on their behalf."[266] His function as spokesman gave rise to speculations about whether Qasim was part of an international network of high-ranking and exiled al-Jama'a al-Islamiya members who continued the fight against the Egyptian regime from their new homelands; yet these accusations were flatly rejected by Qasim: "They are absolute lies. They are an attempt by the Egyptian government to justify its treatment of al-Gama'a's activists and turn attention away from the government's disappointing economic and social policies."[267] Despite this denial, Qasim was linked by people abroad with the activitites of al-Jama'a al-Islamiya, even after he had been granted asylum in Denmark.

MORE VIOLENCE ACROSS BORDERS

With ideological bases in Qutb and Faraj, the militant Muslims initiated a new strategy in 1992 with three main tendencies. First, the groups aimed their attacks at the Egyptian tourist industry. Second, the scope of concrete assassination targets in Egyptian society was widened and, finally, the groups internationalized the fight against the Egyptian regime, which learned that the groups were also active outside Egypt, where they directed their actions against Egyptian interests and authorities abroad.

The most radical and sensational aspect of the new strategy was the decision that tourists were to be targets for the group's actions. Tourism is extremely important for the Egyptian economy, ensuring the livelihood of millions of Egyptians, and terrorism against tourists quickly proved to be effective: the deaths of 11 tourists in 1992 and 1993 in fact resulted in a halving of the income of the Egyptian tourist trade. The attacks against the tourist industry hit a particularly vulnerable spot for Egypt, namely the economy. About 1/6 of the Egyptian work force is occupied in one way or another with tourism and its attendant jobs,[268] so the Egyptian people paid dearly for that strategy. This form of asymmetrical war reached a temporary climax in 1997, when more than 60 people, mostly random Western tourists, were killed and a corresponding number wounded in a brutal terror attack in the Nile city of Luxor. According to the Egyptian authorities, the Afghan veteran Mehat Muhammad Abdel Rahman[269] was the mastermind of the action; however that may be, al-Jama'a al-Islamiya claimed responsibility for the attack, which was carried out to put pressure on the USA to release Omar Abdel Rahman.

The fact that the new strategy was also aimed at new targets within Egyptian society was reflected by the many assassinations and attempts on ministers and other high-ranking politicians in the early 1990s. In 1993 alone there were assassination attempts on the Egyptian Prime Minister, the Ministers of the Interior and Information, journalists and intellectuals: neither were Egyptian cultural personages spared if they came to be at cross purposes with the militant groups' conception of the truth. This cost the Egyptian author Farag Fouda his life in 1992; the reason for his execution could be found in two series of articles in Tal'at Fuad Qasim's *al-Murabitun*, which described Fouda's sacrileges in detail. During his stay in Peshawar, Tal'at Fuad Qasim participated in self-appointed Islamic tribunals, which issued death sentences on Egyptian officials and writers.[270] In 1994 the author and Nobel Prize winner Naguib Mahfouz was the target of an assassination attempt committed by members of the Islamist groups.

THE DANISH CONNECTION

The internationalization of Egyptian terrorism, which was a direct product of the Afghan veterans' global network, meant that the Egyptian government could not feel safe abroad either. On 26 June 1995, President Hosni Mubarak was the target of an assassination attempt in the Ethiopian capital of Addis Ababa, for which al-Jama'a al-Islamiya claimed responsibility. Immediately afterwards, the Egyptian authorities directed strong suspicion toward the authorities in Sudan, who were accused of having trained and granting logistical support to the assassins.[271]

The authorities also criticized the West, including Denmark, for granting asylum to Egyptians wanted for terrorism, on the grounds that the people in question were thereby able to continue their terrorist activity against Egypt from their new homelands. Indeed, Egypt held responsible exiled leaders of the militant Islamic groups for planning and carrying out some of the high-profile actions[272]. These were Ayman al-Zawahiri, who had lived in Switzerland and on 11 September 2001 was in Afghanistan, functioning as Osama bin Laden's chief ideologue; Mustafa Hamza, who resides in England; and Tal'at Fuad Qasim, who lived in Copenhagen until 1995 and preached at the al-Tawba mosque there.[273] The American author Bodansky supports the Egyptian authorities' critique, and in his book *Bin Laden. The Man Who Declared War on America* refers concretely to a meeting between the three leaders in Geneva on 23 June 1995, at which they are said to have gone over the operation in Addis Ababa in detail and given the final go-ahead for putting the plan into action.[274]

Two months later, in September 1995, Qasim disappeared as mentioned earlier during a study trip to the Balkans. On 9 October 2001, the Danish newspaper *Dagbladet Information* published an article that, referring to *The Boston Globe*, included the unconfirmed information that the final destination of Qasim's trip to Croatia was the neighboring country of Bosnia, which he did not manage to enter before being arrested by Croatian authorities and smuggled by American intelligence agents into an American ship in the Adriatic, where he was questioned for several days then handed over to Egyptian authorities.[275] As a reaction to the arrest of Qasim, al-Jama'a al-Islamiya carried out a suicide bombing against the headquarters of the Croatian police in Rijeka in October 1995[276] Qasim apparently had no connection with the three Egyptians who were arrested in Denmark in the fall of 1993 and later charged with planning terrorism against the Israeli embassy in Copenhagen, among other targets. Whether the three were Egyptian Afghan veterans is uncertain, although the Afghan veteran profile fits the two who arrived in Denmark in the fall of 1992 after a fairly long stay in Pakistan. According to the Danish newspaper *Jyllands-Posten*, they both stated they had belonged to al-Jama'a al-Islamiya,[277] were sentenced to death in absentia in Egypt for taking part in terrorism, and had previously been imprisoned in Egypt on charges of participation in terrorist activity.[278] They had apparently managed to flee Egypt, and later went to Peshawar.[279] The third Egyptian had not been in Pakistan, but had also belonged to a militant Islamic group in Egypt. The trial in Denmark against the three Egyptians ended in acquittal in 1996. Life in Pakistan was, however, apparently still appealing for one of the three, who was arrested in 2000 in northern Pakistan, where he was charged with being a member of Osama bin Laden's network.[280]

In November 1995, an Egyptian diplomat was killed in Switzerland, and later the same month Afghan veterans bombed the Egyptian embassy in Pakistan, taking the lives of 16 people and injuring 60. The Islamic groups in Egypt claimed responsibility for the attacks[281] as revenge for the Pakistani-American arrest of Ramzi Yusuf in Pakistan shortly prior to the attacks.[282] These and other attacks documented that terrorism in the 1990s had changed character with regard to both targets and means. First, terrorists were able to operate internationally; second, they were willing to kill even more unscrupulously than before, as seen in the attacks on tourists; third, they made use of both advanced weapons and high-tech communications equipment.[283] Modern communications equipment and network organization were precisely the means the Mujahideen had employed with success in Afghanistan in fighting the Red Army, and it was this, with the return of the Afghan veterans to Egypt, that gave the militant Muslim groups opportunities to modify their terrorist strategies and thereby make the fight against the Egyptian government more effective.[284] Several of the attacks to which the Egyptian society was subjected in the 1990s were thus conceived, planned, instigated and executed by people who had been in the training camps in Pakistan and Afghanistan for shorter or longer periods of time, either in connection with the Mujahideen movement's fight in the 1980s or as newly recruited members of al Qaeda in the 1990s.[285]

A fundamentalist speaks

Excerpt of an interview with Tal'at Fuad Qasim published in the Danish newspaper *Dagbladet Information*.[286]

Tourism – a card in the game
Why does al-Jama'a al-Islamiya commit acts of terror against tourists?

First, tourism is an enormous source of un-Islamic income, which goes straight to the government. That income constitutes financial resources that help the government survive. We believe, on the other hand, that the government ought to be removed. We decided to target tourism in order to deprive the government of this source of income, so that it cannot continue. According to statistics, tourism accounts for 2.2 million Egyptian pounds a year. Limited strikes by members of al-Jama'a al-Islamiya have cost us nothing, but have led to a decrease in these earnings, which are forbidden by our religion.

Second, tourism in its present form is an abomination, because prostitution and AIDS are spread by Jewish female tourists. It is also a despicable way of spreading all sorts of depravation. It is also through tourism that foreign intelligence services collect information about the Islamic movement. Tourism is therefore in our eyes a forbidden activity, which must be stopped. It is for these reasons that strikes against the tourist sector are carried out, as part of our strategy of destroying the government."

But the aim of the violent strikes was murder, because there were tourists who were killed. What does this have to do with the government?

Some of the tourists are guarded against being killed. That is why our slogan is "tourism, not tourists." We took a number of measures to protect the lives of tourists. We sent out various declarations warning tourists against coming to Egypt, because doing so could endanger their lives. We said that those who come put their lives at risk because the tourist trade is a target of attack. We sent messages to the responsible authorities, warning them not to receive tourists for these reasons. On the basis of all these measures, those who come anyway deserve their fate.

The coup plan
In what directions will the work of al-Jama'a al-Islamiya go now?

"There are three directions:
1) A military coup: we are working hard on this plan. The state knows nothing about this. At the same time, the state's security forces have been preoccupied with fighting insignificant forces in the Sa'id.
2) Mass mobilization: when the Islamic revolution occurs, we will need popular support to prevent foreign intervention for at least 18 days, according to our military experts. We have experience with organizing demonstrations.
3) Special missions: this is important work which involves the killing of some leaders. It is a prelude to events to come. The part of the group that will carry out this part of the plan is experienced and capable of seeing it through. The unit for special missions is active and will not stop murdering as long as this is necessary.

The government knows nothing about the military unit that is responsible for planning the military coup, and it doesn't know anything, either, about the unit for special missions. If some of its members are arrested, they only have information about their own cells, and that will not be of much use to the security forces. With regard to the other cells, there is absolutely no connection between them."

I think you are exaggerating in your account of the military work. We have never heard anything about the military units of al-Jama'a al-Islamiya. The Intelligence service has never arrested members of such a group. What is your proof?

My proof is the events of 1981. That time the security forces did not know anything, either, about the military branch of al-Jama'a al-Islamiya. By the way, there were military personnel involved in the Jihad case [trial in connection with the murder of Sadat].

But the military pesonnel who have left the military or who were charged in the Jihad case were low-ranking officers or privates. They have no influence. So assuming that what you are saying is correct, it does not pose much of a threat. What is your opinion?

I disagree. It is the young officers who constitute the real power, since soldiers do not recieve their orders from the generals. We are convinced of the importance of backing from the low-ranking officers. History has shown that they are the ones who are the most mobilized.

Tell us about the coup attempt in 1981.

The plan had different objectives. Militarily, to gain control over the ministries of defense and the interior, and over television and radio, so that we could transmit false declarations of loyalty from different military units in order to confuse the leaders of the army. At the same time, some of the military units were to execute some of the leaders of the government. Finally, a mobilization of the people in large demonstrations to prevent foreign intervention. We had an emergency plan, which we put into effect after the September campaign [in 1981], when many of our leaders were arrested.

The organization had decided to go into action according to the emergency plan, since it was feared that the security forces knew something about our organization after our arrest. The plan was changed after we learned that Khalid al-Islambuli was selected to participate in the military parade. The leaders were uncertain about whether Sadat should be murdered. Other brothers in Cairo decided to go through with the murder of Sadat. Islambuli's burst of bullets was supposed to start the revolution in Cairo and Assiut. It was Usamah Hafez's job to go to the Sa'id-province to inform the leaders there about the plan. But he was prevented from reaching Assiut because of the police road block and had to turn around. Sa'id's leaders were therefore surprised by the murder of Sadat. They thought the attack had been postponed. They waited for two days. But they were not able to gain control over Assiut and the headquarters of the security forces. The security forces, however, were able to regain control over the province after several hours of fighting. And the action in Cairo failed, too.

HISTORY REPEATS ITSELF IN ALGERIA

In Algeria the Afghan veterans were behind the founding of the Armed Islamic Group, GIA, in 1991 to 1992, which entailed a striking radicalization of the Islamic opposition[287] Those behind the establishment of the GIA were former members of the Islamic Salvation Front (FIS) who had fought together in Afghanistan.[288] The founding of the GIA led to an unmistakable escalation of violence after the military coup in 1992, and it is thus GIA, along with the security forces, which has a large responsibility for the bloody civil war Algeria has endured since, and which has cost over 100,000 lives.[289]

In Algeria, neither the Western nation-state model nor Soviet-supported socialism had fulfilled political and economic expectations; it was therefore an almost logical matter of course that, in the vacuum that arose in the late 1980s and early 1990s, the Algerian people more or less spontaneously backed the ideology and program so capably formulated and marketed by the Islamic fundamentalistic party FIS, and especially its leaders Abbasi Madani and Ali Belhadj from 1989 onwards. The great popular backing of FIS was clearly demonstrated during the local elections in 1990, when the Muslim fundamentalists obtained 55 % of the vote and won 853 out of 1,541 districts. Even more remarkable was the FIS victory during the first round of Parliamentary elections in 1991: the fundamentalists won 188 out of 232 seats and stood to have an absolute majority in the second round of elections in January 1992. The military, which was already deeply concerned about the democratic constitution from 1989, used the prospects of an Islamic regime to justify a coup in 1992, and thus effectively put a stop to democratization of Algeria – an act for which the new military leaders received poorly concealed support from the UN and the USA, which by no means desired to see Islamists in power in Africa's second-largest country.

When the Islamists appeared on the political scene in Algeria during the country's crisis, they did not appear out of the blue. They had been present all along, inspired by the Muslim Brotherhood in Egypt and, again, Sayyid Qutb's writings and ideas concerning the Islamic state. The Muslim fundamentalists' most significant contribution was the building of mosques. Early on, the government in Algeria – pursuing a strategy similar to Egypt's – made Islam subject to state control, and the imams were made public employees who would serve the official political ideology. Yet in accordance with legislation, the mosques were not to be turned over to the state until the buildings were finished, so they were simply left uncompleted. Accordingly, many of the mosques were able to defy the government and function as Islamic centers beyond governmental control. It is estimated that in 1980 there were 2,000 unofficial mosques, and that by 1990 the number had grown to 8,000. When the Algerian President Chadli Benjedid permitted the formation of political parties in 1989 with the adoption of the new constitution, FIS was able to mobilize support that can almost be characterized as a popular mass movement, in which long-time frustrations found an outlet in a well-known and simple message. The fact that many different groups could unite around a fairly simple program whose chief goal was the formation of an Islamic state – without a further specification of what this would mean beyond moral prohibitions and regulations – meant that FIS was a very heterogeneous organization. The party numbered everything from Islamic groups who wanted to introduce Islamicization by following a parliamentary path and who were thus prepared for dialogue and negotiations with the regime in power, to radically minded Muslims who saw revolution and armed fighting as the only way forward. Just as in Saudi Arabia, the most radical members came from the Salafiya movement, and in Algeria, too, already had a past, since they had made their dogmatic interpretation of Islam felt in the Algerian freedom movement in the fight against France. The Afghan veterans now insisted on a revitalization of the Salafiya movement, but to a degree which traditional Salafiya followers probably had difficulty recognizing. For the Afghan veterans in Algeria, uncompromising violence was the only navigable way forward.[290] The degree to which the moderate Muslim groups were democratically disposed can be questioned on the basis of the party program published in April 1990 by FIS, in which no will to play by the parliamentary rules of the game is evident; still, tensions between the moderates and the radicals ran high. While the moderate Islamic forces were dominant up until the military coup in 1992 and the prohibition against FIS, the militant groups are the ones who have marked the picture of Algeria since then. Several thousands, including the leaders Ali Belhadj and Abbasi Madani, were imprisoned, under house arrest or had to represent the party from exile in such countries as Germany, the USA, Spain, Belgium, Sweden and France; and the Algerian security forces were able to neutralize many of the local strongholds around the mosques in cities. It was radical Muslims from the militant Salafiya faction who continued the fight. In a way, FIS was sidelined early on, which was reflected in the contradictory announcements that came from the party's spokesmen and leaders. Sometimes they were in favor of an armed struggle, at other times they were against terrorism, demonstrating a willingness to negotiate.

GIA ESCALATES VIOLENCE

This meant that is was the radical groups who determined the direction of the Islamist fight against the Algerian military dictatorship. The most renowned group in this context is the Armed Islamic Group, GIA, which as mentioned earlier started as a group of Algerian Afghan veterans affiliated with FIS. Yet most Afghan veterans opposed the branch of FIS that was willing to negotiate and insisted instead on armed confrontation, which became increasingly more brutal as the conflict intensified. The group, which operated from bases in the poor rural districts east of the capital of Algiers and later throughout most of the country, was established as an independent unit in the summer of 1993 after confrontation with FIS, which, as a result, formed an armed branch of their organization under the name the Islamic Salvation Army, AIS. Yet it was actually back in 1991 that returned Afghan veterans asserted themselves at the end of the year by attacking a police station in the city of Gumhar on the Algerian-Tunisian border, costing a large number of dead and wounded. That action is considered the birth of the GIA.[291] Both operationally and in terms of management, the Afghan connection was important for the GIA. A crucial qualification for a GIA leader was that he had actively taken part in military operations on the battlefield in Afghanistan. This was the case for the founder of GIA, Tayyib al-Afghani, who was the leader of the attack on the police station. He quickly became a unifying symbol for the Algerian Afghan veterans until he was arrested and shot by the Algerian authorities.[292] Tayyib al-Afghani is a cover name, and the "last name" Afghani refers to the fact that he had been in Afghanistan. This was also the case for the later GIA leader, Ja'far al-Afghani, who was killed by security forces in March 1994; the same fate awaited the Afghan veteran and GIA commander Sherif Gousmi in September the same year.[293]

THE UNSUCCESSFUL DRESS REHEARSAL FOR 11 SEPTEMBER

GIA's terrorism was aimed not only at the Algerian state but was also directed against several aspects of Algerian society, just as the civilian population has increasingly been a victim of the group's violence. As in the case with al-Jama'a al-Islamiya in Egypt, the GIA targeted foreigners. Another resemblance can also be seen, namely the international dimension, whereby a commercial airliner was hijacked in Algeria on 24 December 1994 by GIA under the leadership of Djamel Zitouni.[294] The operation itself was carried out by a GIA cell led by the 25-year-old Abdul Abdallah Yahia. It was the first known attempt to use a passenger aircraft to carry out a suicide attack. The aim was partly to force the French government to give up its support to the Algerian government and partly to draw international attention to the conflict in Algeria. The aircraft was an Air France Airbus A-300. Of the 227 passengers, 40 were French nationals. The hijackers released some women and children and killed three other passengers. The Algerian airport authorities then gave the aircraft clearance to leave Algeria and head for France. The operative goal of the kidnapping was apparently to fly the fully-fuelled aircraft into the Eiffel tower in the center of Paris.[295] The French consulate in Oman had received an anonymous warning that the objective of the kidnappers was to blow up the plane over Paris on the evening of 24 December. Fortunately, it never got this far, as the hijackers were given the impression that the aircraft did not have enough fuel to reach Paris, and the French authorities were able to get it onto the ground at Marseilles. There the GIA demanded that the aircraft be loaded with 27 tons of fuel instead of the 10 tons required for the flight to Paris. The French authorities refused to comply with the kidnappers' demands and the group threatened to blow up the Airbus. In interviews immediately after their release, several of the passengers released in Algiers airport had related that the hijackers were in possession of explosives. The aircraft was then stormed by a French anti-terrorist unit that killed all four hijackers and freed 161 hostages and crew members. The terrorists' suicide plan was foiled, and the first suicide attack using a passenger aircraft was delayed by several years. Less than 24 hours after the action in Marseilles, the GIA took revenge by killing one Belgian and three French priests in Algeria.[296] Djamel Zitouni and the GIA also had a share in the responsibility for the campaign of bombings in France in the summer of 1995. It was, however, the kidnapping in Algeria in 1996 of seven French monks, who were later found decapitated, that marked the end of Djamel Zitouni. Shortly after the kidnapping, he was killed by the Algerian army in an ambush. Speculation has been rife ever since about whether his own soldiers informed against him.[297]

The many civilian massacres gave the GIA an increasingly bad reputation in and outside Algeria, where support dwindled in pace with the increasing number of innocent people killed. As in Egypt, there was disagreement as to whether it was justifiable to select civilian rather than military targets, which were perceived as more legitimate. Since the end of the 1990s, the GIA has been split into four smaller groups which operate chiefly in geographically different regions of Algeria. In 1998 the Salafi Group for Proclamation and Combat, GSPC, was founded partly in opposition to the truce AIS signed with the Algerian government and partly in opposition to the GIA's massacres of civilians. GSPC is led by the former GIA commander Hassan Hattab and keeps to the eastern part of Algeria, while GIA's main group is active in the central and western parts of the country.

KABUL — LONDON — AMMAN — ADEN

The Afghan veterans have left their most visible traces in the Middle East in Egypt and Algeria, but other Arab countries such as Tunisia, Morocco, Lebanon, Jordan and Yemen have also felt, if to a lesser degree, the effect of the return of the holy warriors. In Jordan a trial in November 1991 disclosed how Afghan veterans had played a key role in the founding of the militant Islamic group Jaysh Muhammad, Muhammad's Army. It was formed in 1988 in Jordan by an Afghan veteran, Samih Abou Zaydan, who had previously belonged to the Muslim Brotherhood. Zaydan had been inspired at a meeting with Abdallah Azzam. The political and religious goals of Muhammad's Army, to be achieved through jihad, were the reestablishment of caliphates and the creation of an Islamic state in Jordan. The first attacks for which the group was responsible, aimed at people affiliated with the Christian community in Jordan and stores that sold alcohol, were carried out in early 1991, when Muhammad's Army also killed a Greek-orthodox priest in a missile attack.

In 1994, another group of Afghan veterans asserted themselves by bombing cinemas under the leadership of the Palestinian Abu Muhammad Maqdisi. Maqdisi was allegedly one of the men behind the suicide bomb in Riyadh in November 1995 that killed four Americans and two Indians.[298] In 1999, an Islamic terror network led by Abu Hoshar was arrested by the Jordanian authorities. The investigation of the network revealed that the group's targets included the Radisson Hotel,[299] which was used by many Israeli tourists in Jordan. Abu Hoshar had a past in Afghanistan and was one of the founders of Muhammad's Army. In 1993 he was sentenced to a long prison term for planning assassinations but was granted royal amnesty and released some years later only to use the freedom granted him to prepare new attacks.

THE BRITISH CONNECTION I

Iman Abu Qatada, who was involved in the same actions as Abu Hoshar and sentenced in absentia to life in prison for terrorism along with Maqdisi, today resides in London, where newspapers have dubbed him Osama bin Laden's ambassador in Europe.[300] Abu Qatada was interrogated by the authorities in London in November 2001 after it was discovered that he had a number of very healthy bank accounts at the same time as receiving state financial aid. He is still suspected of being one of al Qaeda's financial connections in Europe.[301]

YEMEN: A DEN OF TERRORISTS

Yemen plays a key role in al Qaeda's activities in a number of ways. It has not only served as a country of transit and refuge for the network's members but has also itself been the site of several terrorist attacks, most recently in 2000 when the American destroyer *USS Cole* was blown up in a suicide attack that cost the lives of 17 American sailors. It was in northern Yemen, in the mountains near the city of Sa'da, that the first camp for Afghan veterans was established in 1991.[302] A number of people of different Arab nationalities settled there after their stay in Afghanistan. One of the founders of the Islamic reform party Islah, Sheik Abdul al-Zindani, who played an important role in the recruitment of young Muslims for the war in Afghanistan, mobilized veterans from this base for the fight against the socialist party in South Yemen. Together with veterans from other Arab countries, the returning Yemenites came to play an important role in the political tensions and unrest that marked

Yemen after unification in 1990; likewise, in 1994 they participated in the civil war side by side with the militant Islamic group Islamic Jihad and its leader, the Afghan veteran Sheik Tariq al-Fadhli, on the side of North Yemen's President Salih and his armed forces.[303]

The Islamic groups' support of President Salih quickly ended, however, after the military victory over the Socialist party in South Yemen in 1994, since when the militant groups have challenged the government through a number of violent demonstrations and attacks that have cost many lives.

Yet the militant Afghan veterans had already called attention to themselves before the events of the civil war. In December 1992, militant Muslims placed a bomb in a hotel in Aden where American military personnel had stayed during the military operation in Somalia. The American soldiers had already left the hotel when the bomb exploded, but two people were killed in the attack.[304] Tariq al-Fadhli, who planned the operation, had probably spent some years in Afghanistan during the 1980s and had had contact with Osama bin Laden until he returned to Yemen in 1989. Al-Fadhli's second in command, the Afghan veteran Jamal al-Nahdi, was also associated with the bomb attack in Aden.[305]

THE BRITISH CONNECTION II

In December 1989, a group by the name of Aden-Abyan Islamic Army took 16 Western tourists hostage. The following day, Yemenite security forces attacked, and three Englishmen and an Australian were killed – according to official sources, they were killed by the kidnappers. Great Britain reacted by criticizing the Yemenite authorities' intervention, which the British held partly responsible for the fatal outcome of the hostage crisis. The government in Yemen replied by claiming that the whole affair was led by the London-based Supporters of Sharia (SOS). The leader of SOS is the Egyptian autodidact and self-proclaimed sheik Abu Hamza, who, in the London suburb of Finsbury, had made himself the spokesman for radical Islamic viewpoints. Abu Hamza founded his own group along with other veterans on coming to England from Afghanistan, where he had been for most of the time from 1989 to 1993.[306] According to the Yemenite prosecutors, Abu Hamza had had contact for an extended period with the Aden-Abyan Islamic Army led by Abu Hasan. Hasan had admitted his responsibility in the hostage-taking episode in December, and had allegedly intended to pressure Yemen's government into releasing five British citizens of Middle Eastern origin who had been arrested 24 December 1998. The Yemenites claim that the five British citizens had been financed and sent to Yemen by Abu Hamza in order to make preparations for a terror attack against the British consulate. After the arrest they confessed their guilt but later, when the case began, claimed that their confessions had been given under duress in the Yemenite jail. The Yemenite authorities arrested three other British citizens of Middle Eastern origin and an Algerian in the mountain areas outside Aden that the Aden-Abyan Islamic Army had used as hiding place.

They are charged with having taken part in the hostage-taking and with planning terrorism.[307] Furthermore the Yemenites claim that those who were arrested were sent by Abu Hamza in London. The case is further complicated by the fact that one of the three British citizens, Muhammad Mustafa Kamil, is Abu Hamza's stepson.[308] Abu Hamza, a British citizen, is still living in London, although Yemen has demanded his extradition.

Abu Hasan was executed by the Yemenite authorities in the fall of 1999[309] almost a year to the day before the suicide attack in October 2000 against the *USS Cole* that underscored so vividly the presence of Islamic terror networks in Yemen.

THE FILIPINOS OFFER THEIR SERVICES

It was not only in the Middle East that Afghan veterans found new battle zones after the war in Afghanistan. They also became active in places such as the Philippines, Bosnia, China and Chechnya. Filipino veterans thus went to the Muslim-dominated Mindanao region in the southern part of the Philippines where they began an armed fight against the Filipino government. Until their appearance, two Muslim movements had represented the opposition against the central authorities: the moderate Moro National Liberation Front, MNLF, and the more radical movement, the Moro Islamic Liberation Front, MILF, which was established in the mid-1980s as a result of the truce MNLF signed with the authorities. The truce entailed MNLF toning down its demands for independence in favor of increased self-rule. However, the MILF intensified its activities and at the end of the 1980s, the militant Islamic group Abu Sayyaf emerged and radicalized the armed struggle against the Filipino authorities.[310] The group, which as mentioned earlier is named after the Afghan leader Abdul Rasul Sayyaf, was established in the Mindanao region by Filipino Mujahideen; similarly, a large number of Arab Afghan veterans went along to Mindanao and joined the group[311] which together with MILF has over 15,000 soldiers, 600 of whom are Afghan veterans[312]. The most famous veteran in Abu Sayyaf, Ramzi Yusef, who was the brain behind the attack against the World Trade Center in 1993, was in the Philippines around 1993 to 1994. As early as 1992, the Abu Sayyaf group began its attacks with several bombings, killings and kidnappings targeting Catholic priests, businesspeople and, not least, the Filipino authorities[313] but it was not until 2000 that it became well known known in the West: in April of that year members of Abu Sayyaf kidnapped 21 people, including several Western tourists on the Malaysian holiday island of Sipadan, and took the hostages to the group's bases in the jungle area on the island of Jolo. The group demanded a ransom of $1 million per hostage, but through a series of negotiations in which Libya's leader Muammar Gaddafi played a key role, the release of the hostages was made possible.[314]

The Philippines in general and Mindanao in particular might very well be the next location after Afghanistan where Afghan veterans in the Abu Sayyaf group will be seen in a lengthy conflict with the USA. Not only is the group completely on home ground in the jungle in the Mindanao region, but the USA-led military action against the Taliban and al Qaeda network in Afghanistan can result in members of the network going to the Muslim Mindanao region and continuing their militant activities there or seeking protection with the militant rebels in Abu Sayyaf. So not only could The Philippines become one of the new sources of holy warriors, it could also provide individuals affiliated with the al Qaeda network the logistical capabilities to continue their Islamic terrorism.

AFGHAN VETERANS AND THE DAYTON AGREEMENT

Concurrent with the fall of Najibullah Afghanistan, Serbian President Slobodan Milosevic went to war against predominantly Muslim Bosnia in the spring of 1992. General Ratko Mladic and his paramilitary forces began taking areas in the northern and eastern parts of Bosnia, and the non-Serbian population was driven out and subjected to ethnic cleansing. This involved massacres of the Bosnian civilian population, systematic and brutal sexual offenses against Bosnian women, the establishment of concentration camps, the destruction of crops and the burning down of houses and entire towns. The tragic events in the Balkans and in Bosnia from 1992 to 1995 led to the largest stream of refugees in Europe since World War II.

While Bosnia was the victim of Serbian nationalism and oppression, several highly trained and battle-ready Afghan veterans were preparing themselves both in Pakistan and Afghanistan and in Sudan. The Afghan veterans who had not returned to their homelands or were not already fighting in new zones of conflict and who were ready to continue the fight in Bosnia were flown to Sarajevo. From there, they were driven to Bosnian training camps where they were both involved in the training of Bosnian Muslims and others without combat experience and in establishing militias that attacked the Serbian forces. It is estimated that from 1992 to 1995 there were about 1,000 veterans, chiefly affiliated with the Seventh Mujahideen Brigade, which fought in the region near Zenica.[315] Imam Abu Hamza from London spent a great deal of time in the town of Zenica in central Bosnia before turning his attention to Yemen.[316] The practical and financial aid for the Muslims fighting in Bosnia, including those who came from other places, was arranged by a number of Muslim relief organizations, as had been the case in Peshawar.

The efforts of the Afghan veterans in Bosnia played an important role in the military defense of the Muslim population in Bosnia, securing the political influence that Bosnia needed in connection with the Dayton Agreement in the USA in 1995, which ended the war. But the Dayton Agreement meant precisely that the USA and, to some extent, England put pressure on the Bosnian government to get rid of the many combat-experienced Afghan veterans and other volunteer fighters and mercenaries. The investigation into the bombing of the World Trade Center in 1993 had disclosed the Afghan connection in 1994-95, and in 1995 the USA had become aware of the phenomenon and the risk it constituted. The veterans were simply unwanted in the Balkan and in Europe. It was, however, possible for a number of them to travel on to Kosovo while others were apprehended by CIA and MI6 agents and handed over, for instance, to the Egyptian authorities; several were sentenced in absentia for terrorism against the Egyptian state in and outside Egypt – so for some of them, their efforts in Bosnia meant a one-way ticket to an Egyptian prison.[317]

SALAFIYA FOLLOWERS ESTABLISH THEMSELVES IN THE BALKANS

Still others of those who had traveled to the Balkans were rewarded for their efforts by the Bosnian government with Bosnian citizenship and thus a Bosnian passport. This presented many opportunities to travel to other places and either continue the holy war or take advantage of the possibilities for asylum in a number of Western countries. Finally there were those who married local women and obtained Bosnian citizenship that way. The holy warriors from abroad brought not only their military skills with them to Bosnia, but also a radical Salafiya-loyal concept of Islam and tradition that conflicted with the more tolerant form of Islam practiced for centuries by the local Bosnian population. As in Algeria, Egypt, Jordan, Yemen and Saudi Arabia, the efforts of the al Qaeda members in Bosnia led to a radicalization of and internal divisions among the different Islamic movements and parties. The presence of Salafiya followers in the Balkans thus meant they had firmly established themselves in Europe.

THE BOOMERANG EFFECT IN CHINA

As with the other countries who contributed actively by sending Mujahideen to fight in the Afghan resistance in the 1980s, China also learned that the consequence of attempting to export domestic problems was that the Afghan veterans returned like a boomerang: their homecoming was marked by several attacks at the same time that political unrest flared up in the northwestern Muslim province of Xinjiang. It was precisely here that the Chinese Army in the 1980s had recruited and trained young Chinese Muslims for the Afghan resistance. However, political unrest is not a new phenomenon in the province, where separatist Muslim groups have been fighting for independence and the establishment of the state of East Turkistan, also known as Uyghurstan, off and on since 1950. Such a state actually existed from 1944, when the Xinjiang province used the Japanese occupation of China to declare independence and found East Turkistan. This independence lasted until 1950, when the Chinese again annexed the province into China. The next 40 years were marked by sporadic political unrest that has been intensified since the beginning of the 1990s, giving rise to violent confrontations between Muslim nationalists and Chinese police and security forces.[318] The instability in Xinjiang was not only tied to the growing Islamic fundamentalism that was due in part to the homecoming of Afghan veterans. It was also connected to the political situation in the Central Asian and Muslim neighboring countries, which had become independent with the collapse of the Soviet Union and which, in the 1990s, were marked by the conflict between Islamist movements and the ruling governments.[319] When captured by the Afghan northern alliance, Muslims in Xinjiang related that they had fought with the Taliban, who had recruited them while they were in the madrasas in Afghanistan and Pakistan.[320] In January 2002, the Chinese government issued a report stating that Osama bin Laden's network had supplied arms, money and men to the separatist groups in Xinjiang. The report also includes a list of more than 200 explosions, assassinations and other attacks that had killed and injured several hundred people in the province since the beginning of the 1990s. The authorities in China believe that some 1,000 Chinese Muslims had received training in al

Qaeda's camps in Afghanistan throughout the 1990's. It can be difficult to judge the accuracy of the Chinese information, since the government can be suspected of having its own reasons for exaggerating the situation in order to counter critique of its own often brutal conduct in the province. On the other hand, the Chinese information breaks with the tradition of downplaying separatism within China, where the myth of ethnic unity is an ideological mainstay of the state.[321]

AL QAEDA GETS INVOLVED IN THE CAUCASUS

With the collapse of the Soviet Union in 1991 and the fall of Najibullah in 1992, the North Caucasian and Muslim republic of Chechnya, particularly its capital, Grozny, became yet another rallying point for Afghan veterans, who either directed their military efforts at the Russian presence in Chechnya or used the country as a transit camp and temporary residence on the journey to the West. Those in the latter group might have considered seeking political asylum in a Western country or providing support for the fighting Muslim brothers in Bosnia as aim of the journey.[322]

After the dissolution of the Soviet Union, conflicts flared up in several places; in the Caucasus this meant that Russia was engaged in actual war from 1994 to 1996 following the Chechens' declaration of independence, which the new government in Moscow could not accept. After two years of intense fighting and large losses on both sides, a ceasefire was negotiated by the Russian General Lebed and the Chechen leaders, and in the fall of 1996 the Russian army left the Chechen capital, Grozny, bombed asunder and impoverished. There were, however, also a number of Islamic factions in Chechnya who were in internal dispute, a situation that Salafiya veterans from Afghanistan took advantage of to spread the conflict to the neighboring state of Dagestan.[323] The many alliances led to military confrontations between Russia and Islamic rebels in Dagestan in 1999, and shortly afterwards Russia invaded Chechnya for the second time. There is much to indicate that al Qaeda involved itself directly in Chechnya with the creation of training camps and militia units consisting of former Afghan veterans and new recruits.

FROM BRØNSHØJ, DENMARK VIA GROZNY TO A JAIL IN MOSCOW

Abdul Aziz Wahhab, or "the warrior from Brønshøj [Denmark]",[324] was apprehended by Russian authorities in March 2000 on his stay in Chechnya, where he had been conducting his activities since 1999. When arrested, he was in possession of a machine gun, a grenade and a GPS satellite telephone, which, according to the Danish newspaper *Jyllands-Posten*, was probably intended for use in intelligence tasks for the Chechen rebels.[325] In the fall of 2001, the Brønshøj warrior was sentenced by the Russian authorities to "12 years in prison for fighting as a holy warrior on the side of the Chechen rebels against the Russian central power and for keeping under-aged sex slaves".[326] Illegal arms possession, membership in illegal armed groups, violence and kidnapping are some of the offenses for which Abdul Aziz was sentenced in a Russian court. According to the Russian leader of investigations, Abdul Aziz belonged to "the absolute inner circle in the rebels' highest leadership".[327]

According to *Jyllands-Posten*, Abdul Aziz, who is probably of Palestinian origin, is an Afghan veteran[328] who, during his stay in Afghanistan during the 1980s, was close to the Palestinian Abdallah Azzam.[329]

Since his arrival in Denmark in 1991, Abdul Aziz has made trips to Pakistan, the Balkans, Saudi Arabia and Turkey, to which he traveled in the summer of 1998. He crossed the border to Chechnya from Georgia and there joined the fighting Chechen Mujahideen.[330] Just as in Bosnia and other new battle zones, the North Caucasian republic of Chechnya became a battleground for militant Muslims' fight against an oppressive nationalistic government power that was challenged in particular by the ranks of Afghan veterans who, in their guest appearances, fought alongside local Muslim forces, with a common faith in jihad and the Islamic cause. But as in Bosnia and elsewhere, the character of the conflict in Chechnya is more complex than a focus on militant Islamism reveals at first glance. Nevertheless, al Qaeda's presence there, as elsewhere, documents the fact that the network achieved a global reach throughout the 1990s.

The military training camps in the Afghan-Pakistani border regions gave many thousands of foreign Muslims the opportunity to acquire military skills and qualifications which on returning home or arriving at new battle zones could be used in connection with joining or establishing new militant Islamic groups, some of whose members came to be part of a network ideologically based on the insights of Sayyid Qutb and the Saudi Salafiya movement.

The Diary of Abdul Aziz

During the trial against Abdul Aziz, the Russian authorities produced a diary which he apparently kept during his stay in Chechnya in 1999. Excerpts from the diary were published in the Danish newspaper *Jyllands-Posten*,[331] from which the following passages are taken:

28 April: I met with Sjamil Basajev [internationally notorious terrorist, ed.] in Urus-Martan. He scolded me because I never visit him. He asked for permission to visit me! Later that day he came and visited me at my new house and asked me to work for the Chechen government's intelligence service. He wants to put me in charge of a group of volunteer Mujahideen.

30 April: Arbi (Barajev) came by; he had a conversation with the relatives of our hostages. They offered three [thousand dollars, ed.], but Arbi insisted on ten. He said to me that five would also be fine.

I answered that these were wealthy people and that they easily could pay ten. I said to Arbi, "Let's see what they say when they see the tape."

4 May: Harib came by to ask for a fatwa that grants the right to take prisoners and sell them to states in the Persian Gulf.

- 6 May: We discussed the Russians' security situation in Chechnya and the capture of women.
- 19 May: I gave Murad $200 for expenses in connection with kidnapping.
- 27 May: I drove to Arbi Barajev and asked him to loan me $5,000 in exchange for my car as security. I want to buy a house for the money so that I can place a hostage in it. We discussed how we can transfer the person in question.
- 29 May: I left to study the GPS [Global Positioning Satellite System, ed.]. I got the hostage ready for transfer. We pay 5% of the ransom for transport.
- 7 June: We had a visit by Abu Mujahed. He asked for a fatwa to kidnap a journalist and said that with reference to my words, it is now permissible to kill Russian women in Grozny.
- 26 June: We had a consultation about how we are to conduct ourselves towards (President) Maskhadov. I said that we will accept Maskhadov's repentance on one condition: he must give a speech on TV and say that he was wrong about the armed fight and that the Mujahideen were right.

Maskhadov must also declare holy war on the Russians and demonstrate through his actions his uncompromising position toward the non-believers.

- 8 July: I taught the brothers how according to Islamic law the property of non-believers can be confiscated and given to a Muslim.
- 11 July: We agreed that if we run into problems getting ransom we will cut off the genitals of our hostages.

10. OSAMA BIN LADEN — PORTRAIT OF A LEADER AND HIS ORGANIZATION

This chapter begins with a description of Osama bin Laden the man and follows him from his studies at King Abdul Aziz University to his role as organizer of volunteers for the war in Afghanistan. Then the developments of the 1990s are described, including the building, organizing and financing of al Qaeda, and the fight against the USA up until its culmination – perhaps only for the time being – on 11 September 2001.

After the bombings of the American embassies in Kenya and Tanzania in August 1998, Osama bin Laden was put at the top of the FBI's list of the world's most wanted criminals. Each time a terror attack or threat was directed at the USA, it was his name that turned up in speculations about who might be behind it. This was also the case on 11 September, when attention turned towards the Islamic network in South Asia the moment it became clear that the event was an act of terrorism. However, it is more than likely that few people in the West knew about Osama bin Laden, and many regarded him almost as a figment of the American imagination: similarly, many in Europe interpreted the American theories about new forms of terrorism as exaggeration and, more than anything else, an expression of the American need for a new enemy after the dissolution of the Soviet Union. The events of 11 September changed this perception completely, and today no one would reduce Osama bin Laden to an example of American mythomania. But this does not mean that the person and leader of al Qaeda is identical with the superhuman images out of which American authorities have constructed him. On the one hand Osama is the man behind what is probably the best organized and most extensive terror network the world has ever known, and on the other, endowed by

Americans with almost supernatural powers to make him fit the mold suitable for the man who poses the greatest threat to their country. But who is this man, who for several years now has been able to challenge the world's strongest nation and superpower, the USA?

SOURCE CREDIBILITY

Islamic terrorism is responsible for the largest military losses the USA has suffered since the Vietnam War, and bin Laden's network has been associated with most of the attacks. Many stories have been written about Osama. Many of them are probably modern legends, others a collection of distorted facts, and some definitely in accordance with what we call reality. In this chapter we will attempt to present a coherent portrait of the man. We base it primarily on secondary literature, and some of the material we pass on here might well have been taken from the fringes of fiction. For instance, no one has been able to document the size of his fortune or the number of millions he inherited from his father. Most set the inheritance at $300 million, as do we, because it best explains how Osama was able to live as he did and build up al Qaeda while in exile in Sudan from 1991 to 1996. But the sum could be wrong.[332]

Similarly, very few have concrete knowledge about how al Qaeda is actually organized, how it is financed, how many are involved in the network, what its scope of geographic distribution is, and whether it is capable of regeneration after the death of Osama and the destruction of the camps in Afghanistan, including the loss of that country as a possible refuge. There is, however, a little concrete knowledge gleaned from former members who have been captured and have given information in court or who, for other reasons, desire to communicate what they know. In trials against former al Qaeda members, diaries and similar material have been produced, which has helped create a picture of an organization that is both global and postmodern in its leadership principles. Finally, the organization itself has produced material of which the most known are the two fatwas declaring war against the USA and the videos broadcast by the Arab television station *al Jazeera* after 11 September. But there are also cassette tapes that have been distributed with a view to disseminating al Qaeda's ideology and critique of the USA and the Arab regimes, video tapes that are used in recruiting, and a manual on jihad.[333] Despite the sparce source material and the few accounts, which are either undocumented or reflect a political agenda[334], we will attempt to create a portrait of Osama and al Qaeda as an organization.

BIN LADEN

Osama was born in 1957 in Saudi Arabia as the 17th son of one of the richest construction magnates in the Middle East, Muhammad Awadh bin Laden. Osama was 43 when the USA began to bomb his haunts in Afghanistan, where he was hiding with his four wives and numerous children. He comes from an extremely wealthy family that is known for its strong influence on the Saudi Arabian royal family.[335] Osama's father has roots in the Hadramaut province in Yemen, from where he emmigrated to Saudi Arabia in 1932. The country had just achieved independence and immediately developed into an absolute monarchy in which the Saud family possesses the power and, later, the enormous earnings from the sale of crude oil. Muhammad bin Laden built up a contracting firm from scratch that, with luck and hard work, grew to be one of the Middle East's richest companies. The background to this success was the fact that Muhammad was given the job of building the palaces of the newly established royal family. To this very day, the bin Laden group is one of the most important construction companies on the Arabian peninsula and in 1983 received a contract for $3 billion for the renovation of Islam's holiest areas in Mecca and Medina. Muhammad bin Laden was not only a good businessman, however, but knew how to take care of political interests, and thus formed close friendships at the highest levels in the royal family. At home, he followed the custom for wealthy Arab families and founded a family dynasty: before he died he managed to have 11 wives and 52 children, all of whom were raised in the Wahhabi Islamic tradition. Even after the death of its founder in a plane crash in the early 1970s, the bin Laden group has maintained its close contact with, and influence on, the royal family and is usually represented at the dinner table when foreign leaders or business delegations visit the kingdom.

Osama was 14 when his father died, leaving him approximately $300 million. After a short stay in Beirut, Osama was back in Jedda in Saudi Arabia, where he married his first wife and began his studies in management and civil engineering at the university there.

The image that emerges of the young Osama during his student years in Jedda is of a tall, slim and delicate man with a falsetto voice, who in addition to his studies showed an increasing interest in religious questions. The image also includes a young man who felt overshadowed by his older brother Salim, who represented the company publicly and took over his father's role as head of the family. During his studies he met Abdallah Azzam, a professor at King Abd al Aziz University who spread both his Salafi view of the world and his opinions on the necessity of militant jihad for liberating the Palestinians from the Israeli occupation, and Muslims in general from the dominance of the infidels who, he asserted, were becoming increasingly dominant globally.

Religious identity strengthened Osama's first great mission in life appeared in the form of the Soviet tanks that rolled into Afghanistan in 1979 to secure a loyal government there. The Soviet invasion created a common interest – although with widely differing motives– among the Arab countries led by Saudi Arabia, the USA and Osama bin Laden. Their common interest was simply to get the Russians out of Afghanistan. For the USA and the Arab states it was a question of security policy and oil, while for Osama is was a matter of rescuing Islamic soil from the Communist infidels. As early as a year prior to the invasion, Osama had used his family connections to contact the Saudi Arabian Minister for Intelligence Activity, Prince Turk al Faysal. Then, and throughout the 1980s, Osama obtained the Saudi Arabian government's support and blessing to organize a resistance army against the Russians. While Azzam moved to Pakistan and was behind Maktab al Khidmat in Peshawar, Osama, as right hand to his mentor, became one of the driving forces in the establishment of recruiting offices around Central Asia and the Middle East that were to recruit volunteer Mujahideen for the fight in Afghanistan. He used money from his own private sources but at the same time, with the help of his family and his close contacts with the royal family in Ryadh, he became an effective fund raiser and was able to obtain assistance with travel documents and the like for the volunteer Arabs who came from countries such as Algeria or Egypt to Afghanistan. In pace with the continuing expansion of the organization and the influx of funds from the USA, Saudi Arabia and other sources, banks had to be established to handle the transactions. In 1981, the brother of Prince Turk al Faysal opened the bank Dar al Mal al Islami, and the following year, King Fahd's brother-in-law founded Dalla al Baraka. Both banks channeled the money on to the Islamic social funds that ensured the money was used for recruitment, logistics, arms and training.[336] The arrangement shows that the royal family, to its very core, was deeply involved in the building of the organization that was later to become al Qaeda. It was not just a matter of passive support but active involvement by the Saudi state.

MORE IN SPIRIT THAN IN BODY

It is uncertain whether Osama himself actually took part in any combat, although there are accounts of his sudden appearance on battlefields, just as he himself proudly tells of his efforts in two historic battles: Jaji in 1986 and Shaban in 1987. The fact remains, however, that he excels at establishing and organizing networks; the fact that in 1983 the bin Laden company was awarded the contract for the renovation of Mecca and Medina was seen by many as a reward for Osama's strong commitment and excellent results in the organization of volunteers for the Islamic resistance against the Communists. As early as the beginning of the 1980s he had forged links with Afghan leaders, including the later Taliban leader Mullah Mohammad Omar, who at one time had resided in Pakistan, where Osama both built mosques for him and gave him a residential complex. At any rate, Osama established himself throughout the 1980s within and outside Afghanistan with a large network that includes Arabs, Afghans and Pakistanis and people connected with the governments of Saudi Arabia, Yemen and Sudan and, of course, Pakistan and Afghanistan.

After the Russian withdrawal and the Mujahideen's final defeat of the Soviet-backed government in Kabul, the volunteer Arab soldiers' mission was completed and they began to return to their homelands, partly because of pressure from Pakistan. They carried with them cassette tapes with speeches by Osama bin Laden who, in 1990, had attained the status of war hero and spiritual leader. At least 250,000 copies of tapes of speeches by Osama were made, and he himself returned to Saudi Arabia along with a large number of Afghan veterans.

For both him and his troops, it was a disappointing reality that greeted them on arrival in their respective countries. The contrast between the poor and devastated Afghanistan and the excesses of consumption in Saudi Arabia could hardly be greater. What was worse, American influence could be seen everywhere. Osama has since said of Saudi Arabia that with its luxury goods, extravagant styles in women's clothing and the dominance of the many infidel Westerners on the scene, his country looked like an American colony. His disappointment and disgust towards Western culture left its mark on the cassette tapes he recorded: "When we buy American goods, we participate in the genocide of the Palestinians," it is said in one speech, which continues: "American companies make millions in the Arab world with which they pay taxes to their government. The United States uses that money to send $3 billion to Israel, which it uses to kill Palestinians."[337] The anger felt by Osama and his brothers in arms was not helped by the fact that the returning warriors felt cheated out of recognition for their efforts, rather like many of the American soldiers who returned from Vietnam.

AL QAEDA IS ORGANIZED

The victory over the Soviet Union did not mark the end of Osama bin Laden's activities: it served rather as encouragement for the pursuit of his new goal, which was to liberate the Middle East from Western and Zionist dominance. Such was the rhetoric at least, but it is worth noticing, as Oliver Roy points out, that much of al Qaeda's activities came to lie outside the Middle East.[338] Al Qaeda had been established in 1988 or 1989 as a partial extension of Azzam's organization. The background is somewhat fuzzy but the founding of al Qaeda is probably linked to splits that were beginning to appear among different factions of the Afghan veterans over which of the local warlords should be supported after the withdrawal of the Soviet Union. In this matter, Osama maintained that anyone who had previously been in the Socialist camp should be excluded. Thus al Qaeda can be regarded as a breakaway group, united by its uncompromising criticism of both communism and the West, that will only accept an immaculate Islamic regime.

Around 1990, Osama activated the network and contacted former brothers in arms and veterans who were either still in Afghanistan or Pakistan, or who had returned to their countries of origin, where some of them had joined local Islamist groups.

This made the network's wide geographic distribution possible already from the start, enabling contact with individuals and groups in the Middle East, Central and South Asia and the Far East; likewise, Osama maintained close ties to the groups' leaders, including Ayman al Zawahiri from Islamic Jihad in Egypt, to whom he was very close. As was the case with the Soviet invasion ten years earlier, it was a military invasion that seriously set Osama's plans in motion, namely Iraq's occupation of Kuwait. Osama took part in the critique of Iraq and was clearly opposed to Saddam Hussein's annexation of Kuwait, but argued enthusiastically that Arabs should handle the matter themselves without any Western or American aid and intervention. Accordingly, he was constantly on the doorstep of the Saudi royal family with plans for how the kingdom itself, with help from al Qaeda, could handle Iraq. He therefore regarded Saudi Arabia's appeal for American assistance not only as an outright admission of failure but a betrayal of Islam. Since then, Osama's prime objective has been to get the USA thrown out of the Middle East by fighting Americans everywhere on the planet. At first, however, his anger over the presence of American troops in the Gulf was primarily taken out on the Saudi Arabian regime in the form of support for opposition groups in and outside the country. The critique of the Saudi royal family raised by Osama and opposition groups was then intensified, and as early as 1991 it became too much for the royal family, who pressured Osama to leave the country. In 1994, Saudi

Arabia revoked his citizenship and froze his economic assets inside the country, while the bin Laden family disowned its prodigal son. Osama settled in Khartoum in Sudan instead, and there initiated a friendship with another Islamic leader, Hasan al-Turabi.

Expulsion from Saudi Arabia did not mean that Osama gave up his struggle against the American presence in the Middle East. On the contrary, along with al Turabi and his contacts to the Egyptian Jihad Groups, he made Sudan a center of militant Islamism: first a number of training camps were established; second, approximately 500 al Qaeda members came to Khartoum; and third, several militant groups from Egypt, Palestine, Lebanon, Algeria and Yemen established themselves in Sudan. In 1995, Turabi's movement hosted a famous – or infamous – conference at which Osama bin Laden was introduced to a number of leaders of different Middle Eastern groups: Imad Mughniya from Hizballah and, on the FBI's most-wanted list, Fathi Shakaki from Islamic Jihad, and who was, liquidated later that year by the Israeli intelligence service, Musa Abu Marzuq and Muhammad Nazzal from Hamas, Sheik al Zindani from Islah in Yemen, representatives from al Jama'at al Islamiya and from Iran, Algeria, Pakistan and Tunisia.[339]

THE FINANCING OF TERRORISM

It was also during his stay in Sudan that Osama established his business empire, which was based on monopolizing the production and export of arabic gum, of which the USA is a large-scale consumer as it is needed to make carbonated beverages, among other things. In addition, Osama followed in his father's footsteps and founded a contracting company. He was good at spreading his economic activities to many different areas in different countries. At the same time, he camouflaged his businesses through the extensive use of front men. There is, however, a great deal of uncertainty about where the basic financing comes from and what the economic relations between Osama and Taliban actually were. First there is, as mentioned, uncertainty about just how much money Osama inherited; and even if the sum of $300 million is correct, many believe that most of the money was lost as a result of the freezing of his assets. Furthermore, it can be ascertained that many of the businesses and companies al Qaeda has attempted to run legally around the world either did not produce much profit or simply closed because of deficits. There are indications that a number of companies, including some in European cities like Amsterdam and London, were established more with the aim of sponsoring terror projects than of making a profit. Some of the money for terrorist activities is transferred by regular banks, but al Qaeda has also transported money in other ways, such as cash couriers with suitcases. Since 11 September, it has also become clear that the network has used places like Dubai to launder money. This has been done partly by trading in gold and partly through the transfer of money "hawala," which means that large sums of money are transferred without being registered anywhere.[340] These transactions are conducted by ordinary commercial traders, who are widespread on the Arabian Peninsula. The procedure is for one trader to pay an amount with no receipt other than the promise given by the other trader that he has received the money.

Nevertheless, there is doubt as to whether the inheritance and the legal businesses have been capable of financing the extremely costly activities of running a private army and carrying out acts of terror. So the question arises of where the money actually comes from. The best guess is narcotics smuggling, of heroine from Afghanistan to Europe, through smuggling rings via the traditional trade routes through Dubai, which transfers goods and gold to the peninsula, South Asia and Africa. Added to this is the suspicion that criminal networks such as Abu Sayyaf in the Philippines supply – or have supplied – al Qaeda with money from the many very lucrative kidnappings the group is behind. Finally, it is becoming increasingly clear that the project groups responsible for carrying out concrete acts of terrorism are, to a certain extent, self-sufficient and that they themselves procure financing through credit card fraud, for example. In addition, the militant Islamic networks undoubtedly absorb money from the many Islamic funds that back educational and da'wa projects in South Asia. If this observation is true, it means that the money stems primarily from two sources: crime and Saudi Arabia. After the bombings of the American embassies in East Africa, the Americans stepped up their investigation of the financing of global terrorism by using the National Security Agency (NSA), which has the world's most refined and sophisticated technology for the surveillance of digital communication, including bank transfers. This did not lead to the desired result and, as is well known, neither did it stop the transactions; but much of what was brought to light indicated that the Saudi Arabians were involved in one way or another.[341] After 11 September, a number of people accused by authorities of belonging to al Qaeda have been arrested throughout Europe. In particular, networks with links to al Qaeda have been uncovered in Germany, Belgium, France, Italy, Spain and England. Others have been arrested because they had bank accounts with large sums of money for which no plausible explanation was given; this is the case with Sheik Abu Qatada, whom English media believe has been al Qaeda's contact in Europe.[342] Where the large sums of money come from and what they were to be used for still remains to be investigated. From investigations into 11 September, it is known that considerable amounts were transferred to private accounts for financing the terror attack but authorities have only been able to trace a fifth of the amount that the attack is estimated to have cost.

TO WAR WITH THE USA

The purpose of building al Qaeda was the fight against the USA, which began in October 1993 with the killing of 18 American soldiers in the Somalian capital of Mogadishu, probably by al Qaeda-trained soldiers. Afterwards Osama could gloat and deride Americans for failing in their attempts to establish military bases in Somalia and having to flee the country instead. At that time it was slowly beginning to dawn on Americans what kind of enemy they had created in Afghanistan. The first indications came with the investigation into the first terror attack against the World Trade Center in February of 1993.[343] It quickly became clear that those involved in the act of terror were all Afghan veterans and that they had been in contact with Osama on several occasions.

The leader of the bombing was Ramzi Yusef, who had arrived in the USA the year before and sought asylum. Yusef's actual identity is disputed, but he entered the country with an Iranian passport and lived in New Jersey. An incident with the customs authority revealed that he is the child of a Pakistani-Kuwaiti marriage, had grown up in Kuwait and that prior to the address in Pakistan given in his passport, he had been in Afghanistan as a holy warrior and in England as a student. However that may be, he settled in New Jersey in a radical mosque milieu also frequented by Sheik Omar Abdel Rahman, along with a number of other Afghan veterans. There they formed the group that tried to level the World Trade Center with a homemade bomb on 26 February 1993. While the others in the group, with the exception of an Iraqi who is in Iraq to this day, were arrested shortly after the attack, Yusuf managed to flee to Pakistan, where he became a bombing instructor and bomb maker in al Qaeda's training camps. First this took him to the Philippines, where he was to instruct the Abu Sayyaf group in the use of explosives. Next, the plan was to construct a bomb that could strike Bill Clinton's Air Force One, but as he feared security surrounding the American president would be too tight, he altered his plot to target Pope John Paul II. Yet this was not enough to satisfy Yusuf, who wanted to blow up a number of jumbo jets at the same time as the pope was murdered. This was to be done with the help of small bombs that could be smuggled on board in the heels of shoes. The first attempt failed, however. The bomb had been mounted under a seat, and Yusuf had attached a timer to it before leaving the plane on a stopover; but instead of blowing a hole in the fuselage of the aircraft, the bomb merely killed a passenger and forced the plane to make an emergency landing. Yusuf continued his experiments, though, and during a fire in his apartment, he left behind his PC, containing information that led to his arrest in Islamabad in 1995. At that time he was planning the bombings of 11 American planes on the same day – with a type of bomb reminiscent of the one Richard Reid tried to detonate in an American Airlines plane on the way from Paris to Miami in December 2001.

THE AMERICANS WAKE UP

Both the Somalia affair and the attack on the World Trade Center came as a surprise to American authorities, but as the FBI's investigations increasingly pointed towards some kind of link between Afghan veterans and Islamic networks in Egypt, the director of the CIA, James Woolsey, and 20 of his colleagues traveled to Cairo where Egyptian intelligence officers briefed them about Osama bin Laden's activities. From the summer of 1993, the USA intelligence agency kept Osama's doings under close surveillance, which did not prevent him from expanding his network, continuing his business activities and – according to the American government at least – still masterminding one anti-American act of terror after another. The CIA attempted to develop computer programs to follow and monitor Osama's dealings; his telephones were tapped and information drawn from his electronic communication equipment in the most sophisticated ways. It was not, however, a complete success, partly because Osama is all too well acquainted with American technology – the Americans taught him all about it in Afghanistan – and he could thus take precautions. Important messages were therefore not sent as ordinary e-mails or communicated via telephone or fax machines, but passed on by couriers or, if the internet was used, through temporary chat rooms and fake hotmail addresses.

In addition to the attacks on Washington and New York, the USA holds Osama responsible for bombings of American military bases in Saudi Arabia in 1995 and 1996 and for embassy bombings in East Africa in 1998; similarly, the clues left after the bombings of the American warship *USS Cole* in Aden in October 2000 more or less point directly to al Qaeda. The trial against Ramzi Yusuf, which ended with a life sentence in 1998, did not provide evidence against Osama or al Qaeda. Next, the two terror attacks in Saudi Arabia in 1995 and 1996 were concluded in Saudi manner with the beheadings of a number of people before the case was fully solved. And finally, the attack against the *USS Cole* is still being investigated.[344] Yet during a trial in New York in 2001, evidence was presented for al Qaeda's involvement in East Africa. So it would seem there is much to suggest that the Americans were right

– that Osama is the man behind a global Islamist terror network. The question then arises of how this was possible.

THE ESSENTIAL REQUISITES FOR A NETWORK

There is every indication that al Qaeda is loosely organized in a flat network structure in which ad hoc groups are responsible for carrying out concrete projects, whether they involve toppling the World Trade Center, attacking an American warship, murdering the pope or flying a plane into the Eiffel Tower, which the GIA is thought to have planned at Christmas 1994. Until 11 September, the organization's headquarters were in Afghanistan. However, they were probably mobile, moving around in the various cave complexes. Osama was the leader but relied on a number of people he had come to know during the war against the Soviet Union or who had later joined the organization, possibly after recruitment in Bosnia. Added to this were four committees, each of which was to manage one of the areas of military, religious, financial, or media-political affairs. Finally there were the training camps, where instruction was given in combat technique, the handling of explosives and the like. From the headquarters in the Afghan caves there was contact to Afghan veterans in other countries, for example al Jama'at al Islamiya in Egypt and GIA in Algeria. Yet contact with groups outside the Middle East, particularly in Kashmir, the Philippines, Central Asia and the West, seemed to be increasing. When the information that has come to light from investigations into and trials against al Qaeda's activities up till and including 11 September is analysed, it can be seen that primarily two groups of people are recruited for the network. The first, which can be referred to as "the first generation", consists of individuals who voluntarily signed up for the war in Afghanistan and met each other during combat or in Peshawar. After their discharge they have maintained contact – many of them have no real home and have become instead modern nomads, traveling from one battle zone to another or staying in the camps in Afghanistan. In the words of Olivier Roy they are a brand of globalized individuals who do not belong anywhere, geographically or territorially.[345] The second generation has never fought in Afghanistan and has no past in militant movements, but will often live and be educated in Western countries, where they are attracted for personal reasons to a more pure and true Islam and therefore seek out mosque milieus which cultivate a more anti-Western and fundamentalistic Islamism. From here they can either move on to the Islamic schools in Pakistan or be spotted by talent scouts trying to establish networks in the country in question. The talent scout will typically be a first-generation Afghan veteran who is either engaged in a concrete project, as Ramzi Yusuf was when he organized the World Trade Center bombing in 1993, or who is just establishing a dormant cell of a network. The link between the headquarters in Afghanistan and local networks is unclear, which makes it more difficult to combat the network.

It could be said that the network is oriented both globally and locally at the same time and that what holds it together is an abstract ideology that divides the world into good and evil, us and them, and according to which anyone who is opposed to it is deemed "infidel", regardless of whether he or she is in the USA, Denmark, Egypt or Afghanistan – almost mirroring the Bush doctrine. The community that is created is beyond the limits of time and space and is solely an imagined global community. Both the first-generation Afghan veteran and the second-generation Islamist are nomadic individuals, but where the first is an Oriental warrior with first-hand experience from the war in Afghanistan, the second is a young person with Western schooling, living in the West and often with Western citizenship. The fact that these Westernized young Muslims find a radical anti-globalization ideology appealing is, when it comes down to it, not so strange at all: in the 1960s young people from the university milieus were attracted by anti-imperialism and solidarity with the third world, tiermondism, that sometimes prompted them to join militant movements for the sake of a higher cause. Several of these young people, such as the leaders of the Rote Arme Fraktion in Germany, came from middle-class families and had good prospects for both education and jobs. Still, they acted in solidarity with rebel movements in the former colonies and formed a united front with them in the fight against Western capitalism. The critique of the USA as dominant superpower was the same as that of today. The difference is that today's rebel finds ideological fuel in religion while in the 1970s inspiration was found in Marxist books. In other words, the rebellion for which Osama bin Laden stands today resembles the revolt that Fanon and Jean-Paul Sartre advocated in the 1960s. The difference is that globalization and digitalization has given Osama bin Laden different and more widespread bases for growth than those Fanon had. This chapter has shown that al Qaeda, with simple means and in every way, has been able to take maximum advantage of the opportunities offered by the postmodern world to fight that selfsame world. The question is how the USA and the West will combat the new networks – whether the terrorists will continue with bombs or try a different strategy that in addition to American high-tech weapons also includes policymaking, economics and diplomacy. This is what the next and last chapter will address.

II. PAX AMERICANA — OR "THE AXIS OF EVIL" AS NEW WORLD ORDER

On 11 September 1990, the President of the United States, George Bush, heralded a new world order. The following year the Soviet Union was gone, the alliance against Iraq had emerged from the Gulf War victorious, and both events seemed to hold out the promise that, on the threshold of a new millennium, the UN would come to fulfill the roles it had been intended for from the start: that of guaranteeing that there would not be a third world war and that of resolving conflicts before they develop into wars. In this new world the USA would play the role of sponsor of peace plans in which the superpower would utilize its great potential to encourage cooperation instead of conflict. The sense of optimism lasted for some years, but it became clear as early as the mid-1990s that the new world order would be a long time coming: in the spring of 1996 the Israeli-Palestinian peace process was shaken by violent acts of terror in Jerusalem and Tel Aviv that helped Benjamin Netanyahu, a sworn opponent of the Oslo process, to power.

The Hebron Agreement

The Hebron Agreement was signed by Israel and the Palestinians in January 1997 after the Oslo process had come to a standstill with Benjamin Netanyahu's arrival as Prime Minister in May 1996.

The Hebron Agreement stipulates a withdrawal, but its importance lies more in some of its attached documents, which actually meant a change in the peace process from what was

> referred to as the "land for peace principle" to the "peace for security principle": on the one hand, the Palestinians were now to guarantee Israel's security and on the other the plans for further Israeli withdrawal were made much more loose and imprecise.

Although Netanyahu signed two agreements with the Palestinians, represented by Arafat, namely the Hebron Agreement and the Wye Memorandum, without American pressure on Israel, the Oslo process was put on a collision course that has never been corrected since. In Iraq the USA went it alone and bombed without informing its alliance partners, who were becoming increasingly critical of the sanctions policy, thought by many to be hurting the Iraqi population and strengthening its dictator Saddam Hussein by giving him free propaganda points. The result was that the alliance fell apart over the following years, which meant that since 1998, when Hussein pressed the last of the weapons inspectors out of the country, there has been no international consensus on Iraq policy.

The Wye Memorandum

Israel's withdrawal from the West Bank came to a halt following the Hebron Agreement. In the wake of American pressure, Israel and the Palestinians agreed in October 1997 to meet at the Wye Plantation outside Washington with the aim of resuming negotiations. This led to the Wye Memorandum, which for the second time since the Oslo II Interim Agreement in 1995 set down a plan for Israeli withdrawal from the West Bank and the release of Palestinian prisoners from Israeli jails. At the same time, the Palestinians were to make changes in the PLO's charter, gather up small arms and, most radically, be willing to cooperate with

> the CIA and the Israeli intelligence service in the fight against Palestinian terrorism. The Israeli government fell apart, however, and instead of implementing the agreement, there was a call for elections.

A WORLD OF INTRACTABLE CENTERS OF UNREST

As we discussed in the first chapter, the Middle East and South Asia were marked by war and conflict when Bush became president in January 2001. The American professor Samuel Huntington, who became famous in the early 1990s for his theories on "the clash of civilizations," wrote an article before that decade was out with the brilliant title "The Lonely Superpower". Arguably the USA was and is the only superpower and thus unchallengeable by any state militarily, economically or politically[346] but it is confronted with a world characterized by numerous intractable centers of power that constantly create conflict without there being an overall order into which they can be placed. In other words, the world now finds itself in a period of transition between one world order and another, which in the best case is in the process of being established now, but might not become stabilized for another ten to twenty years. Such a period of transition is marked by conflict, regional wars and instability, which create perfect growing conditions for militant networks like al Qaeda.

On the other hand we have a superpower floating like a giant on waters troubled by minor conflicts and wars. None of them threatens the life of the giant, yet they do create some leeway for those networks who view the superpower as the root of all evil and see this confirmed in what they regard as its arrogant and ignorant policies towards Palestine or Iraq. It is in these conflicts that the networks can find the motives to mobilize opponents of American globalization, and precisely the information strategy of globalization makes the world one big stage for the Wall Street yuppie, the student at the Technical University in

Hamburg, the fundamentalist in Jedda and the Abu Sayyaf member in the Philippines.

Al Qaeda started in Afghanistan and some are of the opinion – and perhaps rightly – that it came to an end during the American bombings of the cave complexes in the Afghan mountains. But history has shown that there were branches of al Qaeda in areas of conflict in the Middle East, Central Asia, the Caucasus, Malaysia, Indonesia, China, the Philippines and Africa, and that they recruited their members for actions in the West, in Europe and in the USA. Dissatisfaction with the USA, with globalization and with Western politics in the Middle East and South Asia, or with Russian politics in Chechnya is not done away with just because al Qaeda's training camps have been bombed out of existence. There will still be a great potential for dissatisfied people in Pakistan who could be thought willing to join newly established networks.

The Kashmir conflict is, as Clinton put it, one of the world's most dangerous conflicts; Afghanistan is very far from being a stable state that will refrain from internal splits and war far into Central Asia; and Saudi Arabia will be a major exporter of conflicts. After the breakdown of the Taliban regime and the capture of al Qaeda members in Afghanistan, states like Yemen, Somalia and the Philippines have been seen to arrest terrorists indiscriminately. But until something radical is done to resolve the numerous conflicts and the huge differences between those who enjoy the fruits of globalization and those who have to be content with its bitter pill, there will be both a basis for the growth of violence and places that, like hidden pockets in the global village, can serve as safe havens for militant networks: the training camps for the terrorists of the future.

The Clinton plan

After the peace negotiations at Camp David in the summer of 2000 ended without results and were followed by a violent conflict between the Palestinians and Israel, Clinton presented a peace plan for the first time in two terms of office. This occurred at a meeting on 23 December 2000 at a meeting of the Israeli interest organization the Israeli Policy Forum, just a few weeks before Clinton was to hand the presidency over to George W. Bush. The plan was therefore seen more as Clinton's personal peace plan than as the USA's. According to the Clinton plan, Israel is to hand over Gaza and approximately 95 % of the West Bank, including East Jerusalem and the Temple Square, to the Palestinians. The Palestinian refugees are to be given the formal right to return to Israel, including those territories that will continue to belong to Israel. Only 120,000 Palestinians will actually be offered the possibility of return, with the remaining 3.5 million or so will receiving some form of compensation. With the resolution, a number of measures guaranteeing Israel's security and sovereignty are to be implemented.

THE RESPONSIBLE SUPERPOWER

After the bombings in Afghanistan two scenarios emerge: in the first, the USA and the West are in an especially advantageous position, in which they hold all the cards for a future international order in the Middle East and South Asia. If these cards are to be played right, the decisions made in Washington must be based on the consideration that in the war against terrorism, bombing raid were only the beginning and that this small but important introductory step must be followed up by economic, political and diplomatic initiatives.

This means that the USA must follow up on its military victory with a political strategy that, on a number of crucial points changes the role of the USA and the West in the region. This is naturally a question of creating opportunities for development in the region, in which economic, social and not least political values are given highest priority. Globally, it is a matter of a more fair and just distribution of the world's wealth. Instead of speculating on whether Iraq, Somalia or the Philippines is to be the next target in the war on terrorism, three unresolved conflicts leap before the eyes as decisive areas that must be addressed if the next steps are to be taken – the unresolved conflict with Iraq, the problem of supporting dictatorial Arab regimes and the war between Israel and the Palestinians.

In all three areas the USA, with its global and regional strength, and the support it has after Afghanistan, could truly make a difference. In Iraq it is a question of removing the ineffective and tragic sanctions on the one hand and reestablishing an effective weapons control on the other. Here, the USA can go two ways: it can either remove Saddam Hussein with military might, as significant powers in the Pentagon would have it, or it can use the new understanding prompted by 11 September between the USA, Russia, China and France to push a diplomatic solution through. Second, the West and the USA could use the opportunity after Afghanistan, just as they did ten years ago, to make demands on its allies in the Middle East, including Saudi Arabia, to implement political reforms and put an end to support of dubious da'wa movements in South Asia. Even before 11 September the USA put pressure on Saudi Arabia to change its policies towards Islamic networks that are unquestionably engaged in terrorism. On the other hand, no American demands that Saudi Arabia should begin a process of political reform were evident, despite the superpower's rhetoric about human rights and democracy. As long as the West and the USA permit Saudi Arabia to export its domestic policy conflicts, it will be difficult to limit the spread of militant Islamic networks. A process of political reform on the Arabian Peninsula would likely remove some of the motivations many have for joining the new Salafiya movements, whose modernistic staging has its origins precisely in Saudi Arabia.

Third, there is the Israel-Palestine conflict, which will only reach a sustainable resolution if Israel's security is guaranteed and the Palestinians achieve their own state on the basis of the principles of the Clinton plan. But the prospects naturally do not stop in the Middle East. There is the conflict in Kashmir, poverty in Pakistan, lack of education in the region and more. This first scenario involves the West and the USA seizing the opportunity they had after the Gulf War, where there was also an alliance, and continuing the war against terrorism with other means, namely politics, economics and diplomacy. In this way something constructive could come out of 11 September – a second chance. In many ways, it was possible to have an optimistic faith in the possibility that this scenario could be realized: for a long period prior to 11 September, the USA had negotiated with governments in Central Asia, and under Bush also with the Taliban, so that diplomatic contacts had actually been established and could be used for something other than merely assisting with the logistics of the war.

In the effort to bring Pakistan into the alliance and help President Musharraf hold hid country together, all sanctions against the country were lifted, the country's debts were cancelled, and promises of future aid were made. In Afghanistan there was a similar will to follow up with aid, and Uzbekistan and Tadzhikistan had already been promised significant American investments. For a period it even looked as though the USA would back the Palestinians' cause more actively, and the USA began paying installments on its debt to the UN. But at the beginning of 2002, there was more that pointed in the direction of the other scenario.

A REVIVAL OF COLD WAR STRATEGY

In this second scenario, the USA uses the war against terrorism to establish the new world order that has not yet come about after the Cold War. The world is divided into those who support the USA in the war against the forces of evil and those who do not, and are therefore automatically considered enemies of the USA and the free world. In other words, terrorism becomes the concept around which a new global order of security is put together and according to which it is systematized. With this, we are back to the structure of the Cold War, and Bush's old guard can pull the Cold War strategy out of the drawer and turn on the military rhetoric.

Unfortunately, Bush's State of the Nation Address to Congress in January 2002 indicated that the administration would use the opportunity to revive the Cold War strategy: where Ronald Reagan spoke in his day of the "empire of evil," in early 2002, his heir spoke of the "axis of evil," by which he meant North Korea, Iraq and Iran. All three nations are on the USA's list of rogue states, and their status as nations that persistently strive to develop weapons of mass destruction was underscored a few days after Bush's speech by the CIA's biannual report, which described the efforts of "the states of concern" to arm long-distance missiles with weapons of mass destruction.

Bush explicitly stressed that Iran supports the Lebanese group Hizballah, which is accused of working together with al Qaeda via its militant branch. There are thus many indications that at the beginning of 2002, the USA was prepared to choose the second scenario, which at best reintroduces a world order in the manner of the Cold War and at worst leads to American military actions in Lebanon, Iran and Iraq. There is little doubt that the USA has the necessary military might to bomb all three countries to oblivion. The problem, however, is that this will not do away with terrorism but more than likely only strengthen the basis for its growth globally.

POSTSCRIPT TO THE INTERNATIONAL EDITION: INTERNATIONAL TERRORISM AND WEAK STATES

While terrorism seems to have been stemmed in the West, it has been intensified in other regions that are characterized as including states that are poorly developed, that is, weak states, or states that are either on the verge of collapsing (becoming 'failed states') or already have, such as Afghanistan, Liberia, Nigeria, Sudan and a number of states in Southeast Asia and Africa. After 11 September, it is particularly in these regions that the world has witnessed terror attacks – in Morocco, Tunisia, Yemen, Kenya, Pakistan, Afghanistan, the Philippines, Saudi Arabia and Indonesia. The world was particularly stunned by a violent attack in October 2002 on the holiday island of Bali that killed over 200 people, most of whom were visiting a disco, in a sophisticated attack that clearly resembled al Qaeda's mode of operation. Later investigations documented that the Indonesian group Jemaah Islamiaya was behind the attack and that it had been in contact with al Qaeda. In August of the following year another bomb exploded, this time in Jakarta, and many saw this attack as linked with the trial against those behind the Bali bombing. There is thus much to indicate that global terrorism has shifted strategy after 11 September to concentrating its efforts on hitting what are called 'soft targets' – discos, hotels and restaurants, instead of government buildings and military targets – preferably in weak or collapsed states.

It has long been known that al Qaeda has close connections to groups and milieus in Southeast Asia. As this book explains, the Abu Sayyaf group has been ravaging Mindanao in the Philippines for some time, with kidnappings and terrorism. And the famous fatwa, or decree, in which Osama bin Laden announces that it is the duty of every Muslim to kill Americans wherever they may be, was issued on behalf of an organization representing Islamists in a geographic area stretching from the Middle East, Central Asia and Pakistan to Bangladesh. Accordingly, one can again and again read in the media that the USA is cooperating with authorities in Georgia in the fight against al Qaeda members who are allegedly involved in the Chechen rebellion against Russia.

Despite two years' intensive hunt for al Qaeda, there are repeated reports of the presence of al Qaeda cells in the mountains of Central Asia, in China and still in Afghanistan and Pakistan. In countries such as Yemen, Georgia and the Philippines, the USA has stationed soldiers to combat al Qaeda cells, and in the past year we have heard about the unravelling of networks in Malaysia and Singapore, as well as increasingly about al Qaeda activity in Kashmir.

AL QAEDA IS BACK IN BUSINESS

Up to the first anniversary of 11 September, and especially up to the first anniversary of the beginning of American bombing in Afghanistan on 7 October, a striking increase in terrorist activity could be discerned. This was followed by unmistakable threats from probably the most influential al Qaeda leader after Osama bin Laden, Ayman al-Zawahiri, as well as Osama bin Laden himself. Most people point to the border region between Afghanistan and Pakistan as the most likely hiding place for the fugitive al Qaeda leaders. The terrain there abounds with hiding places, and the American troops and their allies continuously discover groups of up to 100 al Qaeda members hiding in the mountain caves, only revealed by accident when one of them cannot refrain from using his mobile phone, for example. It is difficult to ascertain how large a capability al Qaeda possesses, yet the fact that the network, or affiliated networks such as those behind attacks in Morocco and Indonesia, choose weak states seems to indicate that al Qaeda has become hard-pressed. But even if this were the case, the network is a dangerous and difficult opponent, which becomes evident by the simple fact that just by making his presence known through threats, Osama bin Laden forces authorities around the world to heighten emergency preparedness.

This example shows with all possible clarity the asymmetry that is at stake in what is called "the war on terrorism," namely that the world's largest and most advanced military machine is not capable of preventing a man with a tape from threatening the Western world to such a degree that preparedness is increased and travel activity, including tourist trips to Thailand and Indonesia, decreases. In this connection, it is worth noting that two years' purposeful military campaign in Afghanistan has neither led to the elimination of al Qaeda, the capture of the network's absolute top leaders and the capture of the previous Taliban leaders, nor resulted in the prevention of major terrorist attacks such as the bombings in Bali, Riyadh, Casablanca and Jakarta. And just as the Israeli army – which is probably the most effective, the most heavily armed and the best organized in the Middle East – despite two years' persistent efforts has not been able to prevent Palestinians from carrying out terror attacks in Israel and attacking the Israeli forces in the occupied areas, the American forces, which must be considered the absolute strongest globally, have not managed to combat the Islamist terror network. A provisional conclusion must be that terrorism, whether national, like the Palestinians', or global, like al Qaeda's, cannot be eliminated through military might.

TERROR AND WEAK STATES

There is much to indicate that the new terror networks seek refuge in weak states and that it is this constellation that constitutes the greatest challenge in the fight against global terrorism today. While it could be ascertained when the archives were opened after the Cold War that left-wing and nationalistic groups enjoyed major support from the Soviet Union and the Eastern Germany, both of which supplied arms, gave economic support and served as actual hiding places, the new networks seek out states that, because of their weakness, offer to provide refuge and may also stand to gain economic and political advantage from the presence of the new networks.

The networks procure their weapons themselves, seek financing themselves, and on the whole operate more as modern, globally oriented businesses, where communication is the most important asset when major terror activities are to be planned and executed. What they need are areas in which they can hide, operate their training facilities and establish centres for the gathering and dissemination of information – all this without interference from a government that is primarily concerned with protecting national interests. Weak states are states that are inadequately developed, where the central government is capable only of balancing between countless interests and conflicts and rarely has territorial control outside the capital – and even there, never completely – and where there is thus a good chance that groups can live undisturbed in, for instance, mountainous areas.

It will often even be the case that the terror network, in exchange for shelter, will offer the central government various services, which as in Afghanistan under the Taliban included providing bodyguards, economic support and actual soldiers for the civil war. In Pakistan, another weak state, al Qaeda provided the training of holy warriors for the conflict in Kashmir, and in other countries it is possible to assist in the smuggling trade, the cultivation of narcotics and other forms of crime.

Sometimes it can seem that the terror networks actually have stronger resources than the weak states that house them. Much indicates that Taliban survived at the mercy and expense of al Qaeda, rather than vice-versa. Yet networks like al Qaeda still need the weak states because despite the unsuccessful character of the latter in a UN context, they appear to be sovereign states in whose internal affairs countries such as the USA cannot permit themselves to interfere. Weak states are, in other words, ideal refuges for networks, whether for the mafia-like narcotics cartels of Central America, or Islamist terror networks such as al Qaeda, who, for their part, seek out areas where the combination of poverty, under-development and Muslim populations create the conditions for fishing in troubled waters and establishing and developing extremist groups.

A MISTAKEN STRATEGY

This is probably the real reason why al Qaeda, despite intense American pursuit, is back in business: there are simply huge areas outside the West that al Qaeda can infiltrate and in which they can hide. The network can both use the contacts that have been established for years and recruit new ones. Interrogations of arrested al Qaeda leaders in Pakistan in September 2002, as well as the unravelling of an al Qaeda cell in Buffalo, New York at about the same time, have revealed that al Qaeda is working very purposefully in Southeast Asia with a view to mobilizing there. The network can establish itself there instead of in Afghanistan, and from there can organize attacks both in and outside the region.

The many terror attacks that have been prevented in the USA and especially in Europe suggest that heightened preparedness works, and that it has become difficult to be a terrorist in the West. On the other hand, one can presume that the motivation to join anti-American and anti-Western networks is greater today than ever before, because in addition to heightened preparedness and police cooperation, the "war on terror" has consisted of military action and not of a will to solve the political problems on which terrorism subsists. If the USA was unpopular in the Middle East and South Asia before 11 September, the war in Afghanistan, remote-controlled liquidations in Yemen, the of war against Iraq, a lack of commitment to the Palestinian cause and a largely uncritical support of Sharon in Israel have not reduced anti-American sentiment. On the contrary.

The combination of weak states, high motivation to join networks and the absence of political solutions to the conflicts that form the basis for the growth of terrorism means that the strategy for combating terror that the West has chosen up to now – that is to protect ourselves with enhanced preparedness at home and bombing attacks abroad – is a Sisyphean task with no constructive prospects. If it is true that the threat of terrorism stems from the combination of weak states and global networks, then it is obvious that it cannot be destroyed by bombs – or entire continents will have to be bombed. Terrorism, in all its bloody cynicism, is a political problem; therefore, military strategies, international police cooperation and heightened preparedness must be supplemented with diplomatic and economic strategies based on political visions for solving the political problems on which terrorism subsists.

BIBLIOGRAPHY

Ahmad, Ashfaq: "The Muslim World Seen from Economic Angle", *Islamic Herald* (Kuala Lumpur), 5, vol. 1 & 2

al-Hawali, Safar Ibn Abd al-Rahman: "An Open Letter To President Bush", *IANA Radionet*, 15 October 2001

Alibek, Ken: *Biohazard: The Chilling True Story of the Largest Covert Biological Weapons Program in the World* (New York: Random House 1999)

Aliboni, Roberto, George Joffé og Tim Niblock (eds): *Security Challenges in the Mediterranean Region* (London: Frank Cass 1996)

Al Qaeda Manual located by the Manchester (England) Metropolitan Police and introduced at the embassy bombing trial in New York in the spring of 2001 (http://www.usdoj.gov/ag/trainingmanual.htm or http://www.usdoj.gov/ag/manualpart1_1.pdf)

Andersen, Kaj Holm, Søren Brøndum, Jan Top Christensen og Gorm Rye Olsen: *International Politik – konflikt eller samarbejde* (Samfundsfagsnyt 1982)

Andersen, Lars Erslev: "Anti-amerikanisme og terror i Aden" in *Mellemøstinformation* vol. 11, 2000

Andersen, Lars Erslev: "Asymmetrisk krig, ny terrorisme og den postmoderne verdens(u)orden – historien om et bebudet terrorangreb" in *Militært Tidsskrift* vol. 1, 2002

Andersen, Lars Erslev: "At sætte lethed ind mod tyngde – offentlighed, islam og politik i forlængelse af De sataniske vers" in *Slagmark* vol. 18, fall 1991

Andersen, Lars Erslev: "Bioterrorismens retorik. Fra anthrax-hoaxes i Kansas til mediemiltbrand i Ålborg", in Lars Qvortrup: *Mediernes 11. september* (København: Gad 2002)

Andersen, Lars Erslev (red.): *EU og Middelhavet* (Odense Universitetsforlag 1998)

Andersen, Lars Erslev: "Den fraværende Supermagt – USA og Osloprocessen", in Michael Irving Jensen (red): *På tærsklen til fred? Al-Aqsa intifadaen og fredsprocessen i Mellemøsten* (København: Gyldendal 2001)

Andersen, Lars Erslev: "Hvem dræber hvem i Yemen?" in *Mellemøstinformation* vol. 3, 1999

Andersen, Lars Erslev: "Islam mellem magt og fornuft", in *Højskolebladet* vol. 12, 1999

Andersen, Lars Erslev: *Muslimske fundamentalister. Militante muslimer i Mellemøsten* (København: DUPI 1997)

Andersen, Lars Erslev: "Den ny terrorisme. Del I: Fra Kairo til Kabul" in *Mellemøstinformation* vol. 8/9, 2000

Andersen, Lars Erslev: "Den ny terrorisme. Del 2: Da'wa og netwar" in *Mellemøstinformation* vol. 10, 2000

Andersen, Lars Erslev: "Oslo-processen: fra fredshåb til krigsfrygt" in *Mellemøstinformation* vol. 8/9 2001

Andersen, Lars Erslev: "USA's Mellemøstpolitik. Del 1: Arven efter Clinton", in *Mellemøstinformation* vol. 1, 2001

Andersen, Lars Erslev & Peter Seeberg: *Iran. Fra revolution til reform?* (København: Gyldendal 1999)

Anwar, Raja: *The Tragedy of Afghanistan. A First Hand Account* (London: Verso 1988)

Arnold, Anthony: *Afghanistan, The Soviet Invasion in Perspective* (Hoover Institution Press, Stanford University 1985)

Arquilla, John & David Ronfeldt: *In Athenas Camp. Preparing for Conflict in the Information Age* (Santa Monica, CA.: RAND and National Defense Research Institute 1997)

Arquilla, John, David Ronfeldt, Michele Zanini: "Information-Age Terrorism", in *Current History* vol. 99, no. 636, April 2000

Bearden, Milton: "Afghanistan – Graveyard of Empires" in *Foreign Affairs*, November/December 2001

Bergen, Peter L.: *Holy War, Inc. Inside the Secret World of Osama bin Laden* (New York: The Free Press 2001)

Berger, Peter og Brigitte Berger, Hansfried Kellner: *The Homeless Mind. Modernization and Consciousness* (New York: Vintage Books 1974)

Berger, Samuel: "A Foreign Policy for the Global Age", in *Foreign Affairs*, November/December 2000

Berman, Marshall: *All that is solid melts into air: The experience of modernity* (London: Verso 1985)

Bill, James A.: *The Eagle and the Lion. The Tragedy of American-American Relations* (New Haven: Yale University Press 1988)

Bodansky, Yossef: *Bin Laden. The Man who declared war on America* (Rocklin, CA.:Forum 1999)

Bradsher, H.S.: *Afghanistan and the Soviet Union* (North Carolina: Duke Press Policy Studies 1985)

Bruce, James: "Arab Veterans of the Afghan War" in *Jane's Intelligence Review*, vol. 7, no. 4, 1995

Burgat, Francois: *L'islamisme en face* (Paris: Éditions la Découverte 1995)

Bush, George & Brent Scowcroft: *A World Transformed* (New York: Alfred A. Knopf 1998)

Carlsen, Jørgen, Hans-Jørgen Schanz, Lars-Henrik Schmidt, Hans Jørgen Thomsen: *Kapitalisme, behov og civilisation* bind I-II (Århus: Modtryk 1980)

Christison, Kathleen: *Perceptions of Palestine. Their Influence on U.S. Middle East Policy* (Berkeley: University of California Press 1999)

Civil Society, January 1994

Cogan, Charles G.: "Partners in Time: The CIA and Afghanistan" in *World Policy Journal*, Summer 1993, vol. 5, no. 2

Cohen, Eliot A.: *Supreme Command. Soldiers, Statesmen, and Leadership in Wartime* (New York: Anchor Books 2002)

Collins, Joseph J.: *The Soviet Invasion of Afghanistan. A Study in the Use of Force in Soviet Foreign Policy* (Lexington 1986)

Cooley, John: *Unholy Wars. Afghanistan, America and International Terrorism* (London: Pluto Press 2000)

Cordesman, Anthony H. & Ahmed S. Hashim: *Iran. Dilemmas of Dual Containment* (Boulder 1997)

Country Profile Egypt 1995-96 (London: The Economist Intelligence Unit 1995)

Davis, Anthony: "Foreign Combatants in Afghanistan" in *Jane's Intelligence Review*, vol. 5, no. 7, July 1993

Dekmejian, R. Hrair: *Islam in Revolution. Fundamentalism in the Arab World* (Syracuse University Press 1995)

Djerejian:"The U.S., Islam and the Middle East in a Changing World", Meridian House International, Washington, D.C., June 1992

Dunn, Michael Collins: "Fundamentalism in Egypt" in *Middle East Policy*, vol. 2, 1993

Dupree, Louis: *Afghanistan* (New Jersey: Princeton University Press 1973)

Eickelman, Dale F. and James Piscatori: *Muslim Politics* (Princeton: Princeton U.P.1996)

Esposito, John L. (Editor in Chief): *The Oxford Encyclopaedia of the Modern Islamic World* (NewYork /Oxford: Oxford University Press 1995)

Fandy, Mamoun: *Saudi Arabia and the Politics of Dissent* (New York: St. Martin's Press 1999)

Fanon, Frantz: *Wretched of the Earth* (New York: Grove, 1968)

Federal Funding to Combat Terrorism, Including Defense Against Weapons of Mass Destruction FY 1998-2001. http://www.cns.miis.edu/research/cbw/terfund.htm

Fukuyama, Francis: *The end of history and the last man* (New York: Avon Books 1998)

Gauss, F. Gregory, III: "Political Opposition in the Gulf Monarchies", Paper at Conference in Qatar October 24th to 26th 1997

Gerges, Fawaz A.: *America and Political Islam. Clash of Cultures or Clash of Interests?* (Cambridge University Press 1999)

Ghaus, Adbul Samad: *The Fall of Afghanistan. An Insider's Account* (Pergamon-Brassey's International Defense 1988)

Global Proliferation of Weapons of Mass Destruction. Hearings before the Permanent Subcommittee on Investigations of the Committee on Governmental Affairs (Washington, D.C.: U.S. Government Printing Office 1996) – 20-875 Vol. 1-3

Goodson, Larry P.: *Afghanistan's endless War. State Failure, Regional Politics and the Rise of the Taliban* (University of Washington Press 2001)

Griffin, Michael: *Reaping the Whirlwind. The Taliban Movement in Afghanistan* (London: Pluto Press 2001)

Gunaratna, Rohan: "Terror in the sky" in *Jane's Intelligence Review*, October 2001

Habermas, Jürgen: *Theorie des kommunikativen Handelns* (Frankfurt am Main: Suhrkamp 1981)

Hammond, Thomas T.: *Red Flag over Afghanistan. The Communist Coup, the Soviet Invasion and the Consequences* (Colorado: Westview Press 1984)

Hegel, G.W.F.: *Vorlesungen über die Philosophie de Geschichte, "Einleitung", Werke in zwanzig Bänden* 12 (Frankfurt am Main: Suhrkammp Verlag 1970)

Hersch, Seymour M.: "King's Ransom. The House of Saud puts Arabia at risk" in *The New Yorker*, October 22 2001

Hobbes, Thomas: *Leviathan* (Cambridge: Cambridge University Press 1991)

Hoffman, Bruce: *Inside terrorism* (New York: Columbia U.P. 1998)

Hourani, Albert: *De arabiske folks historie* (København: Gyldendal 1994)

Huntington, Samuel P.: "The Lonely Superpower", in *Foreign Affairs* March/April 1999

Huntington, Samuel P.: *The Clash of Civilizations and the Remaking of World Order* (New York: Touchstone Books 1997)

Husain, Mir Zohair: *Global Islamic Politics* (New York: Harper Collins College Publishers 1995)

Hyman, Anthony: *Afghanistan Under Soviet Domination, 1964-83* (London: Macmillan Press 1981)

Ibrahim, Saad Eddin: "Anatomy of Egypt's Militant Islamic Groups: Methodological Not and Preliminary Findings" in *International Journal of Middle East Studies*, vol. 12, December 1980, no. 4

Ibrahim, Saad Eddin: "The Changing Face of Egypt's Islamic Activism" in Roberto Aliboni, George Joffe og Tim Niblock (eds.): *Security Challenges in the Mediterranean Region* (London: Frank Cass 1996)

Indyk, Martin: "The Clinton Administration's Approach to the Middle East" (Dual Containment Speech), Washington Institute for Near East Policy, May 15, 1993, in Kenneth Katzman: *U.S.-Iranian Relations. An Analytic Compendium of U.S. Policies, Laws and Regulations.* Occasional Paper, The Atlantic Council of the United States, December 1999

Intelligence Online no. 412 & no. 414

Jane's Document View: Security and Foreign Forces, Afghanistan, al-Qaida, November 21 2001

Jane's Intelligence Review Vol. 13, no. 11, 2001

Jane's World Insurgency and Terrorism, September-December 2001

Jansen, Johannes J.G.: *The Neglected Duty. The Creed of Sadat's Assassins and Islamic Resurgence in the Middle East* (New York: Macmillian 1986)

Jenkins, Brian M.: "International Terrorism: A New Mode of Conflict", in David Carlton & Carlo Schaerf (eds): *International Terrorism and World Security* (London: Crome Helm 1975)

Jerichow, Anders: *Som kongen finder passende: Saudi-Arabien – et land uden for lands lov og ret* (København: Aschehoug 1998)

Jerichow, Anders & Jørgen Bæk Simonsen (eds): *Islam in a Changing World. Europe and the Middle East* (London: Curzon Press 1997)

Joffé, George: "The Islamist Threat to Egypt" in *Middle East and North Africa*, (London: Europa Publications 1996)

Kant, Immanuel: "Beantwortung der Frage: Was ist Aufklärung?, Kant et al: *Was ist Aufklärung?* (Stuttgart: Reclam 1974)

Kant, Immanuel: *Zum ewigen Frieden. Ein philosophischer Entwurf* (Leipzig: Inzel-Verlag 1917)

Kaplan, David E.: "Aum Shinrikyo" in Jonathan B. Tucker (ed.): *Toxic Terror Assessing Terrorist Use of Chemical and Biological Weapons* (Cambridge, Mass.: MIT Press 2000)

Kaplan, Robert: *The Arabists: The Romance of an American Elite* (New York 1995)

Katz, David S. & Richard H. Popkin: Messianic *Revolution. Radical Politics to the End of the Second Millennium* (London: Allen Lane The Penguin Press 1998)

Kepel, Gilles: *The Prophet and Pharaoh. Muslim Extremism in Egypt* (London: Al Saqi Books 1985)

Koch, Henning, professor, University of Copenhagen: *contribution to the hearing of the Danish Folketing on the so called "Terrorpakke"*, 30 January 2002

Koch, Henning: *Demokrati – slå til! Statslig nødret, ordenspoliti og frihedsrettigheder 1932-1945* (København: Gyldendal 1994)

Kornbluh, Peter & Malcolm Byrne (eds.): *The Iran-Contra Scandal: The Declassified History* (New York: The New York Press 1993)

Koselleck, Reinhart: "Sprogændring og begivenhedshistorie" in *Den jyske historiker* no. 50, 1990

Laqueur, Walter: "Postmodern Terrorism" in *Foreign Affairs* September/October 1996

Laqueur, Walter: *The New Terrorism. Fanaticism and the Arms of Mass Destruction* (New York: Oxford U.P. 1999)

Lavoy, Peter R., Scott D. Sagan, James J. Wirtz: *Planning the Unthinkable. Haw New Power Use Nuclear, Biological, and Chemical Weapons* (Ithaca: Cornell U.P. 2000)

Ledeen, Michael: *The war against the terror masters* (New York: Truman Talley Books 2002)

Lewis, Bernard: "License to Kill. Usama bin Ladin's Declaration of Jihad" in *Foreign Affairs* November/December 1998

Litwak, Robert S.: Rogue *States and U.S. Foreign Policy. Containment after the Cold War* (Baltimore: Johns Hopkins U.P. 2000)

"Louis Freeh's Last Case. Who kept the F.B.I. director from closing it?" in *The New Yorker* 14 May 2001

Male, Beverly: *Revolutionary Afghanistan. A Reappraisal* (New York: St. Martin's Press 1982)

Marty, Marty E. & R. Scott Appleby (eds.): *Fundamentalism observed* (Chicago: University of Chicago Press 1991)

McCloud, Kimberly & Matthew Osborne: "WMD Terrorism and Usama bin Laden", http://www.cns.miis.edu/pubs/reports/binladen.htm

Middle East International: 1 May 1992, 15 May 1992 and 20 November 1992

Middle East and North Africa, MENA (London: Europe Publications 1996)

Middle East and North Africa, MENA (London: Europe Publications 1997)

Miller, Judith et al: *Germs. Biological Weapons and America's Secret War* (New York: Simon & Schuster 2001)

Milton-Edwards, Beverley: "Climate of Change in Jordan's Islamist Movement" in Abdel Salam Sidahmed og Anoushiravan Ehteshami, (eds).: *Islamic Fundamentalism* (Westview Press 1996)

Moussalli, Ahmed S.: *Radical Islamic Fundamentalism: The Ideological and Political Discourse of Sayyid Qutb* (Beirut: The American University of Beirut 1992)

Mubarak, Hisham: "What Does the Gama'a Islamiyya Want?" in *Middle East Report* January-March, 1996

Mustafa, Hala: "The Islamist Movements under Mubarak" in Laura Guazzone, eds.: *The Islamist Dilemma. The Political Role of Islamist Movements in the Contemporary Arab World* (Ithaca Press 1995)

Mylroie, Laurie: *Study of Revenge. Saddam Hussein's Unfinished War against America* (Washington, D.C.: AEI Press 2000)

Netanyahu, Benjamin: *Fighting Terrorism. How Democracies can defeat domestic and international Terrorism* (New York: Farrar Straus Giroux 1995)

Newel, Nancy Peabody & Richard S. Newel: *The Struggle for Afghanistan* (London: Cornell University Press 1981)

Nye Jr., Joseph S.: *The Paradox of American Power. Why the world's only superpower can't go it alone* (Oxford: Oxford University Press 2002)

Okruhlik, Gwenn: "Understanding Political Dissent in Saudi Arabia", *MERIP Press Information Note 73*

Pedersen, Carl: *Den sårbare nation* (København: Aschehoug 2002)

Perle, Richard: "How Do We Promote Democratization, Poverty Alleviation, and Human Rights to Build a More Secure World?" Testimony,

Senate Foreign Relations Committee, U.S. Congress, 27 February 2002

Perle, Richard, James Colbert, Charles Fairbanks, Douglas Feith, Robert Loewenberg, Jonathan Torop, David Wurmser, Meyrav Wurmser: *A Clean Break: A New Strategy for Securing the Realm*, The Institute for Advanced Strategic and Political Studies, Jerusalem/Washington, D.C., published May 1996

Pinto, Maria do Céu: Political Islam and the United States. *A Study of U.S. Policy towards Islamist Movements in the Middle East* (Durham: Ithaca 1999)

Quandt, William B: Peace Process. *American Diplomacy and the Arab-Israeli Conflict since 1967* (Washington, D.C.: Brookings Institution Press 2001)

Qutb, Sayyid: *Milestones* (Kuwait: Al Faisal Press 1989)

Qutb, Sayyid: *Maalim fil-Tariq*, (Beirut: Dar al-Mashriq 1986)

Rashid, Ahmed: *Taliban. Militant Islam, Oil and Fundamentalism in Central Asia* (New Haven: Yale U.P. 2000)

Rashid, Ahmed: *Taliban. The Story of the Afghan Warlords* (London: Pan Books 2001)

Rasmussen, Torben Rugberg (red.): *Mellemøsthåndbogen. Fakta om landene i Mellemøsten og Nordafrika* (Herning: Systime 1995)

Reeve, Simon: *The New Jackels. Ramzi Yousuf, Osama Bin Laden and the future of Terrorism* (Boston: Northeastern U.P. 1999)

Roberts, Brad (ed.): *Hype or Reality? The "New Terrorism" and Mass Casualty Attacks* (Alexandria, VA.: The Chemical and Biological Arms Control Institute 2000)

Roy, Olivier: "Bin Laden: An Apocalyptic Sect Severed from Political Islam" in *International Politik*, December 2001

Roy, Olivier: *Afghanistan. Islam, politik og modstand* (København: Eirene 1991)

Roy, Olivier: *Skakmat. Politisk islam. Et alternativ for de muslimske samfund?* (København: Eirene 1993)

Rubin, Barnett R.: "Arab Islamists in Afghanistan" in John Esposito (ed): *Political Islam. Revolution, Radicalism, or Reform* (London: Lynne Rienner Publishers 1997)

Sagiv, David: *Fundamentalism and Intellectuals in Egypt, 1973-1993* (London: Frank Cass 1995)

Schmitz, Charles: "Investigating the Cole Bombing", *MERIP Press Information Note* 67, 6. September 2001

Schweitzer, Glenn E.: *Superterrorism. Assassins, Mobsters, and Weapons of Mass Destruction* (New York: Plenum Trade 1998)

Shah-Kazemi, Reza: "From Sufism to Terrorism. The Distortion of Islam in the Political Culture of Algeria" in Reza Shah-Kazemi (ed): *Algeria. Revolution Revisited* (London: Islamic World Report 1997)

Sharon, Ariel: "Speech" http://www.cnn.com/2001/WORLD/meast/12/03/sharon.transcript/index.html

Shay, Shaul og Yoram Schweitzer: "The "Afghan Alumni" Terrorism. Islamic Militants against the Rest of the World" in *The International Policy Institute for Counter Terrorism*, November 2000

Shultz, George P.: *Turmoil and Triumph. Diplomacy, Power, and the Victory of the American Ideal* (New York: Charles Scribner's Sons 1993)

Skovgaard-Petersen, Jakob: "Moskeer i Egypten" in *Mellemøstinformation*, no. 8/9, 1995

Stern, Jessica: "Pakistan's Jihad Culture", in *Foreign Affairs* November/December 2000

Stern, Jessica: *The Ultimate Terrorists* (Cambridge, Mass: Harward U.P. 1999)

Sørensen, Anne Ingeborg: "Terrorister og frihedskæmpere. At definere terrorisme", in Johnny Laursen, Michael Mogensen, Thorsten Borring Olesen og Søren Hein Rasmussen (red.): *I tradition og kaos. Festskrift til Henning Poulsen* (Århus: Aarhus Universitetsforlag 2000)

Teitelbaum, Joshua: *Holier than Thou. Saudi Arabia's Islamic Opposition* (Washington, D.C.: The Washington Institute for Near East Policy 2000)

Tenet, George J.: "Worldwide Threat – Converging Dangers in a Post 9/11 World". Testimony of Director of Central Intelligence (CIA) George J. Tenet to the Senate Select Committee on Intelligence, 6. February 2002

The Saddam Hussein Sourcebook. Declassified Secrets from the U.S.-Iraq Relationship. The National Security Archive, George Washington University, Washington, D.C.

Urban, Mark: *War in Afghanistan* (Macmillan Press 1988)

Utgoff, Victor A. (ed.): *The Coming Crisis. Nuclear Proliferation, U.S. Interests, and World Order* (Cambridge, Mass: MIT Press 2000)

Voll, John O.: "Bin Laden and the New Age of Global Terrorism" in *Middle East Policy*, vol. VIII, No. 4, December, 2001

Wagner, Don: "For Zion's Sake", *Middle East Report* no. 223, 2002

Watkins, Eric: "Islamism and Tribalism in Yemen" in Abdel Salam Sidahmed og Anoushiravan Ehteshami, (eds.): *Islamic Fundamentalism* (Westview Press 1996)

West Europe Intelligence Report, 8. March 1994

Westerlund, David: *Questioning the Secular State. The Worldwide Resurgence of Religion in Politics* (London: Hurst & Company 1996)

Wienbaum, Marvin G.: "War and Peace in Afghanistan. The Pakistani Role" in *Middle East Journal*, vol. 45, no. 1, Winter 1991

Wiktorowicz, Quintan: "The New Global Threat: Transnational Salafis and Jihad" in *Middle East Policy*. Vol. VIII, No. 4, December 2001

Wilkinson, Paul: "Al-Gamaà Al-Islamiyaa – Egypt and the Challenge of Islam" in *Jane's Intelligence Review*, June 1993

Woodward, Bob: *Bush at War* (New York 2002)

Ya'ari, Ehud: "The Afghans are coming" in *The Jerusalem Report*, 2. July, 1992

Østergaard, Uffe: *Akropolis – Persepolis tur / retur* (Århus: Aarhus Universitetsforlag 1991)

Aagaard, Jan: "Taliban og det regionale spil" in *Mellemøstinformation*, nr. 10, 1998

Newspaper-articles & TV broadcasts

DR: "Horisont", 14. January 2002

TV2: "19-Nyhederne", 15. September 2001

CNN.com: "Rumsfeld: no evidence of al-Qaeda WMD's so far", 16. January 2002

al-Quds 23. March 1998

"Arabere hængt ud for terror", *Ekstra Bladet* 27. December 1993

Burke, J., E. Helmore and R. McCarthy: "How police caught up with the 9/11 mastermind," *The Observer*, 15 September 2002

"Danmark i fokus i global terrorsag" *Aarhus Stiftstidende*, April 1995

"Dansk egypter i baghold" *Dagbladet Information*, 9. October 2001

"Danske muslimer opfordrer til krig", *Dagbladet Politiken*, 27. April 1995
Ekstra Bladet, 22. July 1995

Elliot, M.: "How al-Qaeda got back on the attack," *Time*, 28 October 2002

"En fundamentalist taler ud", *Dagbladet Information*, 5.-6. March 1994

Esmann, Knud: "Den egyptiske forbindelse", *Jyllands-Posten*, 16. September 2001

"EU-terror-stempler grupper og personer", *Berlingske Tidende*, 28. December 2001

Farah, Douglas: "Al Qaeda's Road Paved With Gold. Secret Shipments Traced Through a Lax System in United Arab Emirates", *Washington Post*, 17. February 2002

"FBI går efter dansk dansk spor i stor bombesag", *Berlingske Tidende*, 27. March 1994

"Flere danske spor i terrorsag", *Dagbladet Politiken*, 15. April 1995

"Justitsminister afviser politi-læk om terrormistænkte" *Aarhus Stiftstidende*, 12. July 1994

Lake, Anthony:"Confronting Backlash States", *Foreign Affairs* 73, no. 2, March/April 1994

McGory, Daniel, Laura Peek, Bill Bond: "Bin Laden's 'European ambassador' in London", *The Times*, 21. November 2001

Mearsheimer, John J. & Stephen M. Walt: "An Unnecessary War", *Foreign Policy*, January/February 2003

Mubarak, Hesham: "Trusler sendt fra Danmark", *Dagbladet Politiken*, 26. February 1994

Pan, Philip P.: "China Links Bin Laden to Separatists", *Washington Post*, 21. January 2002

Pedersen, Lars Nørgaard: "Udlændinge-politik: Danmark lukket land for dømt flygtning", *Jyllands-Posten*, 2. November 2001

Rice, Condoleezza: "Shared Values, Interest of U.S., and Allies", *Washington File*, U.S. Department of State, October 15, 2002

Rimington, S.: "Terrorism did not begin on September 11," *The Guardian*, 4 September 2002

Rose, Flemming: "Allahs frontkæmper", *Jyllands-Posten*, 20. December 2000

Rose, Flemming: "Krigeren fra Brønshøj", *Jyllands-Posten*, 17. December 2000

"Saudi royal family in complete panic during recent riots", www.MiddleEast.org / 6. January 2002

Takeyh, R. and N. Gvosdov: "Do Terrorist Networks Need a Home?" *The Washington Quarterly*, vol. 25:3, 2002

"Terrorforbindelse Danmark-USA", *Jyllands-Posten*, 27. March 1994

"Terrornetværk med tråde til Danmark", *Aarhus Stiftstidende*, 18. April 1995

"The United Emirates has positioned itself as the Persian Gulfs freewheeling trade hup, but it is also attracting some unwanted entrepreneurs: money launderes", *Reuters* 10. November 1999

Thomle, Erik og Søren Kragh Pedersen: "Danmark oase for terrorister", *Jyllands-Posten*, 28. June 1995

U.S. News & World Report, "Princely Payments. Saudi Royalty, it is claimed, make out like bandits on U.S. deals" 14. January 2002

"Verdensomspændende terror-net: Dansk Forbindelse", *BT*, 17. April 1995

Westberg, Niels: "Muslimer anklaget for terrorforsøg i Danmark", *Ekstra Bladet* 22. July 1995

Woodward, Bob: "A Course of 'Confident Action'; Bush Says Other Countries Will Follow Assertive U.S. in Combating Terror, *The Washington Post*, Nov 19, 2002, p. A.01

Aagaard, Charlotte: "Allahs mand i Danmark", *Dagbladet Information*, 25. February 1994

Aagaard, Charlotte: "Den afghanske forbindelse", *Dagbladet Information*, 5. May 1994

NOTES

1. Bob Woodward: "A Course of 'Confident Action'; Bush Says Other Countries Will Follow Assertive U.S. in Combating Terror, *The Washington Post*, Nov 19, 2002, p. A.01

2. Condoleezza Rice: "Shared Values, Interest of U.S., and Allies", *Washington File*, U.S. Department of State, October 15, 2002

3. These ideas formed the argument in John J. Mearsheimer & Stephen M. Walt: "An Unnecessary War", Foreign Policy, January/February 2003

4. Thomas Hobbes: *Leviathan* (Cambridge: Cambridge University Press 1991)

5. George W. Bush quoted in Woodward op.cit.

6. Joseph S. Nye Jr: *The Paradox of American Power. Why the world's only superpower can't go it alone* (Oxford: Oxford University Press 2002)

7. Translated by Cindie Aaen from the Danish original Carl Pedersen: *Den sårbare nation* (København: Aschehoug 2002)

8. Dan Quayle quoted from Fawaz A. Gerges: *America and Political Islam. Clash of Cultures or Clash of Interests?* (Cambridge: Cambridge University Press 1999), p. 70

9. George P. Shultz: *Turmoil and Triumph. Diplomacy, Power, and the Victory of the American Ideal* (New York: Charles Scribner's Sons 1993), p. 685

10. Gerges op.cit. p. 69

11. Gerges op.cit. pp. 69ff

12. Peter Kornbluh & Malcolm Byrne (eds.): *The Iran-Contra Scandal: The Declassified History* (New York: The New York Press 1993)

13. *The Saddam Hussein Sourcebook. Declassified Secrets from the U.S.-Iraq Relationship.* The National Security Archive, George Washington University, Washington, D.C.

14. James A. Bill: *The Eagle and the Lion. The Tragedy of American-American Relations* (New Haven: Yale University Press 1988), pp. 306ff

15. Andersen op.cit

16. Alistair Drysdale and G. H. Blake, The Middle East and North Africa: *A Political Geography* (New York 1985)

17 William B. Quandt: *Peace Process. American Diplomacy and the Arab-Israeli Conflict since 1967* (Washington, D.C.: Brookings Institution Press 2001), pp. 307ff; Kathleen Christison: *Perceptions of Palestine. Their Influence on U.S. Middle East Policy* (Berkeley: University of California Press 1999) pp. 256ff

18 It has to be stressed though, that a promise was first given after the defeat of Iraq

19 Christison pp. 242ff

20 Quandt op.cit.; Christison op.cit.

21 George Bush & Brent Scowcroft: *A World Transformed* (New York: Alfred A. Knopf 1998) p. 370

22 Robert S. Litwak: *Rogue States and U.S. Foreign Policy. Containment after the Cold War* (Washington, D.C. The Woodrow Wilson Center Press 2000) p. 24

23 Francis Fukuyama: *The end of history and the last man* (New York: Avon Books 1998)

24 Immanuel Kant: *Zum ewigen Frieden. Ein philosophischer Entwurf* (Leipzig: Inzel-Verlag 1917)

25 Hegel developed his idea that freedom is the founding concept in History in G.W.F. Hegel: *Vorlesungen über die Philosophie de Geschichte, „Einleitung", Werke in zwanzig Bänden* 12 (Frankfurt am Main: Suhrkammp Verlag1970), pp.30ff

26 This argument is developed in details in J. Habermas: *Theorie der Kommunikativen Handelns* (Frankfurt am Main: Suhrkamp 1981)

27 "Aufklärung ist der Ausgang des Menchen aus seiner selbstverschuldeten Unmündigkeit. Unmündigkeit ist das Unvermögen, sich seines Verstandes ohne Leitung eines anderen zu bedienen", Immanuel Kant: „Beantwortung der Frage: Was ist Aufklärung?", Kant et al: *Was ist Aufklärung?* (Stuttgart: Reclam 1974) p. 9

28 Habermas op.cit.

29 Djerejian: "The U.S., Islam and the Middle East in a Changing World", Meridian House International, Washington, D.C., June 1992. See also Gerges op.cit. pp. 78ff

30 Gerges op.cit. pp. 176ff

31 Remarks by President Clinton to the Jordanian Parliament 10 June 1994, here quoted from Gerges op.cit. p. 93

32 Anthony Lake: "Confronting Backlash States", *Foreign Affairs* 73, no. 2, March/April 1994

33 Martin Indyk: "The Clinton Administration's Approach to the Middle East" (Dual Containment Speech), Washington Institute for Near East Policy, May 15, 1993, quoted from Kenneth Katzman: *U.S.-Iranian Relations. An Analytic Compendium of U.S. Policies, Laws and Regulations.* Occasional Paper, The Atlantic Council of the United States, December 1999

34 Attack on *USS Cole* 12 October 2000

35 Bush/Scowcroft op.cit.

36 *The Economist*: "The great exploding tax cut", March 1st. 2001

37 Richard Perle: "How Do We Promote Democratization, Poverty Alleviation, and Human Rights to Build a More Secure World?" Testimony, Senate Foreign Relations Committee, U.S. Congress, 27 February 2002

38 Brian Whitaker: "US thinktanks give lessons in foreign policy", *The Guardian*, August 19th. 2002

39 Laurie Mylroie: *Study of Revenge. Saddam Hussein's Unfinished War Against America* (Washington, D.C.: AEI Press 2000)

40 Richard Perle, James Colbert, Charles Fairbanks, Douglas Feith, Robert Loewenberg, Jonathan Torop, David Wurmser, Meyrav Wurmser: A Clean Break: *A New Strategy for Securing the Realm*, The Institute for Advanced Strategic and Political Studies, Jerusalem/Washington, D.C., published May 1996

41 The founding ideas are developed in one of the most important books outlining the strategic policy of the Bush administration, Eliot A. Cohen: *Supreme Command. Soldiers, Statesmen, and Leadership in Wartime* (New York: Anchor Books 2002)

42 The briefing took place 10 July 2002 and immediately after the briefing RAND posted a notice in *The New York Times* stating that the presented research was not to be identified with RAND

43 Bob Woodward: *Bush at War* (New York 2002), pp. 60ff

44 George P. Shultz: "It is time to think long, hard, and seriously about more active means of defense – about defense through appropriate preventive or preemptive actions against terrorist before they strike", Jonathan Institute 24 June 1984, quoted from Shultz op.cit. p. 647

45 All quotations from Don Wagner: "For Zion's Sake", *Middle East Report* no. 223, 2002

46 Samuel P. Huntington: *The Clash of Civilizations and the remaking of world order* (London: Touchstone Books1998) p. 209

47 The summary is written by Ledeen and published on the homepage of American Enterprise Institute (www.aei.org). In the book he writes: "The main part of the war – the campaign against the terror masters who rule countries hostile to us – is a very old kind of war. It is a revolutionary war, right out of the eighteenth century, and the very kind of war that gave us our national identity. While we will have to act against secret terrorist organizations and kamikaze fighters, our ultimate targets are tyrannical regimes. We will require different strategies in each case. We will need one method and set of tools to bring down Saddam Hussein, another strategy to break the Assad family dictatorship in Syria, a very different approach to end the religious tyranny in Iran, and yet another to deal with Saudi Arabia's active support for fundamentalist Islam and the terror network", *The war against the terror masters* (New York: Truman Talley Books 2002) p. xxii

48 Shultz op.cit. pp. 644ff

49 "19-Nyhederne," [The 7 p.m. news], [Danish] TV2, September 2001

50 A modest selection of headlines from past newspapers: "Terrornetværk med tråde til Danmark" [Terror networkwith threads to Denmark] (*Aarhus Stiftstidende*, 18 April 1995); "Danmark i focus i global terror sag" [Denmark infocus in global terror case] (*Aarhus Stiftstidende*, April 1995); "Justitsminister afviser politi-læk om terrormistænkte" [Minister of Justice denies police leak about terror suspect] (*Aarhus Stiftstidende*, 12 July 1994);"Verdensomspændende terror-net: Dansk Forbindelse" [Worldwide terror-net: Danish Connection] (*BT*, 17 April 1995); "Arabere hængt ud for terror" [Arabs blamed for terror] (*Ekstra-Bladet*, 27 December 1993); "FBI gå efterdansk spor i stor bombesag" [The FBI pursues Danish leads in big bombing case] (*Berlingske Tidende*, 27 March1994); "Danske muslimer opfordrer til krig" [Danish Muslims call for war] (*Politiken*, 27 April 1995); "Flere danske spor i terrorsag" [More Danish leads in terror case] (*Politiken*, 15 April 1995); "Terrorforbindelse Danmark-USA" [Terror connections Denmark-USA] (*Jyllands-Posten*, 27 march 1994)

51 Cf. Anne Ingeborg Sørensen: "Terrorister og frihedskæmpere. At definere terrorisme" [Terrorists and freedom fighters. Defining terrorism], in Johnny Larsen, Michael Mogensen, Thorsten Borring Olesen and Søren HeinRasmussen (red.): *I tradition og kaos. Festskrift til Henning Poulsen* [In tradition and chaos. Essays in honor ofHenning Poulsen] (Århus: Aarhus Universitetsforlag 2000).

52 "EU terror-stempler grupper og personer" [The EU labels groups and persons terrorists] *Berlingske Tidende*, 28 December 2001

53 Cf. contribution by Professor Henning Koch, University of Copenhagen, to the hearing of the Danish Folketing on the "Terrorpakke" ["Terror package" legislation] 30 January 2002

54 Benjamin Netanyahu: *Fighting Terrorism. How Democracies can defeat domestic and international terrorism* (New York: Farrar Straus Giroux 1995)

55 Lars Erslev Andersen: *Muslimske fundamentalister. Militante muslimer i Mellemøsten* [Muslim fundamentalists. Militant muslims in the Middle East] (Copenhagen: DUPI 1997), page 36ff.; Lars Erslev Andersen: "Osloprocessen: fra fredshåb til krigsfrygt" [The Oslo process: from hope for peace to fear of war] in *Mellemøstinformation* no. 8/92001

56 http://www.aipac.org/index.cfm

57 Walter Laqueur: *The New Terrorism. Fanaticism and the Arms of Mass Destruction* (New York: Oxford U.P.1999); Walter Laqueur: "Postmodern Terrorism," in *Foreign Affairs* September/October 1996; Peter R. Lavoy, Scott D. Sagan, James J. Wirtz: *Planning the Unthinkable. How New Powers Use Nuclear, Biological, and Chemical Weapons* (Ithaca: Cornell U.P. 2000); Glenn E. Schweitzer: Super*terrorism. Assassins, Mobsters, and Weapons of Mass Destruction* (New York: Plenum Trade 1998); John Arquilla & David Ronfeldt: In Athenas Camp. *Preparing for Conflict in the Information Age* (Santa Monica, CA.: RAND and National Defense Research Institute 1997); Brad Roberts (ed.): *Hype or Reality: The "New Terrorism" and Mass Casuality Attacks* (Alexandria, VA.: The Chemical and Biological Arms Control Institute 2000); Jessica Stern: *The Ultimate Terrorists* (Cambridge, Mass. Harvard U.P.1999)

58 Brian M. Jenkins: "International Terrorism: A New Mode of Conflict," in David Carlton & Carlo Schaerf (ed.s): *International Terrorism and World Security* (London: Crome Helm 1975), page 16

59 Lars Erslev Andersen: "Asymmetrical krig, ny terrorisme og den postmoderne verdens(u)orden – historien om et bebudet terrorangreb" [Asymmetrical war, new terrorism and the postmodern world (dis)order – the story of a heralded terror attack] in *Militært Tidsskrift* no. 1, 2002

60 Samuel Berger: "A Foreign Policy for the Global Age" in *Foreign Affairs* November/December 2000

61 Press conference on the publication of the National Defense Panel's Report: *Transforming Defense. National Security in the 21st Century* (Pentagon, December 1997)

62 Gurr & Cole op.cit; Walter Laqueur: *The New Terrorism. Fanaticism and the Arms of Mass Destruction* (New York: Oxford U.P. 1999); Walter Laqueur: "Postmodern Terrorism," in *Foreign Affairs* September/October 1996; Peter R. Lavoy, Scott D. Sagan, James J. Wirtz: *Planning the Unthinkable. How New Powers Use Nuclear, Biological, and Chemical Weapons* (Ithaca: Cornell U.P. 2000); Glenn E. Schweitzer: *Superterrorism. Assassins, Mobsters, and Weapons of Mass Destruction* (New York: Plenum Trade 1998); John Arquilla & David Ronfeldt: *In Athenas Camp. Preparing for Conflict in the Information Age* (Santa Monica, CA.: RAND and National Defense Research Institute1997); Brad Roberts (ed.): *Hype or Reality: The "New Terrorism" and Mass Casuality Attaks* (Alexandria, VA.: The Chemical and Biologica Arms Control Institute 2000); Jessica Stern: *The Ultimate Terrorists* (Cambridge, Mass. Harvard U.P. 1999)

63 See for example Stern op.cit., "Introduction."

64 Simon Reeve: *The New Jackels. Ramzi Yousef, Osama Bin Laden and the future of terrorism* (Boston: Northeastern U.P. 1999), page 135ff

65 Reinhart Koselleck: "Sprogændring og begivenhedshistorie" [Language changes and the history of events] in *Den jyske historiker* no. 50, 1990

66 Lars Erslev Andersen: "Asymmetrical krig, ny terrorisme og den postmoderne verdens(u)orden – historien om et bebudet terrorangreb" [Asymmetrical war, new terrorism and the postmodern world (dis)order – the story of a heralded terror attack] in *Militært Tidsskrift* no. 1, 2002

67 David E. Kaplan: "Aum Shinrikyo," in Jonathan B. Tucker (ed.): Toxic Terror. *Assessing Terrorist Use of Chemical and Biological Weapons* (Cambridge, Mass.: MIT Press 2000), page 207ff

68 Victor A. Utgoff (ed): *The Coming Crisis. Nuclear Proliferation, U.S. Interests, and World Order* (Cambridge, Mass.: MIT Press 2000), page 4 ff

69 Ken Alibek: Biohazard. *The Chilling True Story of the Largest Covert Biological Weapons Program in the World* (New York: Random House 1999); Judith Miller et al.: *Germs. Biological Weapons and America's Secret War* (NewYork: Simon & Schuster 2001), page 165ff

70 *Global Proliferation of Weapons of Mass Destruction: Hearings Before the Permanent Subcommittee on Invesigations of the Committee on Governmental Affairs* (Washington, D.C.: U.S. Government Printing Office 1996) -20-875 Vol. 1 – 3

71 Federal Funding to Combat Terrorism, Including Defense Against Weapons of Mass Destruction FY 1998 – 2001.http://www.cns.miis.edu/research/cbw/terfund.htm

72 Cf. Robert S. Litwak: *Rogue States and U.S. Foreign Policy. Containment after the Cold War* (Baltimore: Johns Hopkins U.P. 2000)

73 Kimberly McCloud and Matthew Osborne: "WMD Terrorism and Usama bin Laden, "http://www.cns.miis.edu/pubs/reports/binladen.htm

74 Ahmed Rashid: *Taliban. Militant Islam, Oil and Fundamentalism in Central Asia* (New Haven/London: YaleUniversity Press 2000)

75 Ibid.

76 Ibid.

77 John Arquilla, David Ronfeldt, Michele Zanini: "Information-Age Terrorism" in *Current History* vol. 99, no. 636, April 2000

78 Jessica Stern: *The Ultimate Terrorists* (Cambridge, Mass.: Harvard University Press 1999)

79 Cf. e.g. Bernard Lewis: "License to Kill. Usama bin Ladin's Declaration of Jihad," in *Foreign Affairs* November/December 1998

80 Bruce Hoffman: *Inside Terrorism* (New York: Columbia U.P. 1998), page 67ff

81 John L. Esposito (Editor in Chief): *The Oxford Encyclopedia of the Modern Islamic World* (New York/Oxford: Oxford University Press 1995)

82 The formulation stems from Karl Marx and Friedrich Engels: *The Communist Manifesto* from 1848, but took one pigrammatic meaning with the book by Marshall Berman: *All that is solid melts into air: The experience of modernity* (London: Verso 1985)

83 Cf. also the introductory chapter "Anti-Secularist Policies of Religion" in David Westerlund: *Questioning the Secular State. The Worldwide Resurgence of Religion in Politics* (London: Hurst & Company 1996)

84 John O. Voll: "Bin Laden and the New Age of Global Terrorism" in *Middle East Policy*, Vol. VIII, No. 4, December 2001

85 Cf. Jørgen Carlsen, Hans-Jørgen Schanz, Lars-Henrik Schmidt, Hans Jørgen Thomsen: *Kapitalisme, behov ogcivilisation* bind I – II [Capitalism, needs and civilization vol. I-II] (Århus: Modtryk 1980)

86 Cf. Sarar Ibn Abd a-Rahman al-Hawali: "An Open Letter to President Bush," *IANA Radionet*, 15 October 2001

87 Jean-Paul Sartre: "Preface" to Frantz Fanon's *Wretched of the Earth*. Trans. Constance Farrington 1963, (New York: Grove, 1968) pages 7 – 31

88 Samuel P. Huntington: *The Clash of Civilizations and the Remaking of the World Order* (New York: Touchstone Books 1997)

89 An important source of information for many in the discussion about Islamic fundamentalism is Francois Burgat: *L'islamisme en face* (Paris: Éditions La Découverte 1995) and Olivier Roy: *Skakmat: Politisk Islam: En alternative for de muslimske samfund* [Checkmate: Political Islam: An alternative for Muslim commuininites] (Copenhagen: Eirene1993). Mir Zohair Husain: *Global Islamic Politics* (New York: Haper Collins College Publishers 1995). Gilles Kepel: *The Prophet and the Pharoah* (London: al-Saqi 1995). We should also call to your attention the large "The Fundamentalism Project." Martin E. Marty and R. Scott Appleby (eds.): *Fundamentalisms Observed* (Chicago/London: University of Chicago Press 1991) is just the first volume of a larger series that analyzes fundamentalist movements globally and within all major religions. A general historical survey can be found in Albert Hourani: *De arabiske folks historie* [The history of the Arab people] (Copenhagen: Gyldendal 1994). Finally we refer to the country entries in *The Middle East and North Africa, MENA* (London: Europa Publications 1996) and Torben Rugberg Rasmussen (red.): *Mellemøsthåndbogen. Fakta om landene i Mellemøsten og Nordafrika* [Middle East Handbook. Facts on the countries in the Middle East and North Africa] (Herning: Systime 1995)

90 It is not possible here to give an even slightly comprehensive survey of the stream of literature that addresses the concept of modernity. I will limit myself to a reference to one of the more basic accounts, which includes Max Weber fairly extensively, namely Jürgen Habermas: *Theorie des kommunikativen Handelns* (Frankfurt am Main: Suhrkamp 1981)

91 The very idea that modernity can be controlled, that society can be revolutionized, that one has different options is a thoroughly modern one, cf. Peter Berger, Brigitte Berger, Hansfried Kellner: *The Homeless Mind. Modernization and Consciousness* (New York: Vintage Books 1974), page 177: "If one wishes to control modernization, one must assume one has an option and the ability to manipulate. Thus one may opt against moernity. Thus one will seek to manipulate the processes of modernization. These ideas, however, are modern – indeed, modernizing – in themselves. Nothing could be more modern that man has a choice between different paths of social development."

92 Reference can be made here to the Salman Rushdie case. Cf. Lars Erslev Andersen: "'At sætte lethed ind mod tyngde' – offentlighed, islam og politik i forlængelse af De staniske vers" [Putting weightlessness against heaviness –the public, Islam and Politics in extension of The Satanic Verses] in *Slagmark* no. 18, fall 1991. (Theme issue on Islam and nationalism)

93 "Horisont" [televised news magasine], DR television, 14 January 2002

94 Cf. David S. Katz and Richard H. Popkin: *Messianic Revolution. Radical Politics to the End of the Second Millenium* (London: Allen Lane, The Penguin Press 1998)

95 In his video shown on the Arab news channel *al-Jazeera* October 7th 2001, the same day the USA began its military attack on Afghanistan

96 Quintan Wiktorowicz: "The New Global Threat: Transnational Salafis and Jihad," in *Middle East Policy*, Vo. VIII, No. 4, December 2001, page 20ff

97 Wiktorowicz op.cit. page 22

98 Ahmed Rashid: *Taliban. Militant Islam, Oil and Fundamentalism in Central Asia* (New Haven: Yale U.P. 2000), page 82ff

99 John Esposito (ed.): *The Oxford Encyclopedia of Modern Islamic World* (New York/Oxford: Oxford University Press 1995)

100 Islamic Call Society: Jamaat al-Dawah al-Islamiya established 1972. Reorganized in 1982 as the World Council for Islamic Call: al-Majlis al-Alami lil-Dawah al-Islamiya

101 World Assembly of Muslim Youth: al-Hadwah al-Alamiya lil-Shahab al-Islami established in 1972

102 Ashfaq Ahmad: "The Muslim World Seen from Economic Angle," in Islamic Herald (Kuala Lumpur), 5 no. 1 and 2. Here cited from Dale F. Eickelman and James Piscatori: *Muslim Politics* (Princeton: Princeton U.P. 1996), page 36

103 Cf. Quintan Wiktorowicz and Jessica Stern: "Pakistan's Jihad Culture," in Foreign Affairs November/December 2000

104 Intelligence Online (IOL) 412, page 2

105 Ahmed Rashid: Taliban. Militant Islam, Oil and Fundamentalism in Central Asia (New Haven: Yale U.P. 2000)page 227

106 IOL 414, page 2 and 8

107 IOL 414, page 1 and *The New Yorker* 22 October 2001, page 35ff

108 IOL 414, page 2 and 8

109 Israeli Policy Forum

110 The American Israel Public Affairs Committee (IAPAC): http://www.aipac.org/HillAction.cfm

111 Transcript of Ariel Sharon's speech December 3rd, CNN, http://www.cnn.com/2001/WORLD/meast/12/03/sharon.transcript/index.html

112 Anthony H. Cordesman and Ahmed S. Hashim: *Iran. Dilemmas of Dual Containment* (Boulder 1997)

113 Amnesty International and Saudi Arabia, see http://web.amnesty.org/ai.nsf/countries/saudi+arabia?OpenView&Start=1&Count=30&Expand all

114 Mamoun Fandy: *Saudi Arabia and the Politics of Dissent* (New York: St Martin's Press 1999) page 4ff

115 Peter L. Bergen: *Holy War, Inc. Inside the Secret World of Osama bin Laden* (New York: The Free Press 2001) Chapter 3 and Milton Beardon: "Afghanistan, Graveyard of Empires," in *Foreign Affairs* November/December 2001

116 Robert Kaplan: *The Arabists: The Romance of an American Elite* (New York 1995)

117 *The New Yorker*, page 36. Also cited in *U.S. News & World Report*, "Princely Payments. Saudi Royalty, it isclamied, make out like bandits on U.S. deals" 14 January 2002

118 "King's ransom. The House of Saud puts Arabia at Risk," in *The New Yorker* op.cit., October 2001, page 36

119 Fandy op.cit., page 90

120 Fandy op.cit. and F. Gregory Gauss, III. "Political Opposition in the Gulf Monarchies," Paper given at conferencein Qatar 24 – 26 October 1997

121 Fandy and Gauss op.cit. and Joshua Teitelbaum: *Holier than Thou. Saudi Arabia's Islamic Opposition* (Washington, D.C.: The Washington Institute for Near East Policy 2000) Chapter 1

122 Teitelbaum op.cit. page 17ff; Fandy page 36ff; Lars Erslev Andersen: "Islam mellem magt og fornuft" [Islam between power and sense] in *Højskolebladet* no. 12, 1999 pages 3 – 6; Dale F. Eickelman and James Piscatori: *Muslim Politics* (Princeton U.P. 1996) page 60ff

123 Gwenn Okruhlik: "Understanding Political Dissent in SaudiArabia," in *MERIP Press Information Note* 73

124 Lars Erslev Andersen: "Den fraværende supermagt – USA og Oslo-processen" [The absent superpower – USA and the Oslo process], in Michael Irving Jensen (ed.) *På tærsklen til fred? Al-Aqsa intifadaen og fredsprocessen i Mellemøsten* [On the threshold of peace? The Al-Aqsa intifada and the peace process in the Middle East] (Copenhagen: Gyldendal 2001)

125 Teitelbaum, op.cit. page 39ff

126 The last demonstration was in December of 2001: "Saudi foyal family 'in complete panic' during recent riots," in www.MiddleEast.Org/ 6 January 2002

127 Interview in *The New Yorker* 14 May 2001: "Louis Freeh's Last Case. Who kept the FBI director from closing it?"

128 Gwenn Okruhlik, op.cit

129 Gilles Kepel: *The Prophet and the Pharoah. Muslim Extremism in Egypt* (London: Al Saqi Books 1985), page 94

130 Sayyid Qutb's work is titled *Milestones* or *Signposts* in English editions. Qutb: *Milestones* (Kuwait: Al Faisal Press 1989)

131 Qutb op.cit., page 9

132 Qutb op.cit., page 9

133 Qutb op.cit., pages 8 – 10

134 Qutb op.cit., page 152

135 Qutb op.cit., pages 98 – 99.

136 Qutb op.cit., page 124

137 Qutb op.cit., pages 16 – 17

138 Qutb op.cit., page 18

139 Qutb op.cit., page 258

140 Kepel, op.cit., page 57

141 Kepel, op.cit., page 13

142 Saad Eddin Ibrahim: "Anatomy of Egypt's Militant Islamic Groups: Methodological Note and Preliminary Findings" in *International Journal of Middle East Studies*, vol. 12, December 1980, no. 4, page 431

143 Ibrahim op.cit., page 431

144 Kepel op.cit., page 144

145 Kepel op.cit., page 139

146 Kepel op.cit., page 206

147 David Sagiv: *Fundamentalism and Intellectuals in Egypt, 1973 – 1993* (London: Frank Cass 1995), page 57

148 Kepel op.cit., page 207.

149 Kepel op.cit., page 205

150 Johannes J.G. Jansen: *The Neglected Duty. The Creed of Sadat's Assassins and Islamic Resurgence in the Middle East* (New York: Macmillian 1986), page 1

151 Kepel op.cit., page 193

152 Cited in Jansen op.cit., pages 160 – 61.

153 Cited in Jansen op.cit., page 193

154 Cited in Jansen op.cit., page 192

155 *Dagbladet Information* [The Danish newspaper Information] 5 – 6 March 1994

156 *Middle East and North Africa, MENA*, 1996, page 372

157 *Middle East and North Africa, MENA*, 1996, page 374

158 Jakob Skovgaard-Petersen: "Moskeer i Egypten" [Mosques in Egypt] in *Mellemøstinformation*, number 8/9,1995; Hala Mustafa: "The Islamist Movement in the Contemporary Arab World (Ithaca press 1995), page 184 and Sagiv op.cit., page 156.

159 Roy op.cit., page 42

160 Roy op.cit., page 50

161 Maria do Céu Pinto: *Political Islam and the United States. A Study of U.S. Policy towards Islamist Movements in the Middle East* (Durham: Ithaca Press 1999), page 125 ff

162 Thomas T. Hammond: *Red Flag over Afghanistan. The Communist Coup, the Soviet Invasion and the Consequences* (Colorado: Westview Press 1984), page 38

163 Beverly Male: *Revolutionary Afghanistan. A Reappraisal* (New York: St. Martin's Press 1982), page 57 and Larry P. Goodson: *Afghanistan's Endless War. State Failure, Regional Politics and the Rise of the Taliban* (University of Washington Press 2001), page 51

164 Anthony Arnold: *Afghanistan, The Soviet Invasion in Perspective* (Hoover Institution Press, Standord University 1985), page 63 and Goodson op.cit., page 51

165 Abdul Samad Ghaus: *The Fall of Afghanistan. An Insider's Account* (Pergamon-Brassey's International Defense 1988), page 70

166 Louis Dupree: *Afghanistan* (New Jersey: Princeton University Press 1973) pages 488 – 491

167 Ghaus op.cit., page 77

168 Goodson, op.cit., page 49

169 Hammond op.cit., page 24

170 Goodson op.cit., page 52

171 Hammond, op.cit., pages 38 – 39

172 H.S. Bradsher: *Afghanistan and the Soviet Union* (North Carolina: Duke Press Policy Studies 1985), pages 65 – 66

173 Arnold, op.cit., page 65

174 Arnold, op.cit., page 66

175 Anthony Hyman: *Afghanistan under Soviet Domination 1964 – 83* (London: Macmillan Press 1981), page 76

176 Goodson op.cit., pages 52 – 53

177 Joseph J. Collins: *The Soviet Invasion of Afghanistan. A Study in the Use of Force in Soviet Foreign Policy* (Lexington 1986), page 54

178 Nancy Peabody and Richard S. Newel: *The Struggle for Afghanistan* (London: Cornell University Press 1981), page 72

179 Raja Anwar: *The Tragedy of Afghanistan. A First-Hand Account* (London: Verso 1988), page 153

180 Goodson op.cit., page 56

181 Mark Urban: *War in Afghanistan* (Macmillan Press 1988), page 30

182 Olivier Roy: *Afghanistan. Islam, politik og modstand* [Afghanistan. Islam, politics and opposition] (Copenhagen, Eirene 1991), page 120

183 Hammond op.cit., page 85

184 Goodson op.cit., page 53

185 Collins op.cit., page 71

186 Collins op.cit., page 99

187 John Cooley: *Unholy Wars. Afghanistan, America and International Terrorism* (London: Pluto Press 2000), pages 12 – 15

188 Kaj Holm Anderson, Søren Brøndum, Jan Top Christensen and Gorm Rye Olsen: *International Politik – konflikteller samarbejde* (International Politics – conflict or cooperation] (*Samfundsfagsnyt* 1982), page 238

189 Barnett R. Rubin: "Arab Islamists in Afghanistan" in John Esposito (ed): *Political Islam. Revolution, Radicalism, or Reform* (London: Lynne Rienner Publishers 1997), page 186ff

190 Olivier Roy: *Afghanistan. Islam, politik og modstand* [Afghanistan. Islam, politics and resistance] (Eirene 1991), page 79ff

191 Barnett R. Rubin: "Arab Islamists in Afghanistan" in John Esposito: *Political Islam. Revolution, Radicalism, or Reform* (London: Lynne Rienner Publishers 1997), page 180ff

192 Rubin op.cit., page 180ff

193 John Cooley: *Unholy Wars. Afghanistan, America and International Terrorism* (London: Pluto Press 2000), page 59

194 Ahmed Rashid: *Taliban. The Story of the Afghan Warlords* (London: Pan Books 2001), page 85 and Peter Bergen: *Holy War Inc. Inside the Secret World of Osama bin Laden* (London: Weiderfeld & Nicolson 2001), page 75

195 Rubin op.cit., page 189

196 Larry P. Goodson: *Afghanistan's Endless War. State Failure, Regional Politics and the Rise of the Taliban* (University of Washington Press 2001), page 144

197 Cooley op.cit, page 55 and Rubin op. cit., page 189

198 Roy op.cit., page 142

199 Cooley op.cit., 31

200 Cooley op.cit., page 32 and Goodson op.cit., pages 141 – 44

201 Cooley op.cit., page 34

202 Cooley op.cit, page 70ff. and Goodson op.cit., pages 141 – 44

203 Cooley op.cit., page 76

204 Roy op.cit., page 57

205 Roy op.cit, page 58

206 Cooley op.cit., page 63

207 Cooley op.cit., page 85

208 Simon Reeve: *The New Jackals. Ramzi Yousef, Osama bin Laden and the future of terrorism* (London: André Deutsch Limited 1999), page 142 and Bergen op.cit., page 143

209 Bergen, op.cit., page 58

210 Lars Erslev Andersen: *Muslimske fundamentalister. Militante muslimer i Mellemøsten* [Muslim fundamentalists. Militant Muslims in the Middle East] (Copenhagen, DUPI 1997), pages 42 – 46

211 Anthony Davis: "Foreign Combatants in Afghanistan." *Jane's Intelligence Review*, vol. 5, no. 7, July 1993

212 Bergen, op.cit., page 57

213 Youssef Bondansky: *Bin laden. The Man Who Declared War on America* (Forum 1999), page 11

214 Lars Erslev Andersen: *Muslimske fundamentalister. Militante muslimer i Mellemøsten* [Muslim fundamentalists. Militant Muslims in the Middle East] (Copenhagen, DUPI 1997), page 76

215 Charles G. Cogan: "Partners in Time: The CIA and Afghanistan" in *World Policy Journal*, Summer 1993, vol. 5, no. 2

216 Rubin, op.cit., page 188 and Goodson op.cit., pages 145 – 146

217 Roy op.cit, page 196 and Marvin G. Wienbaum: "War and Peace in Afghanistan. The Pakistani Role" in *Middle East Journal*, vol. 45, no. 1, winter 1991

218 Goodson op.cit., page 68

219 Olivier Roy: *Skakmat. Politisk islam: Et alternativ for de muslimske samfund?* [Checkmate. Political Islam: Analternative for the Muslim communities?] (Eirene 1993), page 144

220 Youssef Bondansky: *Bin laden. The Man Who Declared War on America* (Forum 1999), page 11.

221 221 Reeve, op.cit., page 163

222 Cooley, op.cit., page 81

223 Reeve, op.cit., page 168

224 Cooley op.cit., page 97

225 Reeve op.cit., page 138

226 Cooley op.cit., page 60

227 Goodson op.cit., page 68

228 Bergen op.cit., page 81
229 Cooley op.cit., page 97
230 Bergen op.cit., page 74
231 Cooley op.cit., page 108
232 Rubin op.cit., page 191
233 *Middle East International*, 20 November 1992
234 James Bruce: "Arab Veterans of the Afghan War" in *Jane's Intelligence Review*, vol. 7, no. 4, 1995
235 Rubin op.cit., page 197
236 *MENA*, 1996, page 379
237 *West Europe Intelligence Report*, March 8th, 1994.
238 Jessica Stern, "Pakistan's Jihad Culture" in *Foreign Affairs*, November/December 2000
239 Milton Bearden: "Afghanistan, Graveyard of Empires" *Foreign Affairs*, November/December 2001
240 Goodson op.cit., page 73
241 Michael Griffin: *Reaping the Whirlwind. The Taliban Movement in Afghanistan* (London: Pluto Press 2001), page 1
242 Rashid op.cit, page 21
243 Goodson op.cit., page 73
244 *Middle East International* 1 May 1992 and 15 May 1992
245 Griffin op.cit, chronology
246 Goodson op.cit., pages 75 – 76
247 Rashid op.cit., page 21
248 Rashid op.cit., page 21
249 Goodson op.cit., page 76
250 Griffin op.cit., page 33
251 Griffin op.cit, chronology and Goodson op.cit., pages 77 – 78
252 Jan Aagaard: "Taliban og det regionale spil" [Taliban and the regional game] in *Mellemøstinformation*, nr. 10, 1998
253 Rubin op.cit., page 197

254 Olivier Roy: *Skakmat. Politisk islam: Et alternativ for de muslimske samfund?* [Checkmate. Political Islam: An alternative for the Muslim communities?] (Eirene 1993), page 140 and Roberto Aliboni, George Joffé and Tim Niblock (eds.): *Security Challenges in the Mediterranean Region* (London: Frank Cass1996), page 147

255 Nemat Guenena in Saad Eddin Ibrahim: "The troubled triangle: populism, Islam and civil society in the Arabworld" in A. Jerichow and J. Bæk Simonsen (eds.): *Islam in a Changing World. Europe and the Middle East* (UK: Curzon Press 1997), page 24

256 George Joffé: "The Islamist Threat to Egypt" in *Middle East and North Africa* (London: Europa Publications 1996), page 8

257 Lars Erslev Andersen: "Muslimske Fundamentalister" [Muslim fundamentalists]. Militante muslimer i Mellemøsten (Militant Muslims in the Middle East) (Copenhagen: DUPI 1997), page 15

258 Michael Collins Dunn: "Fundamentalism in Egypt" in *Middle East Policy*, vol. 2, 1993

259 Interview with Middle East Report January/March, 1996. *Dagbladet Information* [The Danish Newspaper Information], 5 – 6 March 1994

260 *Dagbladet Politiken* [Danish newspaper Politiken], 21 April 1995

261 Interview with Middle East Report January/March, 1996

262 Interview with Middle East Report January/March, 1996

263 *Dagbladet Information* [The Danish Newspaper Information], 25 February 1994

264 *Dagbladet Information* [The Danish Newspaper Information], 25 February 1994

265 *Dagbladet Information* [The Danish Newspaper Information], 25 February 1994; translated here from the Danish translation

266 *Dagbladet Information* [The Danish Newspaper Information], 25 February 1994; translated here from the Danish translation

267 *Dagbladet Information* [The Danish Newspaper Information], 25 February 1994; translated here from the Danish translation

268 Saad Eddin Ibrahim: "The Changing Face of Egypt's Islamic Activism" in Roberto Aliboni, George Joffé and TimNiblock (eds.) op.cit., page 34 and Country Profile, Egypt, 1995 – 96, The Economist Intelligence Unit (London1995)

269 John Cooley: *Unholy Wars. Afghanistan, America and International Terrorism* (London: Pluto Press 2000), page 213

270 *Middle East Report* op.cit.

271 *Middle East and North Africa, MENA* (London: Europa Publications 1997), page 380

272 *Middle East and North Africa, MENA* (London: Europa Publications 1997), page 377

273 Yossef Bodansky: *Bin Laden. The Man Who Declared War on America* (Forum: 1999), page 126 and *Jyllands-Posten* [Danish newspaper], 28 June 1995

274 Bodansky op.cit., page 126

275 *Dagbladet Information* [The Danish Newspaper Information] 9 October 2001 and Bodansky op.cit., pages 146,157 and 257

276 *Dagbladet Information* [The Danish Newspaper Information], 19 January, 1996

277 [The Danish newspaper] *Jyllands-Posten*, 18 September 2001. See also the Danish paper *Ekstra Bladet* 22 July 1995, in which one of the accused gives information about his membership in a militant group in Egypt, and *Jyllands-Posten* 28 June 1995

278 *Dagbladet Information* [The Danish Newspaper Information], 27 October 1994

279 [The Danish newspaper] *Ekstra Bladet* 22 July 1995 and [the Danish newspaper] *Dagbladet Information* 27 October 1994

280 [The Danish newspaper] *Jyllands-Posten*, 18 September 2001

281 Bodansky op.cit., page 143 and *MENA*, 1997, page 391

282 Simon Reeve: *The New Jackals. Ramzi Yousef, Osama bin Laden and the future of terrorism* (London: AndreDeutsch Limited 1999), page 236

283 R. Hrair Dekmejian: *Islam in Revolution. Fundamentalism in the Arab World* (Syracuse University Press 1995), page 184 and Hala Mustafa: "The Islamist Movements under Mubarak" in Laura Guazzone, (ed.) *The Islamist Dilemma. The Political Role of Islamist Movements in the Contemporary Arab World* (Ithaca Press 1995), page 183

284 George Joffé op.cit, page 2 and Saad Edin Ibrahim op.cit., page 34

285 Civil Society, January 1994 and Ehud Ya'ari in *The Jerusalem Report*, 2 July 1992

286 *Dagbladet Information* [The Danish Newspaper Information], 5 – 6 March 1994; excerpts of an interview originally published in the Egyptian newspaper *Al Ahasi*. Translated here from the Danish translation

287 Ahmed Rashid: *Taliban. The Story of the Afghan Warlords* (London: Pan Books 2001), page 135 and Barnett R. Rubin: "Arab Islamists i Afghanistan" in John Esposito (ed.): *Political Islam. Revolution, Radicalism, or Reform* (London: Lynne Rienner Publisher 1997), page 199. Roberto Aliboni, George Joffé and Tim Niblock (eds.) op.cit.,page 148

288 Roberto Aliboni, George Joffé and Tim Niblock (eds.) op.cit., page 155 and Dekmejian op.cit., page 208

289 Roberto Aliboni, George Joffé and Tim Niblock (eds.) op.cit., page 155 and Dekmejian op.cit., page 208

290 Reza Shah-Kazemi: "From Sufism to Terrorism. The Distortion of Islam in the Political Culture of Algeria," in Reza Shah-Kazemi (ed.): *Algeria. Revolution Revisited* (London: Islamic World Report 1997), page 197

291 Cooley, op.cit., page 203

292 Cooley, op.cit., page 203

293 James Bruce: "Arab Veterans of the Afghan War" in *Jane's Intelligence Review*, 1995, pages 175 – 76 and *MENA*, 1996, page 271

294 *MENA*, page 271

295 Rohan Gunaratna: "Terror in the sky" in *Jane's Intelligence Review*, October 2001

296 Gunaratna op.cit.

297 *Jane's World Insurgency and Terrorism*, September-December 2001

298 Quintan Wiktorowitcz: "The New Global Threat: Transnational Salafis and Jihad" in *Middle East Policy*, vol. III,no. 4, December 2001, page 29

299 Cooley, op.cit., page 46

300 *The Times*, 21 November 2001

301 *The Times*, 21 November 2001

302 Peter Bergen: *Holy War, Inc. Inside the Secret World of Osma bin Laden* (London: Weiderfeld & Nicolson 2001), page 188

303 Bergen op. cit., page 189 and Eric Watkins: "Islamism and Tribalism in Yemen" in Abdel Salam Sidahmed and Anoushiravan Ehteshami (eds.) op.cit., page 219 and Cooley op.cit., page 125

304 Cooley op.cit., page 124

305 Bergen op.cit., page 189

306 Bergen op.cit., page 189

307 Reeve op.cit., pages 211 – 212

308 Lars Erslev Andersen: "Hvem dræber hvem i Yemen?" [Who's killing who in Yemen?] in *Mellemøstinformation* no. 3, 1999

309 Bergen op.cit., page 200

310 Bergen op.cit., page 237

311 Cooley op.cit., page 254 and Reeve op.cit., page 157

312 Cooley op.cit., page 253

313 Cooley op.cit., page 254

314 Cooley op.cit., page 257

315 Bergen op.cit., page 93

316 Bergen op.cit., page 196

317 Reeve op.cit., pages 208 – 209

318 *Jane's World Insurgency and Terrorism*, September-December 2001

319 Cooley op.cit., pages 75 – 80

320 *Jane's Intelligence Review*, vol. 13, no. 11, November 2001

321 *The Washington Post*, 21 January 2002

322 Cooley, op.cit., page 176

323 Wiktorowicz op.cit, page 25

324 [The Danish newspaper] *Jyllands-Posten*, 17 December 2000

325 [The Danish newspaper] *Jyllands-Posten*, 17 December 2000.

326 [The Danish newspaper] *Jyllands-Posten*, 2 November 1999

327 [The Danish newspaper] *Jyllands-Posten*, 17 December 2000

328 [The Danish newspaper] *Jyllands-Posten*, 1 November 2001

329 [The Danish newspaper] *Jyllands-Posten*, 17 December 2000

330 [The Danish newspaper] *Jyllands-Posten*, 2 November 2001

331 [The Danish newspaper] *Jyllands-Posten*, 17 December 2000; translated here from the Danish translation

332 Since we wrote this in the winter 2001-2002 many new studies with more reliably informations have been published, fx Rohan Gunaratna: *Inside Al Qaeda. Global Network of Terror* (London 2002); As'ad Abu Khalil: *Bin Laden, Islam and America's New "War on Terrorism"* (New York 2002); Jason Burke, Al-Qaeda: *Casting a Shadow of Terror* (London: I.B. Tauris 2003); Loretta Napoleoni: *Modern Jihad. Tracing the Dollars Behind the Terror Networks* (London: PlutoPress 2003); Daniel Benjamin & Steven Simon: *The Age of Sacred Terror* (New York: Random House 2002)

333 Al Qaeda manual found in an apartment in Manchester and used as evidence at the trial in New York in the spring of 2001 against four al Qaeda members who were charged with co-responsibility for the embassy bombings in East Africa in 1998. The manual can be obtained from the home page of the American Department of Justice

334 Yossef Bodansky: *Bin Laden: The Man Who Declared War on America* (Rocklin, CA: Forum 1999) – the bookmakes an argument for Iran's role as sponsor of international terrorism. Laurie Myroie: *Study of Revenge. Saddam Hussein's Unfinished War against America* (Washington, D.C.: AEI Press 2000) – the author makes the argument that Iraq is behind international terrorism

335 In addition to the above-mentioned sources, the biographical data is based on Simon Reeve: *The New Jackals. Ramzi Yousef, Osama bin Laden and the Future of Terrorism* (Boston: Northeastern U.P. 1999); Peter L. Bergen: *Holy War, Inc. Inside the Secret War of Osama bin Laden* (New York: The Free Press 2001)

336 *Jane's Document View: Security and Foreign Forces*, Afghanistan, al Qaeda, 21 November 2001

337 Quoted here from Reeve op.cit., page 170

338 Oliver Roy: "Bin Laden: An Apocalyptic Sect Severed from Political Islam," in *Internationale Politik*, December 2001 (English version)

339 Fandy, op.cit., page 185

340 Douglas Farah: "Al Qaeda's Road Paved With Gold. Secret Shipments Traced Through a Lax System in the United Arab Emirates," in *The Washington Post* 17 February 2002: "The United Emirates has positioned itself as the Persian Gulf's freewheeling trade hub, but it is also attracting some unwanted entrepreneurs: money launderers," *Reuters*, 10 November 1999

341 Reeve op.cit., page 207; *Jane's Intelligence Review* vol. 13, no. 11, 2001, page 8ff

342 Daniel McGory, Laura Peek, Bill Bond: "Bin Laden's 'European ambassador' in London," in *The Times*, 21November, 2001

343 Mylroie op.cit., page 119ff

344 Charles Schmitz: "Investigating the Cole Bombing," *MERIP Press Information Note* 67, 6 September 2001

345 Roy op.cit.346 Samuel P. Huntington: "The Lonely Superpower," in *Foreign Affairs* March/April 1999

346 Samuel P. Huntington: "The Lonely Superpower," in *Foreign Affairs* March/April 1999